In Loving Memory

In Loving Memory

Choosing a Lasting Memorial

CASSANDRA EASON

ROBERT HALE · LONDON

© *Cassandra Eason 1996*
First published in Great Britain 1996

ISBN 0 7090 5815 2

Robert Hale Limited
Clerkenwell House
Clerkenwell Green
London EC1R 0HT

2 4 6 8 10 9 7 5 3 1

Photoset in North Wales by
Derek Doyle & Associates, Mold, Clwyd.
Printed in Great Britain by
St Edmundsbury Press Ltd, Bury St Edmunds, Suffolk.
Bound by WBC Book Manufacturers Limited,
Bridgend, Mid-Glamorgan.

Contents

Introduction

Arranging suitable commemoration in return for a bequest or legacy to a charity or organization may seem to confront prematurely one's own mortality. Yet such memorials may offer a small piece of immortality, whether they consist of an entry in a memorial book, a plaque on a garden seat in a favourite spot, a named building or a university chair. Commemoration can be sought in return for a gift or endowment established during one's lifetime or as an in memoriam gift to a family member or close friend.

I was asked to explore ways in which people could be formally commemorated and discovered forms ranging from elaborate gravestones to a Virtual Memorial Garden on the Internet. The task was not an easy one. I had imagined that if I contacted a charity or organization such as a university, I would be sent a list of memorials a donor could be given in return for a certain sum. This was not always the case but I did receive a fascinating range of replies. For instance, until recently £35 would buy a plank on Yarmouth Pier on the Isle of Wight, with the donor's name inscribed on it. For around £5,000 a memorial seat can be inscribed at the Royal Shakespeare Theatre and £10,000 could put a name on an acre of woodland in Sherwood Forest. A rose can be dedicated to a lost child (The Compassionate Friends), a maternity hospital endowed (Addenbrooke's NHS Trust) or gargoyles can be named at Worcester Cathedral. A particularly splendid book for donors is the Memorial Log, a hand-bound leather book kept on board the *Lord Nelson*, a tall, square-rigged ship built by the Jubilee Sailing Trust so that physically disabled and able-bodied people can sail together. For a seven-figure sum, you could name the new ship that will be joining the *Lord Nelson* in service. Memorials can have interesting spin-offs. When the Hampshire Sculpture Trust erected a commemorative seat on St Giles's Hill on the outskirts of Winchester to a young woman who had died in the early 1990s, it prompted the renovation of the whole hillside. The seat cost £2,300. Half the cost was raised by family and friends and the rest by the trust.

However, I found it incredibly difficult to find charities in any large numbers who did offer a price-list for memorials. Charities prefer bequests without strings because they need the flexibility to adapt to changing circumstances. Equally, some charities believe that such memorials should be discussed on an individual basis and, as long as they were willing to offer memorials, they fell within the criteria of this book. However, some organizations do not offer commemoration in any form other than a letter of thanks and, in one or two cases, I was dismayed by the rudeness or indifference of those who answered the telephone. I have not included these charities or organizations in this book.

Charities are frequently understaffed and desperate for every penny to go to those in need, a commendable aim. However, it may be better for fund-raising in the long term to take £75 or £100 out of a bequest to pay for a small plaque, an engraving on a wall or a calligrapher for an entry in a memorial book. Charities who are aware of this aspect tend to be those whose initial warm welcome is matched by their success at fund-raising. Ingenious schemes to raise money by an unusual commemoration do not show a lack of seriousness by a charity, rather a sense of humanity and warmth that may attract funds in an increasingly competitive market.

This book explores many other aspects of memorials, including financial implications and the costs of formal headstones, as well as ways of starting a memorial charity. However, the book remains a prototype and even as I prepare it for press, charities are exploring new avenues of commemoration for donors, perhaps for the first time. It is hoped that charities will respond with updates of their own work and commemorative opportunities and that readers will share their own experiences in the field of commemorative giving and unusual memorials. *In Loving Memory* is a commemoration of life and an expression of hope for the future.

Part 1

1 Memorials Past, Present and Future

My mother died of cancer when I was nineteen and I was totally devastated. Yet, I could not cry and for two years was unable to speak her name. However, I commissioned a white marble cross which was placed on her grave in the country churchyard she had loved in life. On the cross were inscribed her name, dates and a verse from the Twenty-third Psalm, my mother's favourite hymn. It was the nearest I could come to expressing love, grief and acceptance that my mother had lived and lived no more.

The churchyard is closed now and the cross broken. However, it served its purpose as a memorial on which to focus my loss and as a celebration of my mother's life. This book looks at memorials of many kinds, at their costs and the choices available. There are a number of options in all price ranges, from commissioning a traditional headstone or crematorium urn to inscribing one's name and dates on a cathedral bell or promising young oaks to be harvested a hundred years from now to hold up the roof of a cathedral that has stood for almost a millennium.

Those who have a million pounds or more to bequeath can name a lifeboat or endow a university chair. Those with £50 or less to spare can have a star called after them or have a book inscribed with a memorial name-plate in a university library. For a few hundred pounds a flat in a sheltered housing development can be dedicated to a loved one. For two thousand pounds or more, a guide dog for the blind can answer to a well-loved name and, for less than ten thousand, a Premier League memorial football match can be held to commemorate a relative who loved the sport.

From the dawn of mankind, civilizations have created elaborate tombs and monuments, crammed with the artefacts it was believed would be of use in the next world. Perhaps the most famous are the Pyramids of Giza, across the Nile from modern Cairo. Built between 2,700 BC and 2,500 BC, the royal tombs of the pharaohs were created with great geometric precision, without the use of wheeled transport or beasts of burden. The full astronomical significance of the pyramids is only now being discovered.

China boasts many tombs to the great emperors. Perhaps the most remarkable is the great burial mound of Emperor Qin Shi Huang Di, who by 221 BC had subjected all China to his will. He began planning his monument when he first ascended the throne in 246 BC. Seven hundred thousand conscripts worked for thirty-six years on his tomb while artisans created elaborate grave furniture for his conjectured future needs. It was claimed that an entire palace was created under the artificial mound, and in 1974 the first signs of this kingdom under the earth, once dismissed as legend, were revealed when a vast subterranean pit containing a pottery army of 6,000 life-sized warriors, faces brightly painted with the correct insignia of rank, was uncovered.

The ancient Greeks created the mausoleum, the large sepulchral family monument so beloved of the Victorians, whose remains can be seen today in Highgate, Kensal Green and Brompton cemeteries. The word is derived from Mausolus, Satrap of Caria in ancient Greece, in whose memory his widow Artemisia raised a splendid tomb at Halicarnassus (*c.* 353–350 BC). Some remains of this monument are in the British Museum. Artemisia was so distraught at her husband's death that she drank his ashes and resolved to erect one of the grandest and noblest monuments of antiquity to celebrate his memory. The mausoleum was one of the seven wonders of the ancient world and was created by four different architects. Scopas erected the east side, Timotheus had the south, Leochares had the west and Bruxis the north. Pitis was also employed in raising a pyramid over this stately monument and the top was adorned by a chariot drawn by four horses. The expenses were immense and the philosopher Anaxagoras exclaimed when he saw it: 'How much money changed into stones!'

Such mighty monuments are a testimony to love as well as riches and power. The Taj Mahal was built on the southern bank of the Yamuna River outside Agra in India by the Mughal emperor Shah Jahan in memory of his wife Arjumand Banu Begum. The name Taj Mahal is a corruption of her other name, meaning ('the chosen one of the palace'). She died in childbirth in 1631 after having been the emperor's inseparable companion since their marriage in 1612. The building was started around 1632 to plans by a council of architects from India, Persia, central Asia and beyond. More than 20,000 workmen were employed daily to complete the mausoleum itself by about 1649. The entire complex took about twenty-two years to complete at a cost of about forty million rupees.

The greatest British monument to lost love is perhaps the Albert

Memorial in London, created in memory of Queen Victoria's beloved Albert and now being restored under the auspices of English Heritage. All the statues on the spire, the crowning cross and orb and the enormous bronze figure of Albert are to be fully gilded with new gold-leaf. The restoration will be completed by June 1999. The gilding was there when George Gilbert Scott's original monument was completed in 1876, but was stripped away in 1914–1915. The government has pledged £8 million, English Heritage is putting forward £2 million and expects to raise a further £4 million by a public appeal to reach the total cost of restoration, which is estimated at £14 million. In 1872, it cost £150,000 to build the memorial, equivalent to £5 million in modern prices.

In England the culmination of ostentatious memorials for the general public, at least the better-off classes, was the glorious Victorian Brookwood Cemetery, near Woking in Surrey, that is still used today for burials of the many nationalities who have settled in the south-east of England. The Woking Necropolis Plan, as it was first called, was created around 1850 because of the shortage of cemeteries and involved a grand plan to build a vast necropolis to bury the dead of London and all parts of the country. The cemetery would be state-run and hence would be open to rich and poor. Plans were made to convey the deceased by water and the new, growing railway network. A private company, the London Necropolis and National Mausoleum Company, carried out a modified plan and opened the first 400 acres of the cemetery in 1854. Roman Catholics, Jews, Parsees and Dissenters were to be buried there as well as Anglicans. The London and South Western Railway Company was engaged to convey coffins and mourners from Waterloo to the cemetery. Private stations were provided at both ends of the journey. Two stations at Brookwood served the two halves of the cemetery. The grand Gothic station that was planned was never built and one of the aims of the original plan, to make decent burial available for the poor, was not realized because the costs of plots and transport were well beyond its means.

Since the cemetery was consecrated by the Bishop of Winchester on 7 November 1854, and opened to the public six days later, nearly 240,000 people have been buried there. Plots could be reserved by parishes and organizations as well as individuals. The St Albans Holborn Ground parish plot (within Brookwood Cemetery) is still in use today and has the air of an English country churchyard. The finely carved lich-gate is a memorial to a parishioner who died in November 1892.

The Military Cemeteries were opened in 1917 and extended

during and after the Second World War, serving the war dead of several nations, including America, Canada, Czechoslovakia and those casualties of the British Commonwealth who were killed in Russia during the two world wars.

The most ornate memorials, both at Brookwood Cemetery and throughout Britain, are those of the Victorian era. Such memorials were as important as the trappings of the living, perhaps more so because mortal life could be brief. In 1842, the average age at death of the professional classes was thirty years and only seventeen for the poor. Even in the early years of the twentieth century, mortality rates, especially for children under five years of age, were still very high. Victorian monuments abound beyond the cemetery gates and can still be seen in corners of even the most redeveloped town, recalling a former local hero or magnate, or child cut down in the flower of youth. At Church Litten in Newport, on the Isle of Wight, opposite a new supermarket, stands a monument to Valentine Grey, a nine-year-old pauper from Alverstone who was employed by a Newport sweep, Mr Davis, to climb chimneys. He was discovered dead in an outbuilding of a house in Pyle Street in Newport, where he slept. Unusually perhaps for the time, the boy's bruised body was examined by a surgeon, who declared that the child had died from a massive blow to his head. The sweep and his wife were arrested and convicted of manslaughter. Public sympathy was so great that a monument was erected by subscription in memory of the child. In his case, local reaction helped to swell the tide of opinion against such cruel child labour and led to its eventual abolition. The memorial reads:

> To the memory of Valentine Grey, the little sweep,
> Interred January 5th AD 1822 in the 10th year of his age.
> In testimony of the general feeling of suffering innocence, this
> monument is erected
> by public subscription.

He is also commemorated with a brass plaque in Valentine's Walk about half a mile away, near the scene of his death.

A memorial, whether the simplest wooden cross on a grave or a glittering plaque in an entrance hall as a recognition of a generous legacy to those in need, is a way of acknowledging that a person lived and that life has meaning that lasts beyond the body. The principle remains the same and even in recessionary times, there are few graves that are not marked in some way.

But all memorials were not made of marble. Jeremy Bentham, the great philosopher of ethics, law and government, was not, despite popular belief, the founder of University College, London. However, in line with his utilitarian principles he did endow the college with an unusual memorial, his body 'in the attitude in which I am sitting when engaged in thought'. This 'Auto-Icon' has been in the possession of the college since 1850. The college was also bequeathed over 200 boxes of Bentham's outpourings. This has been described as 'one of the most remarkable monuments to the mind of a single man in all its aspects anywhere.' Since 1959, the Bentham Project has been preparing his collected works and correspondence for publication. Sixteen volumes have been produced and fifty more are anticipated. The 'Auto-Icon' attended the sesquicentennial meeting of the college committee in 1976, the minutes recording Jeremy Bentham present but not voting. His clothed skeleton with a wax head is displayed in a box in South Cloisters. The actual mummified head is kept in a safe in the college.

The Forestry Commission has many fascinating memorials in its forests that hold segments of history and often a personal cameo. There is a sixty-foot monument to Alexander Murray on Forestry Commission land, in memory of a self-educated man who went on to become a professor of languages, speaking more than twenty-six foreign tongues; it is at Talnotry, in the Newton Stewart Forest District in southern Scotland. Murray served as Queen Victoria's expert on Chinese languages and adviser to the Chinese emperor before the advent of communism and his monument provides an instant history lesson for walkers and picnickers.

But another more poignant memorial to Alexander Murray exists in the forest. John Davies, the former Conservator in South Scotland, planted a Chinese rowan-tree to commemorate the great man of British politics who had risen from such humble beginnings as the son of a poor shepherd. The tree was planted about 1974 at the centre of the ruined walls which are all that remain of the shepherd's cottage.

The spot where a famous character died can be marked with a memorial stone. For example the Rufus Stone stands in the New Forest near Ringwood, marking the spot where an arrow fired at a stag glanced off a tree and killed William Rufus, William the Conqueror's son, on 2 August 1100. The king's body was loaded into a hand-cart belonging to Purkin, a peasant who made the two day journey with the body to Winchester Cathedral for burial. However, the Benedictine monks were not at all impressed as they considered him a bad king and prophesied disaster if he were buried in the holy of holies, close to the high altar. William Rufus's memorial was short-lived. Seven years later, the central tower came crashing down, destroying his tomb. There are many alternative theories about William Rufus's death; that he was accidentally killed by Sir Walter Tyrell, murdered by a dispossessed Saxon at the behest of his younger brother Henry, or as part of a strange pagan ritual, allied to the sacrificial slaying of the Corn King. Whatever the cause, his only memorial, the Rufus Stone, is itself a replacement of the original stone that was vandalized. The new, more durable metal monument was erected in 1841 using the original inscription and it is disappointingly small and utilitarian.

On a different level, near the cliff edge on Afton Down in West Wight is a small grey and rather more picturesque stone monument. The inscription reads:

E.I.M. aged 15.
'He cometh forth like a flower and is cut down.
He fleeth also as a shadow and continueth not.'
Erected in memory of a most dear and only child who was suddenly removed into
eternity from the adjacent cliff on to the rocks beneath. 28 August,
1846.

The cliffs have eroded in the passing century and a half, but local youngsters as well as tourists still scramble along the wild, remote, beautiful but dangerous coastline.

In Victorian times, it was easy to erect a monument at the place a person died but even today it is possible to erect a tree or stone to mark such a place. One in Marwell Zoo Park in Hampshire was planted by the staff to commemorate the spot where a visitor died. His relations have visited and been comforted by the living memorial in the park. Bulbs are sometimes planted at the roadside where a traffic accident occurred and every spring are a reminder of new hope.

Though it is often the great whose monuments receive attention, a memorial to a loved family member is, as I found in my own life, part of the healing process for those remaining, as well as commemorating the life of a unique human being. Harriet Frazer founded the company Memorials by Artists partly because she realized that choosing and helping to create a memorial served as therapy at a time of grief. She set up the company after her own difficulties finding a suitable memorial for her stepdaughter Sophie. Bereaved families are put in touch with artists and letter-cutters and together they plan and design a personal memorial.

Peter Burman, secretary for the Council for the Care of Churches, sees the value of even a modest hand-crafted memorial stone, 'as a quiet and distinctive work of art, visible in a public place'. He comments: 'For most people the commissioning of a headstone or other form of memorial will be the only or one of the rare opportunities in their life for commissioning a work of art from a living artist or craftsman. The relationship which develops between the bereaved person and the artist-craftsman can be a part of the healing process.' (*Memorials by Artists* booklet, 1993). Harriet Frazer also regards the epitaph on a stone, like the memorial itself, as a way of commemorating the unique qualities of the person who has died. For her, an epitaph should not attempt to be an obituary but to evoke a person's unique achievements and character. She cites the example of a soldier killed at the Somme. His parents used as his epitaph the words of an eyewitness who described how the young man would go up and down the trenches encouraging his men and 'when danger was greatest, his smile was loveliest'.

One of the most pragmatic epitaphs is to be found in Highgate Cemetery in London on the grave of Dr Michael Pratelli. Mounted at the head of his grave is his professional plaque: Dr Michael Pratelli, Dental Surgeon. By Appointment only. Telephone: 01 485 3752.

Though the grandeur of Victorian memorials has largely been replaced in the modern world of neatly lawned graves and ordered rows of crematorium memorabilia, there are still people who follow the idea of an elaborate, almost gaudy, commemorative stone. Traditional gypsy families tend to be buried in the area around which they travel and they may use a particular cemetery over many years. Often the favoured memorial stone is a huge black-granite heart with gold lettering. Memorial vases from different branches of the family will be set along the grave surround. The Arabs and other Middle Eastern people also continue the tradition of elaborate memorials, as do those from the Mediterranean.

Beyond the cemetery walls, imaginative modern memorials can create for the present and future generations a perfectly preserved piece of history that encapsulates the lives of those who created it; for example, a 93-year-old grocery shop is to become a museum, in accordance with the will of its late owner. The business in Fore Street, Saltash, in Cornwall has not been trading since its owner, Francis Elliot, retired fifteen years before his death in June 1995 aged ninety-seven and left the business to the Tamar Protection Trust as a memorial to himself, his deceased twin brother and his father who opened the shop in 1902. The condition was that the shop should be preserved as a historical display of a grocer's. To this end Francis had been collecting items of interest for the Elliot

Museum he wanted to be founded on his death. The shop is
perfectly preserved with gas-lamps hanging from the ceiling, tins
of Ovaltine from the 1950s standing on the shelves and Marmite
still advertised at two shillings and sixpence per jar.

Another form of memorial was raised to Jessie Hurlstone, a
27-year-old stable girl who was stabbed to death at Jimmy Frost's
stables near Buckfastleigh, South Devon, in 1995. The Jessie
Hurlstone Memorial Handicap race is to be held annually at the
Devon and Exeter Racecourse on Haldon Hill, near Exeter. Mr
Frost, a Grand National-winning jockey, devised the race as the
best way to remember Jessie because she was devoted to the
horses in her care.

Living memorials are perhaps the most exciting of all and it is
not just the exalted halls of Eton or Harrow that receive legacies of
property or land. For thirty years Phil Drabble, the naturalist,
author and television presenter has owned a ninety-acre nature
reserve in Staffordshire. Two local children wrote to him asking if
they might visit his herons (two per cent of Britain's herons nest in
his trees). From this regular visits were instituted by the children
of Richard Clarke First School in Abbots Bromley, Staffordshire,
and the older children planted trees on the reserve in what is now
called Clarke's Copse. In June 1995, Mr Drabble decided to
bequeath the nature reserve to the pupils of the village school,
saying: 'If I can give children a taste of the joy I found in nature as
a child, I shall be happy. I do get a feeling of satisfaction when I
look out of the window and know it's all going to be here in a
hundred years but I shall haunt anyone who ruins it.' He has the
pleasure of seeing children sharing what will be his legacy to them.
Bath University also recommends that, where possible, benefactors begin the endowment of a university chair or department
during their lifetime to enjoy the pleasure of setting it up and
having a hand in its organization.

Another recent in memoriam gift involved hiring the Royal
Albert Hall in the autumn of 1995 for a private concert in memory
of the late George Cathcart. Joanne Millet, Cathcart's great-niece,
paid about £50,000 for the hall and the Royal Philharmonic
Orchestra. George Cathcart, a doctor and honorary laryngologist
to the Royal Academy of Music, provided during his lifetime
money to stage the first Promenade Concerts in 1895. As a
laryngologist, he saw that the singers had vocal strain and insisted,
as one of the conditions of the donation, that the pitch was
lowered. He paid for a complete set of new instruments for the
orchestra to allow for the change in pitch and also provided money
for the garlanded fountain that is still the centre-piece of the
Albert Hall arena. However, it was his second stipulation that

indirectly led to his obscurity after his death. Mr Cathcart had insisted that Henry Wood should become conductor and such was Wood's fame it was his name, not Cathcart's, after whom the Proms were named.

Even if we cannot afford to hire the Royal Albert Hall, there are universities and music societies who will put on a memorial concert for a more modest cost or a young musician could be sponsored for a specific performance in memory of a loved one.

With conventional memorials, too, new avenues are opening. The vast majority of present-day funerals involve cremation, and crematoriums, lawn burials and churchyard regulations have led to a standardization of memorials. However, there is a new development towards natural woodland burials with trees and flowers as memorials. Ken West of Bereavement Services in Carlisle pioneered the first green burial ground in the UK in 1991. He has established within the local authority cemetery an area that is to be oak woodland and a red squirrel reserve, where graves are marked not with traditional headstones but an oak sapling and a profusion of bluebells. He comments:

> Some psychologists argue that conventional memorials such as headstones are essential as part of the grieving process. It may be that for some people they are, but for others a natural site and more natural form of memorial, such as a tree, offer a chance to be remembered by recreating an environment that has disappeared, such as the oak woodland in Carlisle.

At present there are only sixteen woodland sites with eleven more about to open, and about forty are in the early planning stage. These are in a sense a legacy for the future. However, the future may well not lie in traditional memorials or even tangible ones but in microchips. The Internet Virtual Memorial Garden is perhaps an indication of how an increasing number of people will be commemorated in the twenty-first century. It was set up in 1995 by Dr Lindsay Marshall, a lecturer in the computing department of Newcastle University, and by the end of that year already had well over 300 names from all over the world. Up to six new names are added each day. The bereaved can include a photograph or lines of verse. Dr Marshall does not use crosses on his Internet site because he wishes to make it culturally neutral. He has pledged that so long as the facilities remain, the garden will operate twenty-four hours a day.

Like memorials ancient and futuristic, the idea sprang from a human need to have loved ones commemorated publicly. It began with Dr Marshall's interest in obituaries and a page containing them which he created on the Internet to commemorate the deaths of celebrities. But he found that many contributors were sending details of deceased friends and family. So he decided to create the Virtual Memorial Garden for everyone who wanted to contribute.

Users can sign a visitors' book, which is already filled with messages from people, comforted by browsing in the garden. Entries come from all over the world, stored in alphabetical order in the way chosen by family or friends. Some entries resemble conventional headstones in content but others lead to another computer where a full life story, poems and even photographs may be included. One example is that of Corporal Mark Isfeld who was killed in 1994 clearing mines in Croatia. His father has, via the Virtual Memorial Garden, created a memorial on his home computer with photographs of his son as a boy and man, reminding people that Mark died to make Croatia safe. Memorials in future will open up the possibility of sound and images, perhaps clips from home videos and memorials to whole families. Already one memorial is a passage to an exhibition by a dead artist, the paintings stored in the memory of his own computer.

The modern world shows no abatement in the universal and timeless desire to be commemorated after death. *In Loving Memory* begins in this modern world and is primarily a practical manual, suggesting cost-effective ways of perpetuating one's name. The next chapter offers detailed information about the financial considerations of making a lifetime gift, in memoriam donation or legacy to a charity or organization and negotiating a suitable memorial in return.

2 Giving to Charity: Financial Considerations

Generally speaking, there is very little financial difference between lifetime gifts and those made after death, since gifts and legacies to recognized charities are free of tax. However, personal financial circumstances may make one method more beneficial to you and the charity in terms of additional tax concessions.

There are three main ways of giving money to a favourite charity: as a gift during your lifetime, as a legacy on your own death or as an in memoriam gift for a loved one or given by family members on your behalf.

Although this chapter offers general strategies, it is best to consult your accountant about your individual finances, especially if substantial amounts of money are involved. This is especially so since the Conservative government committed itself in November 1995 to the eventual abandonment of inheritance tax. However, a change in government could result in a complete turnaround of both inheritance taxes and lifetime giving. While up-to-date information can be obtained from the Inland Revenue (The Inland Revenue, FICO (Financial and Intermediaries Claims Office), Charity Division, St John's House, Merton Road, Bootle, Merseyside L69 9BB. Tel: 0151 472 6000) or any chosen charity, there is no substitute for sound financial advice to maximize any gift both to the donor and beneficiary.

Equally a solicitor is necessary to draw up a will in such a way that after your death your wishes are followed and money can be used by the charity of your choice in the way you intended. This can ensure not only that any legacy can be used but also that any memorial you request is an integral condition of your gift. A solicitor is well worth the expense and should not cost much above £100, perhaps less if matters are straightforward and you have your wishes drafted in advance.

Many charities do have special legacy leaflets and have trained legacy officers to offer advice about the most cost-effective way of benefiting a charity. Yet, you may not wish to reveal your financial status or personal situation to a stranger, however professional and courteous. They are also concerned with maximizing the benefits to their charity (they would be failing in their duty to the charity if they did not). You may also find it difficult if you are undecided about the charity to choose or if you wish to bequeath your money to several different causes, although again legacy officers are well used to this situation. Therefore, involving your own professionals may be worthwhile, especially where property or substantial bequests are involved.

One or two of the organizations in this book do not have charitable status nor do they qualify for tax concessions as being beneficial to the nation, as do universities and heritage organizations. Such non-charitable organizations may have altruistic purposes but may not qualify either because they are quangos, like the harbour authority listed, and so are required to pay their way or because they are not sufficiently sound financially to meet the stringent criteria of the Charity Commissioners, like one zoological garden mentioned that is struggling for survival.

Giving to charity

To find out in detail how to obtain tax relief for setting up a memorial through a charity, see leaflets IR65, *Giving to Charity – How Individuals Can Get Tax Relief*, and IR113, *Gift Aid – A Guide for Donors and Charities*, from the Inland Revenue. There are three main ways of getting tax relief on gifts to charity during one's lifetime. These are:

Payroll giving

This is a scheme whereby employees can give to charity directly from their pay and get tax relief on their payments. It is not run by every employer but where it is, provides a cost-effective way to the donor since the amount given to charity is deductible from the gross salary before PAYE tax is calculated. So tax is payable on the net salary only, after the gift has been deducted.

An employer needs to be told how much should be deducted each pay-day and to which charity or charities it should be given. Relief is given at the highest rate of tax being paid on the salary, on gifts of up to £1,200 (from April 1996) in any one tax year. A husband and wife who both pay tax under PAYE can each give up to £1,200 in any tax year and get tax relief.

Pensioners can use the scheme if tax is deducted from the pension under PAYE. The maximum contribution at 1996 figures was £1,200 per annum but the figure may vary in the light of different budgets and any changes in government. Contact the Inland Revenue, either a local office or the Charity Division, for current figures. There may be a minimum donation under the particular scheme an employer uses.

Payroll giving and memorials

The major problem with this method of giving is that it would be necessary to negotiate with the charity separately over the way the money is to be used, since the scheme passes money to the charity through a charities' agency.

Also, a charity may be reluctant to make a long-term commitment to an ongoing memorial, such as a prize, on the strength of payroll giving since it can be terminated at short notice either through design or if the donor leaves the firm. However, the personal financial saving to the donor may make any difficulties worth overcoming.

Deeds of Covenant

This is a way of giving on a long-term basis and is a legally binding way of giving away part of one's income every year. Most charities will supply a deed of covenant form. The covenant must be paid for more than three years if the giver and charity want to get tax relief. Most charitable covenants tend to be for four years and are renewable. Deeds of covenant do not provide tax relief at source as payroll giving does. Tax relief is obtained by the donor subtracting tax at the basic rate when paying the gift to charity. Providing the donor is paying at least that amount in tax, tax relief is obtained by keeping the amount that has been deducted. The charity can claim back the tax from the Inland Revenue so that it is not out of pocket.

The usual method is to pay a 'net of tax' covenant. If a donor wishes to give a charity an amount which at 1996 rates would cost £76 after taking basic tax relief (twenty-four per cent at the time of writing) into account, the first step is to sign a covenant under which the donor undertakes to pay the charity every year 'such a sum as after the deduction of tax is equal to £76'. The next step is to pay the charity the £76 a year. But this is really worth a payment of £100, from which the donor has deducted basic tax at twenty-four per cent, or £24. As long as a donor is paying tax at the basic rate, he or she need do nothing more. The charity can claim the full tax back and so it gets the full £100, £76 from the donor and £24 from the Inland Revenue. Some people choose to pay the full amount to the charity, in effect increasing the value of the gift to the charity, in the case of the hypothetical £100, to £124 after the charity has claimed tax relief.

This method is of real value to the donor if he or she pays the higher rate of tax. In this case the tax office should be informed of the deed of covenant and the net amount entered on the tax return. The tax office will arrange for the extra relief, usually through the donor's PAYE or tax assessment. Deeds of covenant are, however, only viable for tax-payers, for if a donor is not paying tax, he or she must pay the Inland Revenue any tax deducted from the payments to charity. It is easier just to give donations directly to the charity. It may be better for a husband or wife who is paying tax to make the deed of covenant instead. In the case of joint covenants, the husband and wife are generally treated as paying half each for tax purposes. If the wife is a non-taxpayer, the husband will not get higher rate relief on her half of the covenanted payments. Tax relief can be obtained under both payroll giving and covenanting if a person subscribes to both methods of giving to charity. However, covenanted payments cannot be made through payroll giving.

Covenanting and memorials

Covenants are an effective way of making regular lifetime gifts to a charity and in memoriam gifts. Since a covenant is fixed for a period of more than three years and cannot be stopped like payroll giving within a reasonably short period, this may make it a more suitable form of giving for in memoriam gifts and living memorials such as prizes or awards, so long as the rate of inflation on the value of the prize is considered.

Gift Aid

Gift Aid gives tax relief for single cash gifts made to charities by UK residents. Each gift must be at least £250 net of basic rate and charities are able to claim back tax at basic rate. Higher rate tax relief is available to donors if applicable. There is no upper limit on the amount that can be given in any one tax year, but there must be at least as much income charged at the basic rate of tax as the amount of the gross donation. If the donation exceeds this amount, the Inland Revenue may ask the donor to make up the difference.

Gift Aid and memorials

The advantage of these lifetime gifts is that a donor can enjoy seeing his or her gift in action. Gift Aid can be used as many times as required in a tax year to make gifts to the same charity or different charities so long as each gift is at least £250. However, if Gift Aid is used for an in memoriam gift, any token by the charity must not be worth more than 2.5% of the net gift and the total benefits received from any one charity must not be worth more than £250 in any tax year.

Therefore, it may be important to specify that only a plaque on the item purchased is to be paid for in this way. A Gift Aid tax certificate, form R190(SD), can be obtained from the charity direct or from the tax office at Bootle. This should be filled in and is best sent with the payment to the charity as they will need it to claim tax back on the payment.

Other lifetime gifts

Outright gifts to charity made before a person's death are not liable for inheritance tax, no matter how soon after the gift a person dies. This can be a way of giving a substantial amount of capital to be invested by the charity to fund a prize or fellowship. Normally there is a seven-year rule, with taxation on a sliding scale. This exemption also includes gifts for the benefit of the nation, such as to universities or heritage organizations like the National Trust, the Natural History Museum, the National Heritage Memorial Fund or the Historic Buildings and Monuments Commission for Britain.

Other assets to charities, for example land or stocks and shares, are not liable for capital gains tax when a donor makes the gift. If the asset is worth more than was originally paid for it, the gain is carried forward until the charity sells the asset. Usually the charity will then be exempt from tax on the total gain which has accrued since the date the donor bought the asset.

Legacies

A legacy to a registered charity is also free of inheritance tax. In April 1996, this was set at £200,000. Although the Conservative government then pledged to abolish this tax, set at forty per cent of money above the threshold, a change of government could radically alter the limits of exemption.

The value of this legacy is subtracted from the net value of the total estate, leaving the family with a smaller sum liable to tax.

Deeds of variation

For family members who have been left money in an estate, the amount of inheritance tax due to be paid can be reduced by diverting some of it to a charity favoured by the original testator. If all other beneficiaries agree, a deed of variation can divert some of the inheritance to charity, tax free. The beneficiaries could pay less tax on the estate or give the extra money to the charity. The solicitor handling the will can arrange this but must do so within two years. A similar method is used whereby a benefactor leaves money to a relation or friend on the understanding that he or she will pass a proportion of it on to charity, thereby also attracting double the tax concessions. Consult an accountant or solicitor as the two have slightly different procedures, although the principle and tax benefits are the same.

The gift is, within the two years, regarded as made by the deceased and so avoids inheritance tax of forty per cent. However, in addition, if the legatee is liable for income tax on at least the grossed-up equivalent of the gift, he or she should gift the sum to charity as a net amount under the Gift Aid provisions (see restrictions on Gift Aid above) and the charity can claim the extra from the tax office. If the legatee is subject to higher rate tax on the equivalent of the charitable sum, the tax advantage is even greater and can, divided between the three parties and two different taxes, exceed ninety per cent of the donated sum.

The advantage of after-death gifts made by the family is that any memorial or chosen project can be tailored to the current needs and resources of the charity. However, it does depend on having good family relations or trusted friends who will give the money in a way the deceased person would have wished.

Planning a legacy

Once you have decided on a charity, its legacy officer or relevant leaflet can advise you on the different kinds of legacies. However, it may well be worth while, as with any will, going to a solicitor. Then you can be certain that you are leaving money to be spent as you wish by the charity. It will also give you an opportunity to insert a clause about a memorial while making sure that the terms of your will are not so restrictive as to make the legacy invalid (see next section for suggested wording). This is an area where it is important to talk to the relevant charity to be sure that it is happy and able to follow your wishes regarding the project area and memorial, perhaps some years hence.

Examples abound where legacies have been lost because of clauses that could not be followed. Few are as bizarre as that in 1827 when Edinburgh University Senate received notification of a bequest by a John Farquhar of £200 a year 'to each of the Arts Professors in the Scottish Universities' on condition that they would agree to teach 'the whole year without any other vacations than those established by law and fourteen days about Midsummer'. It is doubtful whether any of the arts professors would have felt able to accept the legacy on those terms, let alone whether they would have found an eager audience of students for this continuous teaching. In the event, the question never arose as the will was declared invalid, the testator having been of unsound mind at the time of its execution.

Unusable legacies are still a common problem. Linda Norgrove, head of the Legacy Department at the RSPCA, points out one difficulty of leaving a legacy specifically for a memorial:

> The Charity Commissioners, to whom as a registered charity the RSPCA are accountable, frown upon the establishment of separate restricted funds for specific purposes. This is partly because once the purpose of the fund is achieved, any monies remaining in the fund cannot be used for any other purpose and partly because this would involve greatly increased administration costs and charities must ensure that these are kept to a minimum. Registered charities are obliged by law to expend their funds only upon their strict charitable purposes being, in the case of the RSPCA, the promotion of kindness and prevention of cruelty to animals.
>
> It would not therefore be proper for the society to spend its funds on such projects as the planting of memorial trees, nor would it be proper for us to advertise for bequests specifically for such purposes.

Restricted legacies not discussed beforehand can also be problematic. Mrs Cynthia Zur Nedden of Cheshire devoted her life to caring for sick animals and strays. She was well known for feeding the wild foxes, squirrels and garden birds. On her death, she left her former home, Stapeley Grange, and a bequest to the RSPCA 'to establish an animal home and refuge with a clinic if they so desire at Stapeley Grange.' The proviso was that if the RSPCA was unable or unwilling to utilize the bequest in this way, the bequest should pass to another animal welfare charity. If that charity also refused the bequest on these terms, it would pass to a third and so on.

This bequest, although a great and much appreciated act of generosity, put the RSPCA in a difficult position. Once costings were obtained for planning permission, architects' fees and the alterations and rebuilding, etc. which would be necessary to convert the country house into an animal home, it was evident that these costs would run into millions of pounds. This was far in excess of the bequest without the further huge continuing commitment to running/staff costs. In the event, the RSPCA trustees decided to accept the bequest and the property is now complete and up and running as a wildlife/rescue centre and hospital with facilities for domestic animals as well. The gross cost of setting up the hospital was three times that of the original bequest and annual running costs are over £400,000 a year. This has proved a very large drain on RSPCA resources (see chapter 7 for exact costs). Stapeley Grange was opened in 1994 and is expected to deal with thousands of wild-animal casualties and hundreds of stray cats every year.

Another case again involved a lady who left the society a bequest 'provided the RSPCA takes care of any pets which may survive me for the rest of their natural lives.' The lady had left a dog but it was in a dreadful condition and terminally ill. Had the RSPCA accepted the bequest this would have been contrary to the society's animal-welfare policies, as the kindest thing to do was to have the animal humanely destroyed. It was suffering and its pain would only increase if it were allowed to live out its natural life.

The overall advice from many societies is for potential benefactors to talk through with administrators the implications and likely overall costs of carrying through a major project. The vast majority of charity officials, like those at the RSPCA, are courteous, helpful and aware that it is legacies that make much of the work possible.

Wording a will

Because it is difficult to predict exactly how much money will be available in a will years hence, many people leave a residuary legacy to charity, i.e. all or part of the money that is remaining after debts and other bequests have been paid. A pecuniary legacy is the gift of a fixed sum of money in a will and a specific bequest is the gift of a particular item in a will.

It is important to word carefully any specifications for commemoration in a will and it is worth getting your solicitor to show the draft of this clause especially early on in negotiations to the chosen charity. It is worth finding charities that are happy to accept reasonable conditions so long as there is room for flexibility; over time many more will realise that the offer of tangible commemoration is a way of securing funds in an increasingly competitive market for legacies.

The Royal National Lifeboat Institution has suggested wording in its legacies leaflet that does agree to a specific use of the money bequeathed and appropriate commemoration. This could perhaps form the basis for other named bequests, such as naming a building (see chapter 21 for sample costs).

Sample wording for the provision of a lifeboat
'I give tax-free to the Royal National Lifeboat Institution of West Quay Road, Poole, Dorset BH15 1HZ the sum of £ ... and I declare that the receipt of their Treasurer or other proper officer shall be a full and sufficient discharge. It is my wish without creating a binding trust that the RNLI use this gift for or towards the provision of a new lifeboat to be named ...'

Sample wording for requesting a commemorative plaque
'I give free of tax to the Royal National Lifeboat Institution of West Quay Road, Poole, Dorset BH15 1HZ the sum of £ ... and I declare that the receipt of their Treasurer or other proper officer shall be a full and sufficient discharge. It is my wish but without creating a binding trust that the RNLI provide a plaque or some other suitable commemoration to mark this bequest.'

How much do you need to leave for an endowment to be effective?

Edinburgh University suggested possible figures, based on 1995 prices, and although these may not apply to other institutions precisely, they do provide guidelines against which possible costs can be measured:

> The policy of the Edinburgh University Development Trust is to spend only the income of such gifts unless it is or has fallen to a level that would not allow the purpose of the gift to be achieved. In such circumstances, the capital would be used providing the terms of the gift do not prohibit its use.
>
> Gifts or legacies with continuing purposes are usually invested in one of the university's trusts, managed by professional fund managers. At 1995 rates, to provide an annual income of £8,000 for a postgraduate scholarship, an investment of £200,000 capital would

be required. It would be possible for an award of this kind to be made only where there is sufficient accumulated income e.g. once every three years.

Anthony Burns, executive director of CORDA, the heart research charity, estimates that a new hospital would cost up to £25 million to build and that £5 million would be necessary to fully endow a medical research chair unless costs were being shared by another body such as a university. However, some universities and medical establishments would be happy to name a chair for about £1.5 million. Of course, even a few thousand pounds can endow a modest prize in music or writing and arts boards can offer scope for personal interests to be reflected.

Personal charitable trusts

For donors with cash or assets worth £10,000 or more that they wish to give to charity, an alternative to personal negotiations is a personal charitable trust, arranged through the Charities Aid Foundation, itself a charity established to help the flow of money to other charities.

Sylvia Baig, trust manager of the Charities Aid Foundation comments:

> Generally memorials are set up by family and friends in memory of a recently departed person. However, there are a few people who set up Trusts or Foundations in their lifetime which act as a memorial to their lifetime's work. The advantage of setting them up during a lifetime is that they can ensure that the trust is used in accordance with their wishes and a pattern of grant-giving is established before they die.

If the donor feels insecure in releasing a lifetime gift because of possible unforeseen eventualities and financial commitments, he or she can set up a trust by the will to be administered by trustees. If this is to have the benefit of charitable status, it will have to be applied for via the Charity Commissioners.

However, a Charities Aid Foundation trust can be established by will. Relatives or friends can set up a trust fund in memory using either a similar CAF trust or a private charitable trust registered with the Charity Commission. A CAF trust is a simple way of establishing a memorial fund (see chapter 4 for other ways of setting up a memorial charity). People donating to the trust can use Gift Aid to make payments of £250 or more, if they have taxed income to cover the payments. A trust account with the Charities Aid Foundation usually involves nothing to set up, and operating it costs one per cent annually of the capital value as a contribution towards the foundation's overheads.

As well as a suitable method of setting up a memorial charity, it can be a simple way of making lifetime gifts to more than one charity. The trust account can be personalized with a person's name or a title of their choosing, so that the name of a loved one can be remembered. Money can then be given in his or her name and, where required, commemoration can be negotiated by the Charities Aid Foundation. The trust can be made for a specific number of years or a lifetime, with the residual capital being distributed on termination to a chosen charity. The trust can also be continued after death by a named relative and there can be up to three signatories for the named cheque book. The foundation (Mrs Sylvia Baig, Trust Manager, Private Charitable Trusts, Charities Aid Foundation, Kings Hill, West Malling, Kent ME19 4TA, Tel: 01732 520000) deals with all tax matters; it also deals with other forms of giving such as Gift Aid on a client's behalf.

Can you claim tax relief on the cost and upkeep of churchyard/crematorium memorials and in memoriam donations?

Tax relief is not available on private memorials and indeed VAT is payable when you initially purchase the stone. Although gifts for the maintenance etc. of churches are generally charitable, bequests for the upkeep of graves and tombs are only charitable if the grave or tomb concerned forms part of the fabric of the church, which is very rare in modern times. The upkeep of a cemetery as a whole may be charitable but not that of the individual graves in it.

If a family member wishes to buy a headstone, this would not normally be a charitable gift. A donation to charity in lieu of flowers or a donation to a charity in memory of endowing, for example, a hospice bed in memory of a relation, would be charitable but not because of the association with the deceased. It would be charitable exactly in the same way as money put in a collection tin. The charitable status of a gift is related to the purpose of the gift rather than to the reason why it is being given.

Expatriates and charities

Those living abroad permanently can leave money to British charities but their bequests may be subject to tax in their country of residence, as many countries do not allow inheritance tax relief on charitable bequests. This would not apply to someone working abroad temporarily who has voting rights in this country.

Quite a few countries avoid the complexities of the charity concept by using a category of 'non-profit making organizations' that includes charities, pressure groups, sports clubs, etc. Tax and other concessions may not be as generous as those available to charities in the UK. Equally, many international charities providing aid abroad are registered with the Charity Commissioners in this country and as such are exempt from inheritance tax. If a foreign charity is not recognized in this country – those listed in this book are unless stated otherwise – money can be left to it, but there would be no relief from inheritance tax. In practice, money can be bequeathed to any cause anywhere in the world.

3 Choosing and Buying a Private Memorial

Who will supply a memorial?

Memorials in cemeteries, churchyards and crematoriums are usually arranged through a funeral director. It can be quite daunting for some people to telephone round and negotiate prices with a stone-mason at a time of stress, but at a funeral parlour a family can discuss different memorials in comfort, with a familiar member of staff who helped with the initial arrangements. The total price of a particular memorial will include all necessary permits (each diocese and local authority, even individual crematoriums, have their own regulations about memorials). Some funeral directors do not charge directly for arranging a memorial but the headstone costs naturally tend to reflect this extra work. This should be clarified early on. Even if you are not using a funeral director for the main ceremony, it is often possible to get one to arrange a memorial, although in such a case the memorial would probably need to be prepaid.

Dealing directly with the stone-mason can lower costs and may make it easier to arrange an individualized memorial. However, a funeral director will undertake negotiations about personal touches to a headstone with the stone-mason on a client's behalf. It is not true that modern headstones are all mass produced and many stone-masons of quality will offer personalized memorials for little more cost than those in a funeral director's catalogue.

When should you arrange a memorial?

Some people prefer to discuss memorials before the funeral and in some cemeteries the kind of grave purchased can affect the kind of memorial that can be erected at a later date. Some crematoriums have quite a stringent memorial system and any memorials must be purchased from the crematorium. In such a case there is usually a wide choice, but the range on offer needs to be considered before the crematorium option is taken, if a non-standardized memorial is important to the family of the deceased. A local funeral director can discuss this in an informed way. However, if you are satisfied with the range of options at a crematorium, there is no need to rush into a decision. Cremated remains may often be held at the crematorium for a period of three months to allow time for reflection on the most appropriate form of placing the ashes and the kind of memorial preferred.

Since the ground in a churchyard or cemetery needs about six months to settle, there is no urgency in ordering a memorial, although some graves of the lawn type, where there is a fixed plinth for the memorials, can have a memorial earlier. Obviously the time gap does not apply in a crematorium unless remains are buried. Memorials can be arranged and installed in about six weeks, sometimes less, although they can take much longer, up to a year where an artist or craftsperson is creating a memorial. This again is a subject to discuss before an agreement is made as a slower job does not necessarily reflect a more craftsmanlike product; and if a firm claims to be so busy that it can give no dates of estimated delivery, it may be that the owners are taking on too much work.

Making your choice

Insist on courtesy and lack of pressure in deciding what may be a major purchase of £1,000 or more. Among stone-masons and funeral directors there can be one or two who make clients feel uncomfortable and this should not be accepted. The majority will take infinite trouble and not demand fast decisions. The firms I have used as examples in this chapter are very client-friendly, courteous and generous with their time to clients.

If money is a real consideration, shop around, for even memorial masons in the same area do vary in price. It is not always a question of getting what you pay for. Sometimes a newer firm may be owned by someone trained in traditional ways but with a flexibility and creativity that an established firm with higher overheads and more lavish premises may lack.

However, it is important, if you are shopping around, to visit the stone-mason and look for one who has a variety of memorial forms and does not push you towards the highest in cost. Equally, at a funeral parlour, ask if the firm deals with stone-masons other than the one featured in the main catalogue and compare designs and prices. Although London and the South East are traditionally more expensive, certainly in terms of cemetery and funeral costs, a backwater with only one stone-mason may have artificially high prices. In such a case, use Yellow Pages to ring round a wider area and you may find that a mason even fifty or more miles away regularly visits your area and may offer not only better prices but also more choice.

As well as personal preferences in memorial type, the burial ground will have its own regulations about type of material, size and inscription. Churchyards tend to be more specific about the type of stone used and some will not permit black, shiny materials if they are not in keeping with the church and churchyard, or allow familiar inscriptions, such as 'Dad' or 'Nan'. The final decision rests with the vicar, who is answerable to his diocesan office.

It is recommended that people making a will containing stipulations about their funerals and subsequent memorialization seek the advice of their local cemetery and crematorium department or funeral director in order to ascertain that their proposals are possible.

Costs of permits

Churchyards

Apart from the cost of a headstone, there are fees for erecting a memorial in a churchyard that are set nationally by the Church Commissioners, as are burial fees. The costs from 1 January 1995 for a permit to erect a memorial on a grave in a churchyard are as follows: a monument of a small cross of wood – £10; a small vase (12" by 8" by 8") – £21; a tablet (21" by 21") erected either horizontally or vertically – £37; any other headstone or memorial larger than 21" by 21" – £85. There are no restrictions as to who can be buried in a Church of England churchyard, unlike weddings and funerals where church membership may be a requirement. In Catholic churchyards either the deceased, or his or her spouse, must be a Catholic. The sole requirement for burial in a C. of E. churchyard is that the deceased lived within the parish. In practice it is very difficult to be buried in a church of choice outside the actual parish, as space is far more limited, but where it is permitted then the price will usually be doubled. A plot in a churchyard can be bought at the vicar's discretion for a set period usually between fifty and seventy years. A fee of £20 is payable for extra inscriptions to be added to an existing headstone in a churchyard.

Cemetery costs for headstones

Cemeteries charge non-residents more not only for burial but also to erect a memorial, sometimes twice the fees charged to residents of a borough (see examples below for details of sample costs). The costs of a headstone vary and it is possible, although not necessary, to pay well over £1,000 for a quality product. A traditional, inscribed headstone including fitting and permits would be around £700+. It would be difficult to buy, inscribe and fit even a small headstone in any area for much under £400. Some cemeteries and churchyards do permit a memorial vase, which could cost as little as £150. If you have little money a simple wooden cross can be placed in most churchyards as a memorial.

A sarcophagus, a box-type stone, costs £2,000–£2,500. Some churchyards still accept this traditional design as do cemeteries. Very large memorials, such as the kind often found at grander cemeteries, i.e. Brookwood Cemetery near Woking, are even more expensive; an area 12' by 15' might cost upwards of £8,000 for a single burial. An elaborate memorial built to personal specifications could cost £20,000 or more.

Crematorium memorials

Whereas a headstone tends to be a once-and-for-all purchase, apart from any optional restoration costs at a later date, crematorium memorials do not generally last for more than a set number of years, sometimes as little as six, and payment must be made for renewal after this period, which family members may be unable or unwilling to do.

However, an entry in the book of remembrance is invariably permanent and the burial of cremated remains within a special area of the crematorium grounds does also offer more permanence. For example, a commemorative double wall plaque might cost £240 for six years and a steel plaque on a commemorative bench would be £508 for a six-year period of dedication. The cost of most crematorium memorials is not increased by having to obtain a permit and renewal fees are usually lower than the original fee.

Getting help with costs of a memorial

While the Department of Social Security will pay for a basic funeral for those who are on benefit and cannot afford to pay, it will not contribute towards the cost of a memorial.

Advance payments

It is possible to order a headstone many years in advance at current prices, although this is a service which you would need to negotiate directly with a stone-mason. Some will store headstones free of charge and the only cost will be for the final inscription, which at 1990s prices would be no more than £20–£30. The advantage of prepayment is that you can choose your own headstone and save family or friends the expense. It is also possible to pay in advance for a headstone as part of a prepaid funeral plan (see end of chapter for details).

However, it may be that if you do buy a headstone when you are relatively young, by the time you die your own ideas may have changed, circumstances may be different or a particular churchyard for which it is intended may have closed or its regulations altered.

In the case of woodland burials, full payment can sometimes be made beforehand and a chosen plot reserved for about £500, which includes the price of a memorial tree. The fifty-year or sometimes seventy-five-year deed would run from the date of burial. This is suitable for clients who are alone, with no near relatives, who wish to know everything will be taken care of exactly according to their wishes. Husbands or wives may wish to arrange everything in advance so that their loved ones are spared an additional worry. A visit to choose a plot is usually welcomed and it would be possible to request a certain type of tree.

Insuring your headstone

There is an insurance policy called StoneGuard that many stone-masons and funeral directors can arrange, where for a premium of from £15 for five years a headstone or monument can be insured against damage from many causes, including storms, falling trees, theft and vandalism. New and existing memorials can be covered (see end of chapter for costs). This is well worth the expense in view of the rising problems with vandalism in cemeteries and churchyards even in rural areas.

Alternative graveside memorials

There has been a sharp rise in the popularity of natural or

woodland burials in a nature reserve burial ground, run by a farmer, local authority or wildlife trust, where a tree is planted as a memorial instead of a formal headstone. This costs from £250 upwards. The tree is placed on or close to a grave, sometimes with wild-flower bulbs, and the price is almost always included in the cost of the plot, making it cheaper than a headstone.

Another advantage is that where most graves are leased for fifty years, woodland burials on nature reserves, although not woodland graves in local authority cemeteries or on private land, tend to be protected almost indefinitely. By law cemeteries cannot sell an individual the right to have a grave protected forever, although in practice it would be unlikely that a memorial would be removed after fifty years, especially in a churchyard of a church that continued in use. The tree is placed on the grave within a year of the burial and often much sooner if placed at the grave head. The settings tend to be more aesthetically pleasing than some newer cemeteries.

However there are disadvantages; once a wood has grown up, the exact spot can be hard to locate even though some do have markers near the tree and a location map. The woodland itself becomes the memorial, which can be difficult if you want a lasting personalized memorial.

Other memorials

It is not as difficult as might be imagined to obtain a personalized memorial that is not intended for a churchyard. Some stone-masons can offer alternative forms of memorial, perhaps to stand as a garden memorial or on a patio or, if accepted by the local planning authority, in a nearby beauty spot or favourite park.

A small fountain made from Portland stone to be put in a garden, perhaps in a favourite spot, could be as little as £300. A statue about three feet high in stone could be created to the client's specification and inscribed for about £800, while a bench in Portland stone would cost less than £1,000. If a particular stone-mason does not offer alternative memorials, try others who will almost certainly oblige. Like a headstone, a garden memorial is a major purchase and should not be rushed or dismissed as impractical. Andy Raitt of Stonecrest Memorial Masons, who offers a range of alternative personalized memorials, says that in practice it is possible to make anything, even standing stones, if you can get planning permission.

For materials that are not necessarily stone, Harriet Frazer of Memorials by Artists in Suffolk encourages the creation of personalized memorials for other kinds of settings, such as house or garden memorials from a variety of materials, for example a single ceramic memorial tile, a pane of stained or engraved glass, a wooden bench, a sculpture, a fountain, a sundial or some object in silver.

Useful contacts and examples of services

Advance payment

Chosen Heritage, Customer Information Supervisor, Funeral Plans Limited, Farringdon House, Wood Street, East Grinstead, W. Sussex RH19 1EW. Tel.: Freephone 0800 525555 or 01342 312266
Chosen Heritage offers a plan whereby people can pay in advance for their funeral either as a lump sum or up to sixty monthly instalments.

It is also possible to pay in advance for memorials through Chosen Heritage. This may be helpful if a person has no close relatives to erect a headstone at a future time. The money would be put into the general trust fund as part of additional costs and would be index linked, as other expenses such as cemetery costs are, to ensure there would be sufficient funds for the chosen kind of headstone. A local funeral director or stone-mason could supply current costs at the time of applying for the scheme. If a person then wished at a future time to have a more elaborate memorial stone than the one originally chosen, additional money could be paid to Chosen Heritage at any time to make up the difference.

Cemeteries

Lewisham Cemeteries, Julie Dunk, Assistant Head of Cemeteries and Crematorium Services, Verdant Lane, London SE6 1TP. Tel.: 0181 697 2555
While prices reflect the cost of living in the South East, they are fairly representative of the costs and services in local authority cemeteries generally. The Cemeteries and Crematorium Services of the London Borough of Lewisham are responsible for the administration and management of the crematorium and four cemeteries, two of which are still in frequent use. The administrators wish to offer as wide a range of memorials as possible and so offer a choice of grave space within the cemeteries.

The service is efficient and comprehensive.

Graves in full memorial sections can accommodate headstones and kerbsets or landings over the grave space, as well as sundry grave furniture, such as vases and plaques. There are restrictions on the dimensions of memorials and the way they are fixed and they must be made of natural stone. Graves in lawn sections can only accommodate a headstone, although the space at the head of the grave may be planted with garden-type plants.

A recent request for the erection of a mausoleum was declined as it was felt that its security could not be guaranteed because of possible vandalism in the cemeteries.

Private grave

Buying a private grave ensures a more lasting memorial. The cost varies according to the type selected, which affects the kind of permitted memorial, and whether the purchaser was a resident of the borough or lived outside its boundaries. Burial in full memorial sections costs £395–£448 for residents, according to whether it is a border plot, and £1,580–£1,792 for a non-resident. These fees are for the purchase of exclusive rights of burial for a period of fifty years. Lawn memorials vary from £288–£341 for residents to £1,152–£1,364 for non-residents of the borough.

Public grave

The only fee for the burial is the grave preparation fee which is free for children under two years of age and £166 for residents. Cremated remains may be buried in both public and private graves for £56 regardless of residency.

Memorials

Subsequent to burial, memorials may be placed on a grave subject to permission from the grave owner. Masons must submit an application to the cemetery office, detailing the type of memorial, the dimensions, the method of fixing and the proposed inscription. The only restriction imposed on the inscription is that it must not be offensive to anyone, i.e. swear-words or overtly racist or sacrilegious comments would not be allowed. The use of nicknames or 'Dad' instead of 'Father' are permitted.

The cost of a permit to allow the erection of a memorial varies according to the type of memorial and the residence of the grave owner. Fees for the lawn section (headstone only) are £44 for residents and £176 for non-residents.

In the full memorial section, a headstone will cost only £44 for

residents and £176 for non-residents for a permit. A headstone and
other memorials, such as vases, will cost £75 for residents and £300
for non-residents. A permit to erect a full kerb plus headstone and
other memorials costs £138 for residents and £552 for
non-residents. Additional inscriptions to an existing headstone
cost £17 for residents and £64 for non-residents.

Memorials on public graves

The only memorials allowed on public graves are small tablets
placed flat on the ground, which may only remain in place for
fifteen years from the date of burial. There is no fee for placing
such a memorial but an application must still be made.

Erecting a memorial

For graves in full memorial sections, it is recommended that a year
is left following the burial before a memorial is erected to allow for
settling of the soil. Temporary memorials may be placed on the
grave following burial, either in the form of a wooden cross or a
specially designed small marker, sold through the cemetery office
at a price of £45. Memorials in lawn sections may be placed
immediately following burial as they are fixed on a concrete beam
which sits in undisturbed ground at the head of the grave.

Memorials in crematoriums

Lewisham Crematorium, The Crematorium Counsellor, Verdant Lane, London SE6 1TP. Tel.: 0181 698 4955

The costs and services reflect those of local authority
crematoriums generally. The crematorium offers a wide range of
memorials, all of which are obtainable only through the
crematorium office. A very tasteful illustrated brochure explains
the options for memorials and also the arrangements for a service
and music. In addition every summer, on the first Sunday in July,
an annual service of remembrance is held at the crematorium.

Prices are effective from April 1 1995, including VAT where
applicable. There is a crematorium counsellor to offer advice,
although funeral directors will arrange memorials if requested.

The book of remembrance: this is located off the cloister. It is open
at the page for the day, although a particular entry may be viewed
on request. An entry is a permanent memorial.

The volumes of hand-bound vellum are made by craftsmen and
lettered and tooled in gold. The inscriptions and motifs are written
and illuminated in medieval style. Emblems and badges are hand
drawn and coloured individually by artists. Entries can be made

under the day of death or some other anniversary and names can be added at any time after death. Emblems and badges can be set with five or eight line entries. There is a maximum of forty letters and spaces per line.

A permanent entry costs from £30 for two to eight lines and a coat of arms is £130.

Roses: there are both standard roses and rose bushes available for a dedication period and the crematorium counsellor can advise about the different colours and types. A six-year dedication, with the name and date of death on a name-plate is £140 for a standard rose and £128 for a rose bush. An additional name-plate can be added for £18.

Wall tablets: these are placed in the cloister overlooking the floral tribute area and are engraved commemorative plaques on the wall. A six-year single dedication costs £120 for a maximum of sixty letters over four lines. A double plaque costs £240, giving 120 letters over eight lines.

Kerb tablets: these are situated along the paths and it is often possible to have an engraved tablet close to the spot where a loved one's ashes were strewn, ensuring that family and friends can return to the exact spot on days of significance. A ten-year dedication, giving a maximum of seventy letters costs £138 and a replacement can be made for £30 once the period has expired.

The garden of remembrance: these informal gardens, like the rest of the crematorium, have become an oasis for wildlife and ashes can be strewn here.

Memorial seats: these are situated in specific places throughout the garden of remembrance. The option of dedicating either the whole or a one-third share of a seat includes the provision of a stainless-steel name-plate bearing the name of the person to whom the seat is dedicated plus two lines of verse. For six years' dedication, including the name-plate, a whole seat costs £508 and a third share £170.

Burial of cremated remains: this offers a specific place where family can be close to their loved one's remains. It consists of a granite stone in a choice of colours, engraved and lettered in gold. The memorial provides for up to four burial spaces and a flower-holder has been designed into the memorial. The dedication fee includes the cost of the stone, the first burial and engraving with the name of a loved one and his or her dates. A longer inscription can be provided if required (ask the crematorium counsellor for further details). The overall fee for exclusive rights of burial for twenty-five years, a permit for the erection of the memorial, a granite memorial stone, inscription of name and dates and digging fee, is £561.70, of which £298.45 is for the granite memorial stone. This stone can hold up to four names and dates. This fee is for residents of Lewisham Borough. Those who live outside pay an excess of £249 for exclusive rights of burial, making a total of £810.70.

Funeral directors

Contact Frances Lowe, Twymans Funeral Directors and Monumental Masons, Avenue Road, Freshwater, Isle of Wight PO40 9UU. Tel.: 01983 752169
Twymans are a typical example of a high-standard funeral director and the services offered in the field of memorials. This is a tasteful, warm and friendly establishment where the wishes and care of clients are paramount; if someone felt uncertain about choosing a formal private memorial, he or she would be eased and advised through the process without the necessity to make telephone calls or extra visits to stone-masons. There is no pressure towards high-cost memorials. Indeed the emphasis is on finding something affordable, such as a small vase. Twymans offer beautiful vases for £247 in marble and £292 in stone materials. There is help with writing an inscription if needed.

A simple basic upright headstone from their funeral parlour catalogue costs from £700+ for grey or white marble and about £800+ for stone materials. The cost for arrangements is reflected in the memorial price. A book with an angel would cost from £1,210 for grey or white marble and from £1,410 for stone materials. An elaborate double stone with a surround enclosing a vase in marble would cost from £2,100 and £2,220 for granite. There are many beautiful designs on offer, such as a Madonna beneath an arch, a headstone in the shape of a heart, a Celtic cross for £1,300 in marble and £1,560 in stone, an open book and several stones with gold engraving of leaves, flowers, angels or a Madonna etched on the headstone. Individualized touches can be arranged.

The costs of headstones include the inscriptions and VAT, although letters that are gilded or lead filled cost £35 extra in total.

Home memorials

Yvonne Malik, Sweet Briar Cottage, 52 Hornby Road,
Wray, Lancs., LA2 8QN. Tel.: 01524221767
Yvonne Malik created the idea of memorial boxes as a tool for
reminiscence. They quickly developed into memorial boxes to
help bereaved families and individuals.

Yvonne said: 'Headstones stay in the cemetery, flowers soon
wither. How necessary then to look for an activity that runs in
tandem with the traditional services of the funeral director, which
has both private and intimate meaning and is something which can
be done by ourselves. Filling something like a memorial box either
before the funeral or at the church or crematorium can be a shared
activity without the necessity of religious overtones. Friends and
relations could feel free to place something in the box such as a
small memento, photograph, poem, etc., which would afterwards
be taken home and kept as a memorial by those closest to the
deceased. The contents would be a personal ritual and focal point
which we can carry out ourselves. The memorial box offers a
continuing shared and easily accessible unique memorial.'

The memorial box can be marked with the name and dates of
the deceased. Contact Yvonne for further information on
memorial boxes and details of the workshops she holds on the
subject at her cottage in Wray, Lancashire. Yvonne also paints
designs on coffins and can be contacted for commissions on
individual memorials.

Individualized memorials

Memorials by Artists, Harriet Frazer, Snape Priory,
Saxmundham, Suffolk IP17 1SA. Tel.: 01728 688934
Memorials by Artists is not for those who want an instant
memorial but is ideal for those wishing to be closely involved in its
creation. Although very fairly priced, the company will match a
client to a suitable artist or craftsperson and so must charge over
and above standard memorialization. Harriet Frazer set up
Memorials by Artists after her own difficult search to find a
suitable memorial for her stepdaughter Sophie in 1985. Since then
she has built up a nationwide register of quality artists,
letter-cutters and craftspersons in Britain and Ireland, who do not
charge much more for a personalized, hand-crafted memorial than
you will pay for a modern mass-produced headstone.

Harriet provides an illustrated booklet, containing many
photographs of a range of well-designed contemporary

headstones, plaques and tablets as well as memorials in other media. There are articles on memorial design, choosing stone, epitaphs, the cleaning of memorials and advice on commissioning a memorial; these make useful reading for anyone planning a memorial for a loved one. The booklet costs £5 including postage and packing. Alternatively, telephone for a free leaflet and more information.

Harriet will talk first to a potential client about the kind of memorial he or she would like and any ideas for designs and inscriptions. Initial arrangements for a memorial can be made by letter or telephone and visits to Snape Priory are always welcomed. Harriet Frazer will discuss a client's suggestions with a suitable artist and the client will be given his or her address so that a meeting or detailed discussion can be arranged. The design becomes an interaction of the client's ideas and the artist's vision. Many artists like to know about the person whose memorial he or she is designing and perhaps have a photograph, so that the memorial will be appropriate not only for its setting but also for the person in whose memory it will stand. Because the rules for memorials in churchyards and cemeteries vary between dioceses and local authorities, Memorials by Artists will apply for these rules at the beginning of the commission and normally obtain necessary permission.

The time period from discussing a possible memorial to its fixing in the chosen place can last from four months to more than a year. The memorial will be placed either by the artist or through Memorials by Artists. The costs of headstones begin from £1,000 (1993 prices) including delivery, fixing and the Memorials by Artists fee. However, if less money is available, Harriet says that Memorials by Artists will do its best to help.

Insurance of headstones

StoneGuard Insurance Cover, Bridge Insurance Brokers (Manchester) Ltd, Indemnity House, Chatham Street, Manchester M1 3AY. Tel.: 0161 2366969
StoneGuard Insurance is a special insurance scheme, usually arranged through the stone-mason providing the memorial, covering the full value of replacing or repairing a headstone or monument and third party liability up to £2 million. It can also be arranged direct. The policy lasts for five years and can be renewed each successive period of five years for as long as is required. The memorial stone is index-linked at five per cent per annum. It covers all risks, accidental and malicious, apart from damage by

normal weathering and subsidence.

Insurance for headstones was, at 1995 prices, from £3 per annum on a renewable five-year term for a headstone of current value of up to £300. A headstone worth between £750 and £1,000 would be £50 for the five-year period. A stone worth £1,251–£1,500 would be £75 for the period, while stones of over £1,500 can be insured for five per cent of their value to cover the same period. Damage cover includes falling trees, storm damage, lawnmower impact, a stolen plaque or statue, vandalism or graffiti. Established headstones and monuments can be insured provided that prices are based on the current replacement value. The scheme is approved by the National Association of Memorial Masons.

Memorial Plaques

These are examples of quality suppliers who can provide brass memorial plaques both for private usage and for memorial benches etc.

Falon Nameplates, Kenneth and Fiona More, Units 10–12 Stephenson Court, Barrington Industrial Estate, Bedlington, Northumberland NE22 7DQ. Tel.: 01670 530136
A family-owned firm, Falon Nameplates have been trading for over forty years and specialize in cast-bronze memorials, for humans and animals. They are happy to supply memorial plaques for private individuals and will take orders from anywhere in the world. They also work in cast aluminium, engraved wood, Perspex, plastic, metals and plastic 'mock stone'. Quotations are available on request and their prices for cast-bronze memorials start at £20 plus VAT and postage. The most expensive memorial they have so far created cost £1,800 and they can create individual designs as simple or complex as required and in any language. For this reason orders should be written or faxed (01670 530102).

Sula Products, Peter Brining, 41 High Street, Cowes, Isle of Wight, P031 7RS. Tel./fax: 01983 295750
Peter has been running this firm for nineteen years and uses traditional craftsmanship. He offers good old-fashioned service. A small black plastic memorial plaque for a simple wooden cross, perhaps faced with gilt alum, or a plaque with a simple message such as 'In Loving Memory' and the dates the person was born and died, would cost about £13. The same in brass would be about double the price but the letters are engraved in the brass to last

forever. A larger memorial plaque on a bigger memorial, built specially to commemorate an organization or special individual, would cost between £40 and £90. Peter Brining also engraves on slate and in this case will work on a client's own materials or artefacts.

Orders can be taken from all over Britain and indeed the world. Orders from abroad should be paid in sterling or by banker's draft. He is happy to accept orders from anywhere in the world and only needs a rough draft of the dedication. Peter suggests that potential customers phone or fax him for specific prices and details of methods and materials.

Stone-masons

Stonecrest Monumental Masons, Andrew Raitt and Peter Smith, Mead Lane, West Street, Farnham, Surrey GU9 7DY. Tel.: 01252 717750

These stone-masons typify reasonably priced and high-quality memorial masons in Britain. They are relatively young but full of enthusiasm for their work and are highly adaptable as well as experienced in all forms of stone-masonry. Their area covers Surrey, Buckinghamshire, Hampshire and the Isle of Wight but they will make monuments anywhere, although in this case travel costs will be incurred. The stone-masons can be contacted through a funeral director, but they also accept commissions directly and will arrange permits with the local vicar in the chosen area and make sure that the chosen stone fits with the specifications of the cemetery or churchyard. For this service they make no charge. Visits to their premises are very welcome.

The firm offers personalized memorials; for example, a three-foot-high simple headstone, engraved with a deer for someone who loved the countryside, might cost as little as £500–600 in stone direct from Stonecrest. They point out that while some people may want an artist to design a memorial, a firm such as Stonecrest can produce fine lettering and carving in a much shorter time and for less cost.

The stone-masons are happy to add personal details or symbols very reasonably. For example, a keen sports fan had a footballer engraved and a cricketer who collapsed and died on the pitch had a memorial depicting a cricketer. A thirteen-year-old guitarist's memorial was engraved with a replica of his guitar, carved from a photograph, then painted red and white with a single golden note. The family sent a picture of the guitar and an exact replica was carved. Andrew Raitt says that he finds such work rewarding and might charge as little as £40 for such an addition. He states that their stones are not mass produced but are individually made, and they will make absolutely any memorial.

Inscriptions cost from £1.20 per letter in black enamel to £1.40 per letter in 23- or 24-carat gold-leaf. The firm can arrange for a picture of the deceased to be included in the memorial. A photograph, about 8″ by 10″, is baked on ceramic in Italy and can be attached to the headstone – this costs about £80.

Woodland memorials

This section contains several examples, since the idea of a memorial burial tree is relatively new and information is hard to find.

The Natural Death Centre has information available on several forms of natural burial and simple memorials. A regularly updated information pack covering inexpensive green, family-organized funerals with trees as memorials is available for six first-class stamps from the Natural Death Centre. Contact Nicholas Albery, Director of the Natural Death Centre, 20 Heber Road, London NW2 6AA. Tel.: 0181 208 2853. Specific woodland sites include:

Carlisle Cemetery
Ken West, Bereavement Services, Cemetery Office, Richardson Street, Carlisle, Cumbria CA2 6AL. Tel.: 01228 25022.
The approach is very friendly and helpful and out-of-area burials are possible.

The first green burial ground in the UK was established within the local authority cemetery at Carlisle, set on a peaceful site looking towards the river. Memorials in the conventional sections incur a fee for registering the memorial, checking the inscription and ensuring the stone is placed on the correct grave. This fee does not apply to woodland burials. There is also a fee of £176 which gives right of burial for fifty years. Only these private graves can have memorials placed on them.

There are three kinds of grave on offer and the kind chosen will affect the memorial to be erected. The lawn grave allows for any kind of memorial to be placed at the head, up to three feet in height. The rest of the grave is turfed and mown regularly. On a traditional grave, a memorial must cover the grave and this can be of any height, material and design. Ideally the cemetery authorities would like to see more memorials in wood, since these are biodegradable. In these first two types, a headstone will need to be obtained from either the funeral director or memorial mason.

The woodland grave involves the same cost of right of burial but, in this case, a tree will be provided in the cost of the grave. The burial ground is seen as a living memorial to future generations. Two family members can be buried side by side. After the first burial a very small oak tree is set at the head of the grave and 200 bluebell bulbs planted on the grave as a memorial. The woodland graves are carefully recorded on plan, each grave being individually numbered.

Each grave number, cast in metal, is set on a concrete block and placed a few inches below ground on each grave. This is to ensure that graves can always be identified as trees grow. Since the grave area needs to be protected from disturbance during growth, traditional granite plaques can be placed as memorials on the adjacent wall. Alternatively, an entry can be made in the book of remembrance in the nearby crematorium (apply for details). It will take ten to fifteen years to transform the field into an oak wood. Because trees are planted, people are encouraged to use a biodegradable coffin that is sold by the cemetery. Oak trees are planted because the area was originally ancient oak woodland. Prices are £176 for woodland burial including memorial tree and flowers.

Corstophine Hill Woodland Burial Ground in Edinburgh, Scotland

This woodland burial ground, the first in Scotland, was opened in November 1995 by the Edinburgh District Council at Corstorphine Hill crematorium. The cost is £200 for residents and non-residents alike. There is room for 500 graves. Silver-birch trees will be planted along with bluebells and wild flowers. Contact George Bell, Bereavement Services Manager, Morton Hall Crematorium, Howden Hall Road, Edinburgh EH16 61X. Tel.: 0131 225 2424.

Greenhaven Woodland Burial Ground Ltd at New Clarks Farm, near Rugby

This is a two-acre site, just off Junction 18 of the M1. The plot fee is £200 if reserved in advance, £250 for normal plot fee. Wild flowers, such as bluebells, anemones, wild daffodils and primroses may be bought at small cost and planted on the grave. Families are welcome to picnic on the site which will become a wildlife habitat.

Initially the graves are reserved for seventy-five years but eventually they will be protected in perpetuity when the ownership passes to a wildlife trust. The costs include a choice of tree planted on each site at no extra charge, including alder, ash, crab-apple, silver birch, hazel and rowan. The trees are those native to Northamptonshire. Contact Christine Atkin and

Nicholas Hargreaves, Yelvertoft Road, Lilbourne, Rugby, Warwicks CV23 0SZ. Tel.: 01788 860604.

Hinton Park Woodland Burial Ground Trust

Mike Hedger, Hinton House, Hinton, Christchurch, Dorset BH23 7EA. Tel.: 01425 273640. This is an environmentally friendly burial place in a meadow that will become a woodland. All forms of faith may use the burial ground. Plots can be consecrated if that is the wish of the loved one or family. Families who wish to do everything themselves will be welcome to do so. The trust keeps a register of the people buried at Hinton Park Woodland.

A plot may be reserved on payment of £300. A deed of ownership for fifty years will be forwarded. In all cases this period begins from the time of burial. This method assures the applicant that he or she will be buried at Hinton. A visit to choose a plot is welcomed. Full payment can be made beforehand for the fee of £500. The trust does intend to provide seats though these will not be memorial seats. Neither will there be sculptures – just a woodland. There will be no form of memorial other than a native English tree. The provision of the tree and the planting in the next season of planting will be carried out by trained staff and is included in the original fee. Gradually a wood will extend across the burial ground, although some plots will be left as grass. Wild flowers such as cowslips, primroses, bluebells, cornflowers and foxgloves may be planted and cutting the grass will be left to the discretion of the staff.

Each plot will be marked with a cast letter and numbered metal plate that will be placed at the foot of each plot. Where the tree has a stake, the number will be repeated on the stake. A careful drawing of the whole site will be kept at the office of the woodland burial ground and a complete reference of the numbers and the names of those buried will be kept and made available to visitors and relations.

Since transport costs for the deceased within a twenty-five-mile radius are included, the burial ground is suitable for those of limited means in Hampshire or Dorset, or for those from further afield who are prepared to pay the costs of extra transportation.

Oakfield Wood Memorial Burials at Manningtree, Essex

A farmer who manages a seven-acre burial ground overlooking the River Stour has given ownership of the land to the Essex Wildlife Trust. It costs £259 per grave including digging, tree and wooden plaque. Children under ten are buried with no charge. Contact the agent for the site, Peter Kincald, 256 High Street, Dovercourt, Essex CO12 3PA. Tel.: 01255 503456.

Stapenhill Woodland Burial Ground, Stapenhill Cemetery,
Burton upon Trent, Staffordshire

This local-authority woodland burial area is sited within Stapenhill Cemetery in a quiet spot, looking down the hillside, where there are many old trees. There is a choice of native trees as memorials, including ash, oak, cherry, hazel and birch, and the graves will also be planted with bulbs. The cost of a grave, including digging, is £850 for local residents, but double for outsiders. Contact Pauline Smith, 38 Stapenhill Road, Stapenhill, Burton upon Trent, Staffs., DE15 9AE. Tel.: 01283 508572.

4   Memorial Charities

When a loved one, especially a child, dies from an illness that has a high mortality rate, relations or close friends of the family may decide to start a charitable fund in the name of the deceased, aimed at helping towards research into the disease and the care of other sufferers. Dr David Flavell, honorary director of Leukaemia Busters, a children's leukaemia research charity based in Southampton that was inspired by the death of his own son Simon, sees such an aim as entirely positive (see chapter 8 for details of the charity's work): 'It is the motivation provided by personal difficulty and tragedy that makes possible change in a positive direction,' he says. 'The creation of Leukaemia Busters and the work it does is just one example of this.'

The Ben Hardwick Memorial Fund for Liver Transplants in Children, the Anthony Nolan Bone Marrow Trust and the Malcolm Sargent Cancer Fund for Children are three other memorial charities that have succeeded in perpetuating the name of a sufferer while helping others.

The Malcolm Sargent Cancer Fund was set up in 1967 as a lasting and practical memorial to the conductor Sir Malcolm Sargent, who died that year. He became known internationally, particularly in the choral field, where he was called 'the Ambassador with the Baton'. The fund was started through the enthusiasm of the Promenaders who were determined that his name would live on (see chapter 8). The Malcolm Sargent Fund had a sufficiently high profile to attract donations from music lovers all over the world, but fame is not necessary to succeed with such a project. An ordinary parent or spouse can, given determination, move mountains.

The stories of the success of two such memorial charities may offer pointers and encouragement to other ordinary men and women who may wish to establish such funds but are daunted by the idea. Anthony's and Ben's funds were started by mothers who were desperate to save their children's lives by any means and who continued the work after their children's deaths.

The Anthony Nolan Bone Marrow Trust manages the world's first and largest fully independent register of bone marrow donors. It was set up in 1974 by Shirley Nolan to try to save her son's life by establishing a register of unrelated bone marrow donors. Anthony was born in 1971 suffering from Wiscott-Aldrich syndrome, a rare bone marrow disease which left his immune system unable to fight infection. It was diagnosed as incurable. In 1973, the first successful bone marrow transplant using an unrelated donor was performed, and Anthony's mother realized that he had a chance of life if a matching donor could be found. She brought her son to London and the search for a suitable donor began. However, Shirley discovered that there was no major donor register and no facilities for establishing one. She began her appeal for bone marrow donors in 1974, realizing that thousands needed to be found because of the high odds against matching donor and patient.

Anthony was a patient at Westminster Children's Hospital, where Shirley met Dr David James, a consultant pathologist who was responsible for the existing, very limited donor testing programme for bone marrow transplants. He was eager to increase the volume of tests. However, he told Shirley that a major problem would be the funding of the tests needed to match the tissues. A laboratory technician working full-time could manage only five of the complex tests each day and, in 1974, £3,000 per year was needed to fund such a role. Shirley vowed to raise the money for a technician and to establish a voluntary register of donors. Her local paper in Thanet first published her story and offers of help came, among others, from the Round Tables of Ramsgate, Margate and Broadstairs. They began fund-raising and established the first donor clinic at Margate Hospital. Television helped to publicize Anthony's story and several stars from the world of entertainment offered their support.

The money was found for a technician and a small space in the basement of Westminster Hospital with a large broom cupboard served as an office. Dr James, a technician and Shirley started the first register of volunteer bone marrow donors from there. By 1978, six people were working on the register but the accommodation was proving increasingly awkward. No government grant was available and many bureaucrats and members of the medical profession saw little value in the project. In 1979, Anthony died before a successful match could be found. Shirley vowed that, if it was humanly possible, no other child would suffer a similar fate. The National Round Tables of Great Britain and Ireland and many other organizations and individuals supported the venture, and the culmination of their efforts was the permanent Anthony Nolan Research Centre, completed in August 1990 at the Royal Free Hospital in Hampstead. Shirley succeeded because of her determination and because there was a very real need for the fund.

The same determination helped another mother to pioneer liver transplants in children. The Ben Hardwick Memorial Fund was set up in memory of the first young child to receive such a transplant in Britain. Ben's case was the pioneer for liver transplantation in children and has resulted in countless other lives being saved. However, like Shirley Nolan, Ben's mother, Debbie Jackson, faced what seemed at first an impossible task.

In January, 1984, she telephoned the BBC to say that her two-year-old son had only a few weeks to live. He suffered from biliary atresia, a liver disease, and his only hope of life was a liver transplant. However, Debbie had been told that no transplants had been performed on toddlers and that there were no donors. Ben's story was broadcast on BBC television's *That's Life* show and the same week a family who had lost their son agreed that his liver could be donated. The operation at Addenbrooke's Hospital in Cambridge by Professor Roy Caine gave Ben another year of life before he died. However, in the same year a dozen more children had the same operation and their lives were saved.

Viewers round the country began to raise money because of Ben and awareness of his case led to a great increase in organ donation. The money from fund-raising events was used to staff and equip the Ben Hardwick Room, an intensive care room in Addenbrooke's Hospital, and to pay for a special doctor's post, called the Matthew Fewkes Fellowship after the little boy whose liver was used to try to save Ben. This post was specifically to work with children suffering from liver disease.

Not all memorial funds concentrate on medical issues. Another form centres on the commemoration of a local historical personage, to keep his or her memory alive for future generations. The Julia Margaret Cameron House Trust in Freshwater Bay on the Isle of Wight was formed to save the derelict former home of Julia Margaret Cameron, the Victorian photographer. As a detailed example of the day-by-day steps from dream to achievement, I include here the experiences of the group who eventually became trustees. The rest of this chapter explains the practical considerations involved in forming a memorial charity, the relevant agencies to contact and the regulations governing their establishment, whether for a loved teacher, historical personage or family member.

I met Ron Smith, the chairman of the council of management, a down-to-earth Midlander, local councillor and former local businessman, in the panelled tea-room at Cameron House. He described how the trust not only saved and restored the beautiful house, with views over the Downs that Tennyson loved so much, but also created in it a centre of photographic history and a museum of the literary and artistic figures of Victorian times who were photographed there. These included Tennyson, Darwin, Watts and Thackeray, Lewis Carroll, Robert Browning, Holman Hunt, Palgrave, Edward Lear and Ellen Terry. Photographs of these, and friends and servants attired in classical garb and Shakespearean pose, can be seen on the newly restored walls of the Upper Gallery. Ron explained the trust's quest to create a living memorial to Julia Margaret Cameron and to keep her art alive for present and future generations:

A group of dedicated enthusiasts including my wife Audrey were desperately trying to save the unoccupied Cameron House from being demolished for holiday flats. Although they attracted donations, progress was slow and time was running out. Therefore it was decided to make a more focused effort by establishing a charitable trust. I took over as chairman and we were initially given £250 from the county council towards postage, as well as other small donations.

With the help of Dr Brian Hinton, a local historian and expert on Tennyson, the original brochure was republished. At the same time a solicitor drew up the necessary documents to form a charitable trust. The Charities Commission do supply booklets and information on how to apply for charitable status, but it is better to use a solicitor to avoid possible pitfalls. It is often possible to find an honorary solicitor, someone local and sympathetic to the cause, who will provide his or her services free of charge. An accountant is also necessary for a professional presentation, but again a local figure may give services free.

A professional presentation is essential when approaching a grant-making trust or local authority for funding so it is worth concentrating on this, even if such a brochure or proposal seems expensive. Again there may be designers, artists, even a local printer who will offer a cheap or even free service perhaps in return for publicity in the final brochure. The new appeals brochure of the Julia Margaret Cameron Trust was in full colour with sepia prints and was sent worldwide.

Becoming a charitable trust is vital for ongoing serious fund-raising in order to establish serious intent and stability and to get tax concessions. It is not as hard as it sounds, given that you follow all the necessary steps set out in the literature provided. The

Charities Commission are looking for reasonable aims and organised management to grant charitable status.

The key to success in achieving the goal is patience and perseverance throughout, especially when the going gets hard. The holding company who owned Cameron House eventually dropped the price right down to £120,000 from the original £300,000. But the trust offered £100,000 which had been promised by the Foundation for Sports and Arts in Liverpool as a result of our appeals to grant-making trusts.

However, we decided to obtain back-up funds in case we had to pay the new full asking price. During the three months we waited for a decision from the holding company, the trustees sent out a fresh appeal to raise the additional funding. When the lower offer was accepted, this left a core of £23,000 to begin restoration work.

Another hint for achieving the goal is to follow any possible lead, however unlikely and to use any contacts who may arise in other contexts. For example, the wife of a man who ran the gallery for Olympus Cameras, herself worked for the Royal Photographic Society who were placing plaques on 12 homes of notable photographers, one of which was Cameron House. When she visited Cameron House to arrange this, I talked to her about our needs on the restoration front and she and her husband decided to stop off in Winchester on the way home to visit the chairman of Olympus, the camera makers, to see whether he could help us with funding. Olympus Cameras gave £45,000 as a result.

Then the house next door, part of Julia Margaret Cameron's original Dimbola Lodge, was offered to us by the owner whose wife had recently died, at an interest-free mortgage. He also later gave the trust a similar deal to buy a bungalow at the side of the property, built in the original grounds.

These strokes of fortune and unexpected altruism helped the dream to come true far quicker than we could have hoped. A trust in Switzerland provided £20,000 for equipment and the Esme Fairbairn Trust £5,000.

The work continues and the main source of income is, as well as admission and money from the tea room, donations and the Friends of Julia Margaret Cameron Association. Seminars of photography and musical soirees with readings from the Victorian poets and writers who were photographed at Dimbola, are enjoyable ways we have raised income.

The trust to establish a living memorial to Julia Margaret Cameron succeeded where some other charities fail, because it persevered, used local professionals to help with the work, presented the project professionally and explored every avenue, however unlikely. Above all, the activities of fund-raising and the work were made pleasurable. Finally, the project remains open-ended, important even if a single financial target is the initial aim, as the costs of maintaining equipment and providing ancillary services and comforts remain. Indeed it is vital to consider this ongoing funding almost from the planning stage.

Starting a memorial charity

Should you start a new charity or join an existing one?

The first question to ask is whether there is an existing body that already attracts funds for a very similar cause and so would prevent your own charity from succeeding. A memorial fund that can break new ground offers the greatest chance of success, as with the Anthony Nolan Bone Marrow Trust, which filled a real gap in the provision of medical services.

Another area likely to succeed is where a memorial charity concentrates on a local need, as with the Julia Margaret Cameron Trust. Successful personal appeals often have a strong local target, for example establishing a library in memory of a well-loved deceased head-teacher or councillor.

If your own field does overlap with an existing successful cause, it might be worth making initial enquiries to see whether one of the larger appropriate charities would name a local unit or vital piece of equipment, such as a body scanner, after a loved one in return for concentrated local fund-raising. You should ascertain the kinds of sum you would need to raise for such a tangible memorial. The entries in this book give a general idea of the ongoing needs of national charities that lend themselves to local projects. It is as well to enter into personal negotiations with the appropriate charity appeal officers before launching a major effort. You may decide after such discussions to go it alone.

Joining forces

Another alternative is to graft the projected memorial fund on to a local hospital or research unit in a hospital, or on to a local school in need of major funding, perhaps for a hall, gymnasium or music block. Such direct links may make negotiation easier than with a charity, since you will already be tapped into local needs. This can make fund-raising simpler by giving your appeal an existing local focus and by allowing access to existing facilities from which to work. With the money raised by Leukaemia Busters, the Simon

Flavell Leukaemia Research Laboratory was built and equipped within the Faculty of Medicine at Southampton General Hospital, where Simon's parents are researchers. Many of its supporters are parents of children who were treated at the hospital for leukaemia.

Simon, the son of Drs Simon and Bee Flavell, died from leukaemia, his parents' field of expertise. He died in June 1990, having given Leukaemia Busters its name and logo. Simon's illness provided the catalyst for the creation of Leukaemia Busters as a fund-raising charity. He was aware of the impetus his illness had given his parents' work and in his few final weeks at home, being fully aware of the fact that he was dying, insisted that David and Bee continue and intensify their antibody work as a means of improving the chances of children who relapse, the problem faced by Simon who died during his third relapse.

Although a memorial to Simon, the laboratories formed the focus as a memorial to other children, who were treated for but died of leukaemia and whose plaques may be seen around the unit. Indeed, the laboratory's inauguration plaque reads: 'These laboratories are dedicated in memory of all children who lost their lives to leukaemia so that the work carried out in them will provide a better chance for those children who come after.' Leukaemia Busters became an official charity in 1992, enabling it to continue fund-raising to maintain and expand research.

But remember, even if you can raise the million or so pounds to establish a unit or animal centre in a loved one's name, you have to have some assurance of funding from your charity to run it in the years ahead, and costs could run to thousands of pounds a year. Alternatively, you would need to establish that the local authority or another organization, such as a health trust, would underwrite it for the foreseeable future. It is worth talking with the school or hospital you wish to benefit in order to clarify exactly how your needs would fit into their future plans.

This may sound discouraging but if the hospital or institution of your choice is uncertain – and given budget cuts, promises of future funding are like gold dust – try other places. If the cause is feasible, someone somewhere will share your enthusiasm and accept your generous offer with gratitude.

What is a realistic target for a fund?

While it may be impressive to set a target of £1 million, many lesser targets can be reached without applying for charitable status, such as a holiday for the family of a local child who was tragically killed or equipment for a local health centre, dedicated to other sufferers. Unless you are certain of local support over time and/or a cause that will extend to national level, it may be easier to start an open-ended appeal rather than a fixed huge target and to be flexible as to the kind of memorial towards which you are working. Even if, for example, you cannot raise enough to establish a full memorial library, you could purchase several sections of books for an existing library or collection that could be dedicated to a loved one. It is better to compromise and achieve some success than become overwhelmed and give up or, worse still, never begin.

If the idea of a separate fund is daunting, you could organize a memorial day for a loved relative and give the proceeds to an existing charity. For example, events commemorating the names of other children who died from leukaemia have been held under the auspices of Leukaemia Busters; an all-day fund-raising event was held in memory of Mark Browning at his former school, Wallands School in Lewes, East Sussex, that raised more than £5,500. A dedicated sports day or a performance at the local amateur dramatics or orchestral society could be a suitable commemoration of a beloved child, parent or partner. You could even make it an annual event, perhaps on the anniversary of the death.

Organizing a memorial charity

What resources are needed to organize a memorial charity?

Whether you are organizing a fund in memory of a relation or for a local figure, past or present, a great deal of time is the most vital resource required by the founder, perhaps several hours or more a week, not only in the early days but over months or even years. At some point you might be able to afford professional assistance, but there are still meetings and fund days to attend and phone calls to answer, and unless you can hire a venue for meetings and contacts, you may need to use your own home telephone over a long period and have access to or purchase a fax and photocopier. Local office bureaux can be horrendously expensive unless you can persuade them to offer their services in return for publicity.

In addition, you will need secretarial skills or help, ideally a computer and good-quality printer for preparing handouts and publicity material, a telephone that is manned for some part of most days, a contact address that will hold good until you are able to rent premises and money for initial phone calls, stamps and paper. Charges soon mount up and until you get a grant – it is worth contacting your local council and pestering for this – you will have to make the initial outlay. Remember to keep all receipts, even for small items, and to buy stationery in bulk and see if a local printer will offer cut-price services.

You need a good organizer and business head working with you, even before you reach the stage of recruiting a solicitor and accountant. A treasurer is needed almost at once to take charge of funds and open a special bank account, and to liaise with a local accountant. Above all, you need to find support from a fund-raising group, such as the Lions, Rotarians or Round Table, as Shirley Nolan did. The earlier you can get such backing, the swifter a fund can grow and the more attractive your fund becomes to other backers. The local branches of such fund-raisers are a resource you need to harness and, as Shirley Nolan found, this interest can swiftly spread to the national level of these organizations.

Publicity and a memorial charity

You will need to be or find a good communicator, for the secret of success is publicity, whether on local radio or TV (as with Ben Hardwick's mother who appealed on *That's Life*), in newspapers or by persuading personalities to sponsor your cause initially for very little return. Shirley Nolan began with her local paper. Unusual stunts can attract the interest of local radio and papers, and you will need to tell your story over and over again. Attractive publicity material can offer a key but a personal appeal may work wonders.

Commercial as well as BBC local radio has a great deal of airtime to fill and you should send a brief proposal to the researcher of a chat-show (get the name from the switchboard, as general approaches get lost in the system) concerning any major fund-raising events or milestones. If you do not hear within a few days, telephone the station and try to speak to the researcher.

It is the first line of your proposal that will attract the attention of the reader. Try to individualize the proposal, as circulars tend to go in the bin. When you get airtime, take along a cheat sheet with relevant facts and figures, and remember that you are concentrating on explaining your cause to the presenter – forget the thousands listening. Keep comments and anecdotes short and try to introduce a note of humour, no matter how serious the topic. If you are good entertainment (remember radio and television are first and foremost about entertainment) and can talk about a few campaign banana skins, you will get repeated invitations.

Personalities are a sure-fire winner. Scan cuttings – you may find a star who shares an interest in your cause; you can contact them through their agents in *Spotlight*, via a programme they appear on or through their publishers. Explain that you are a new charity and that expenses are short – avoid the circuit publicity merchants, who charge £500 to leave their front doors, as they are rarely value for money. You may, via local radio, find an up-and-coming presenter. Make friends with unknowns – they may remember you when they are famous. Tap every source. Many people have a friend of a friend who went to school with a personality. Be shameless for your cause.

The Julia Margaret Cameron House trustees were able to attract several personalities from the high-profile photographic world, such as Koo Stark and David Bailey, and this attracted the local and national press and media. It is always worth alerting a local news agency (found in Yellow Pages) if a personality is coming to open a fête. The agency will publicize it nationally. A high public profile, even for a local project, is vital. People need to know not only what you are working for but also where to contact you. They will rarely search, so leave your contact number and name with everyone from the Citizens' Advice Bureau to the local town hall and the local library. Above all you need a core of reliable supporters who will turn out to serve at coffee mornings, jumble sales, etc., when the first wave of enthusiasm is past. Should you decide to go ahead, then you will have incredible satisfaction in knowing that each step forward is a memorial in itself.

Practicalities

What is a charity?

Charities have been classified by law into four categories: the relief of poverty; the advancement of education; the advancement of religion; and other purposes beneficial to the community, such as the provision of recreational or leisure activities. All charities must exist solely for the benefit of the public.

The Charity Commissioners (London Office, St Alban's House, 57–60 Haymarket, London SW1Y 4QX. Tel.: 0171 210 4477) are the officials who will decide whether you can register as a charity. All charities in England and Wales that are not specifically exempt or excepted from registration are required to be registered with the Charity Commissioners. Exempt charities include universities, grant-maintained schools and many of the national museums and galleries and heritage organizations. An excepted charity is usually a small one that does not have a permanent endowment, the use or occupation of any land (including buildings) or an annual income of £1,000 or more. This category can be useful if you are planning a very small memorial fund, perhaps for an annual memorial prize.

Certain charities cannot be registered at all and so do not qualify for tax benefits. These include funds set up for the benefit of an individual person, bodies which have political aims, members' clubs, including sports clubs, which benefit their own members rather than the general public and closed religious orders, except those that say public masses.

Why register a memorial charity?

It is incredibly difficult, as Ron Smith at Cameron House pointed out, to raise a substantial amount of money over time without charitable status. As well as tax benefits that prevent your losing any profits to the Inland Revenue, the belief is held certainly by grant-aiding organizations and indeed by the general public that if you are registered, you are reliable, serious about your intent and unlikely either to flounder at the first stage or to run off with the profits. In practice, it is also very difficult to raise money without charitable status without also having to prove your honesty to everyone from the local police to the little old lady sorting through your jumble.

Registering a memorial charity in England and Wales

The Charity Commissioners have jurisdiction over all charities operating or whose head office is in England or Wales. The first thing a charity needs to get up and running is trustees. These are the people under the charity's governing document who will be responsible for controlling and managing the charity. This council or committee will probably be the original core of enthusiasts, plus one or two sympathetic local experts gathered on the way. A charitable trust is the most usual form of organization.

To simplify the process of setting up a charity, the commissioners have a set of draft documents for a trust deed and other forms of charitable documents. These forms are available on request and, if followed, can speed the process of registration. When an organization applies to be registered, the commission will need the charity's governing document and will ask for a questionnaire to be completed to decide whether its purposes are charitable in law. Once the commission is satisfied that an organization's objects are wholly charitable and its activities are in accordance with those objects, the charity will be required to complete a formal document of registration. A friendly local solicitor may be useful in helping to draw up the deed, usually with the help of someone who is good at filling in forms and can work with the solicitor in checking everything is in order. It is worthwhile taking trouble to make sure this paperwork is complete and accurate first time.

When the application is returned, the charity will be entered on the register of charities, which is kept on computer. Once a charity is registered, it is recognized by other bodies such as the Inland Revenue, which encourages potential donors to leave legacies or give money to a cause, as they can save on their own tax bill as well as benefiting their chosen charity (see chapter 2 for full details of tax benefits that a charity can use, such as deeds of covenant, Gift Aid, etc.).

Trustees have to notify the Commissioners of any changes to the charity's registered details, must submit their annual accounts and may be asked periodically to complete a return or supply additional information. A local accountant, who may offer services in return for free publicity, will be of infinite help in seeing that the money side is on an even keel. The Charity Commissioners offer much helpful material to those who wish to set up a charity. Leaflets are free of charge. Leaflet CC1 lists the full range of Charity Commission publications and gives a list of useful leaflets, reports and audio and video cassettes. Leaflet CC2 'Charities and Charity Commissioners' is also useful since it describes the work and responsibilities of the charity commissioners. Leaflet CC21 provides essential information on starting a charity.

The Charity Commissioners have three offices which serve three broad geographical areas. Information and leaflets can be obtained from any office but correspondence about a particular charity should be addressed to the relevant office.

The Charity Commissioners, London (St Alban's House, 57–60 Haymarket, London SW1Y 4QX. Tel.: 0171 210 4477) deal with all national and overseas charities, based in the Greater London boroughs. The office is also responsible for local charities in Bedfordshire, Buckinghamshire, Cambridgeshire, East Sussex, Essex, Greater London, Hertfordshire, Kent, Norfolk, Northamptonshire, Suffolk, Surrey and West Sussex.

The Charity Commissioners, Taunton (Woodfield House, Tangier, Taunton, Som. TA1 4BL. Tel.: 01823 345000) deal with national and overseas charities based in Bedfordshire, Buckinghamshire, East Sussex, Hertfordshire, Kent, Surrey and West Sussex. The office is also responsible for local, national and overseas charities based in Avon, Berkshire, Cornwall, Devon, Dorset, Dyfed, Gloucestershire, Gwent, Hampshire, Hereford and Worcester, Isle of Wight, Mid-Glamorgan, Oxfordshire, Somerset, South Glamorgan, West Glamorgan and Wiltshire.

The Charity Commissioners, Liverpool (2nd Floor, 20 Kings Parade, Queens Dock, Liverpool. L3 4DQ. Tel.: 0151 703 1500) deal with national and overseas charities in Cambridgeshire, Essex, Norfolk, Northamptonshire and Suffolk. The office is also responsible for local, national and overseas charities based in Cheshire, Cleveland, Cumbria, Denbighshire, Derbyshire, Durham, Flintshire, Greater Manchester, Gwynedd, Humberside, Lancashire, Leicestershire, Lincolnshire, Merseyside, North Yorkshire, Northumberland, Nottinghamshire, Powys, Shropshire, South Yorkshire, Staffordshire, Tyne and Wear, Warwickshire, West Midlands and West Yorkshire.

The Inland Revenue, (FICO), Charity Division, St John's House, Merton Road, Bootle, Merseyside L69 9BB. Tel.: 0151 472 6000) has a very helpful charities' pack and will also answer queries about individual problems.

Establishing a memorial charity in Scotland

There is no system for registering a charity in Scotland, although the Scottish courts have decided that English charity law should apply in deciding whether a body is a charity for tax purposes and therefore offers tax benefits to donors. No Scottish charity can call itself a registered charity, as this term applies only to charities in England and Wales registered by the Charity Commissioners. However, a charity can apply to the Inland Revenue (FICO (Scotland), Trinity Park House, South Trinity Road, Edinburgh EH5 3SD. Tel.: 0131 551 8127) for recognition as a charity for tax purposes. If the application is successful, the body can then call itself a Scottish charity and enjoy similar status to charities in England and Wales. All charities in Scotland must have formal documents which show their purpose and organization. It is recommended that a draft copy is sent so that the Scottish Inland Revenue can identify any difficulties and say whether approval will be granted. The relevant documents must be sent when the charity is formally set up. Because the documents are complex, it will probably be necessary to consult a solicitor, as the Scottish Inland Revenue, unlike the Charity Commissioners in England and Wales, is unable to help draft these.

However, the Scottish Council for Voluntary Organizations may be able to supply, for a small charge, an information pack for anyone thinking of setting up certain types of organizations.

Contact the Scottish Council for Voluntary Organizations, 18–19 Claremont Crescent, Edinburgh EH7 4RD. Tel.: 0131 556 3882.

A recognized Scottish charity will normally be exempt from income tax, corporation tax and capital gains tax on most of its income and gains. The tax exemption is always subject to the condition that the income or gains are used solely for charitable purposes. Repayment of tax on behalf of a recognized charity should be claimed on a special form from the taxation office.

For detailed information on the effect of charitable status on inheritance tax in Scotland, contact the Capital Taxes Office, Edinburgh, Mulberry House, 16 Picardy Place, Edinburgh EH1 3NB.

Memorial charities in Northern Ireland

The Charities Branch of the Department of Social Security in Northern Ireland has similar functions to the Charity Commissioners in England and Wales, the main difference, as in Scotland, being that there is no register of charities in Northern Ireland.

The definition of a charity is standard throughout the UK, as is the system for tax relief. Therefore, organizations in Northern Ireland qualify as charities if they are established solely for charitable purposes. Their charitable status is recognized (not registered) for tax purposes by the Inland Revenue. In practice, the Northern Ireland Charities Office spends most of its time dealing with applications from charities for power to sell properties, altering the purpose of charities that can no longer function in their present form and providing general advice. Contact the Charities Branch of the Voluntary Activity Unit of the Department of Social Security (Annexe 3, Castle Buildings, Stormont, Belfast BT4 3RA. Tel.: 01232 523203) for free publications, such as the very comprehensive and clear *Northern Ireland Charities, a Guide for Trustees*.

For advice on tax affairs contact the Inland Revenue's Charity Division at Bootle (see above for address).

The Northern Ireland Council for Voluntary Action (127–131 Ormeau Road, Belfast BT7 1SH. Tel.: 01232 522780) is itself a charity and provides various publications to help with the formation of charities in Northern Ireland, including the particularly helpful *So you Want to Be a Charity*.

Memorial charities in the Republic of Ireland

Contact the Commissioners of Charitable Donations and Bequests for Ireland, 12 Clare Street, Dublin 2, Ireland. Tel.: 00 3531 6766095.

5 Commemorative Giving

Non-financial considerations

Each form of memorial giving offers satisfaction in different ways that rank alongside the financial considerations.

Lifetime gifts allow you to become involved with the development of your project and receive positive feedback. This is especially true of a named research project or university chair or even a small prize in a favourite topic. Although Phil Drabble made a lifetime promise rather than gift (see chapter 1), he talks of the pleasure he derives from sharing his beloved nature reserve with the school-children who will, after his death, inherit it.

Equally, a memorial gift commemorating a loved one, whether a tree, a favourite artefact donated for exhibition in a museum or the endowment of a prize, can be a tangible part of the healing process of grief. Some people find it far more comforting than visiting a graveside to visit a place where the person was so happy in life, for example a particular donkey sanctuary to see a plaque or new dedicated stable, or a bench on a well-loved sea-front.

Legacies are still the most usual method of commemorative giving. The only possible disadvantage of making a bequest or lifetime gift is that as the years pass, the charity's specific projects or memorial you have chosen may no longer be practical. This can be avoided either by beginning payments towards a project during your lifetime, with the final more substantial gift coming from the residue of your estate, or by making a more general legacy so that the charity can use your money to fit the current need in the area you have chosen and provide a memorial in accordance with the spirit rather than the letter of your wishes. However, if you are closely involved with a particular charity, you can update your will every few years to adapt to new areas of work and need, and likewise keep abreast of changing commemorative opportunities.

The majority of people who make wills favouring charities do in fact keep them updated. Bernard Sharpe of Smee and Ford Legal Consultants sees both sides of the coin and offers a balanced view of the question of legacies. Smee and Ford are the foremost experts in almost every aspect of this field and view every will in probate, over 1,000 a day. Now Scotland is to have its own repository similar to Somerset House, they will also examine Scottish wills from early 1996. They collect data on all estates, either where there are wills or when a person has died intestate, and produce a heritable wealth survey. They also produce the General Charities Wealth Report, breaking down the charities into fourteen categories so that each can see how well it is performing in its own category in terms of number of bequests. Mr Sharpe comments:

> Charities are naturally cautious especially where a bequest is made in middle years for by the time the legacy is realised the services to be endowed may no longer exist.
>
> However, twenty-five per cent of charitable bequests will mature within a year and forty-nine per cent within three years because many people in their eighties and over are still interested in charitable concerns. Charitable bequests increase as people live longer and there are more single people in late old age who may not have family obligations and also perhaps as extended family ties are weakened. Leaving to charity avoids dying intestate and thus having one's money pass to the Treasury and so is a very positive memorial.

Smee and Ford can be contacted at 2nd Floor, St George's House, 195–203 Waterloo Road, London SE1 8XJ. Tel.: 0171 928 4050.

Is it reasonable to expect tangible commemoration in return for a legacy or in memoriam gift?

It is entirely reasonable to expect commemoration and a say in how your money will be spent in return for a bequest or in memoriam gift. Some people prefer to remain anonymous in their giving but this is no more virtuous than those who wish their name to live on, merely a different attitude. The Victorians were great ones for memorial plaques and even monuments to their largesse, but in the post-war period there was a return to the almost biblical attitude of giving without any expectation of thanks.

However, in modern recessionary times, there is much more awareness that donors should have their hard work recognized and their name perpetuated. Often the most generous donors are not necessarily those with inherited wealth but those who have perhaps lived more frugally to benefit a worthy cause after their death.

In the spring 1995 issue of the *Lifeboat* magazine, produced by the Royal National Lifeboat Institution, is the story of Sam Webber who died in Plymouth aged ninety-four. He was an inshore fisherman for many years and continued his love of fishing and crabbing, often giving away his catch in later years. Sam and his wife lived very frugally and, having known great poverty in his youth, he saved secretly and on his death bequeathed £300,000 to the RNLI, a great surprise to those who assumed he was as poor as his modest appearance and lifestyle suggested.

Is it possible for a charity to provide tangible commemoration without detracting from its work?

Naturally charities prefer to receive 'no strings' money and some find it difficult to give as much money as possible to those they represent and to satisfy the wish for a tangible memorial by a testator. But the fact remains that some do both very successfully – the Royal National Lifeboat Institution and Edinburgh University are but two examples that offer a variety of commemorative schemes in all price ranges. It is perhaps no coincidence that the RNLI, which positively encourages commemoration of donors, is consistently one of the most successful charities.

The issue of commemoration needs to be discussed in advance with the charity concerned, and suitable wording put in the will (see chapter 2) to allow the legacy to be workable and at the same time to ensure that a memorial will be provided. There are many forms of commemoration that will be practical even perhaps forty or fifty years on and charities are increasingly aware that this is an area that at least needs consideration and forward planning, especially in the area of sponsorship. For example, the Wessex Children's Hospice has a scheme to sponsor a nurse.

Of the legacy and administrative officers to whom I have written or spoken, the majority are courteous and helpful and where they have been reluctant to suggest prices, it is because they have been afraid that those who can only give a little will feel unappreciated if faced with a price-list of memorials. They stress that any donation, however small, is valued. Many of those societies listed as offering unspecified prices will, if asked, try to find a suitable memorial or project feedback for a relatively modest donation, especially for long-standing supporters.

Memorial books are becoming an increasingly popular way of

commemorating those who can afford only a little and sometimes entries are entirely free. However, almost all the charities ask that potential testators talk to them first before making a will, so that any questions can be answered and common ground established. The organizations listed in this book are not, of course, the only helpful ones but I feel happy to recommend any that are listed.

Are memorials usually offered by charities?

As I said in the introduction, it was far more difficult than I had expected to find charities and organizations able or willing to offer tangible commemoration for donations and to give prices for these. Fewer than a quarter of the charities I contacted have any formal system for commemoration, although more than half were able to suggest costs of projects and to suggest that donors negotiated with them directly about memorials.

On the whole, the areas of conservation, the arts, religion, medical research and animals offer the most opportunities for commemoration, while overseas aid organizations, for example, found memorials difficult to offer as foreign agencies often supervised projects *in situ*. However, given imagination even in this area, one or two have managed to find a way round the question (see Part 2).

In practice, if you give a large donation, £500,000 or more, the vast majority of charities will agree to some form of commemoration. However, I was astonished in an isolated case to hear that a million pounds would merit only a letter of thanks. For a small donation, the most readily available tangible form of commemoration can be found among nature conservation organizations. Memorial tree planting represents excellent value, as woods may be subsidized by heritage organizations or local authorities.

If you are interested in a particular area of the country or cause, try more than one charity and see which seems closest to your needs, feels right and can suggest suitable commemoration and an approximate cost after an informal discussion. Most charities welcome visits and there are some legacy officers who will even visit you at home.

Some charities and organizations are very structured – if this approach is one you welcome, then there is a good selection of charities in the book that are prepared to be specific. However, if this seems too formalized and regimented or you want a personalized memorial, look at the entries where charities welcome individual negotiations and are willing to adapt to any reasonable suggestion. This is, as I have said, the approach of the majority of charities but, because of the nature of the book, I have tried to include rather more of those who do offer a formalized approach. My research found that for every anonymous benefactor, there are ten who want their name on a memorial, whether a plaque, a scholarship or a restored tram, and I believe this is the way forward.

How do I know my gifts will be honoured after my death?

In general, charities will do their very best to honour gifts and will only accept artefacts into collections if they are able to care for them in perpetuity. However, the donation of artefacts to a museum or gallery can be problematic when a gift appears to have been abandoned. It can be very distressing to go to a museum or art gallery and not see the in memoriam gift to a relative or their prized bequest on show. This does not necessarily make the museum a villain. Tony Conder of the National Waterways Museum explains:

> There are things that museums cannot guarantee and the most important is that any work bequeathed or donated is not guaranteed display space. It is a frequent lament of relatives that a much loved item is in store and not displayed. This is partly because of a lack of understanding of museum work. An item just being in a collection has such a value for future generations that consideration of display or storage here and now are not as important as the fact that the gift is available, although understandably this may be upsetting. What a museum should be able to guarantee is that an item which exists now will continue to exist into an unknown future, carrying the memory of the donor with it.

However, there have occasionally been cases where a memorial has been sadly neglected or a donor's wishes ignored. Donor Watch is an organization that proposes 'to attract the membership of donors, testators and their heirs in all the fields in which gifts are made for the public benefit, of those who support the sanctity of testamentary provisions, of lawyers interested in this branch of the law and anyone else concerned about the issues of ensuring that the wishes of benefactors are followed after their death for as long as the terms specified in the gift'. Donor Watch is envisaged by Dr Selby Whittingham, its founder, as providing a body of strength and expertise to challenge infringements of trusts and to right any imbalance between donor and donee, which Dr Whittingham believes is heavily tipped in the donees' favour after the donation is made and time has elapsed. It was suggested in October 1995 that membership might require an annual subscription of £10, but funds are urgently needed to get the organization in place and higher donations are very welcome.

One example that concerned Dr Whittingham was brought to light by Erica Gibbs of Brighton, who reported in a letter to a national newspaper the case of Basil Austen, who died in humble circumstances. She wrote: 'He was terribly proud of his grandfather, the scientist Sir Robert Mond, son and heir of industrialist Dr Ludwig Mond, founder of ICI. Sir Robert built the Mond Mausoleum in East Finchley as a memorial to his father.' As a trustee Basil Austen constantly fought against the lack of care the mausoleum received. He was determined to come from Brighton to London to sort out promises of a better future for the mausoleum despite being wheelchair-bound and relying on oxygen tanks and other aids. However, the effort proved too much for the old man and he died in early October 1995.

Contact Dr Selby Whittingham, Donor Watch, Turner House, 153 Cromwell Road, London SW5 OTQ. Tel.: 0171 373 5560.

Organizations and charities suitable for bequests

Almost every organization would accept £1 million and would put no upper limit on in memoriam gifts or bequests. Equally, most have no lower limit for in memoriam gifts and bequests and welcome small donations of less than £50, although this can make commemorative opportunities more limited.

Therefore, the prices quoted below and used in chapters 6–21 refer only to sample special projects that have or are suggested as commemorative opportunities or to established memorials on offer within certain price ranges. They are not intended to indicate the only commemorative opportunities offered by a particular charity – rather key areas that may be of special interest to donors.

Up to £100
Up to £500
Up to £1,000
Up to £5,000
Up to £10,000
Up to £50,000
Up to £100,000

Up to £250,000
Up to £500,000
Up to and beyond £1 million

'Per annum' will be inserted next to any price that represents an annual contribution. A memorial book, wall, etc., where offered, is indicated under each relevant entry. The term 'Unspecified' indicates organizations unwilling or unable to supply general prices or to list specific memorials, but willing to consider in memoriam gifts and legacies. They either offer to discuss suitable commemoration on an individual basis or, in the case of overseas projects, offer follow-up contact on projects that are sponsored. This price category can offer a rich source of memorials and so should not be regarded as unfruitful. Some charitable areas do not lend themselves so easily to advance costings.

This category is also used for museums that mainly receive artefacts, rather than money gifts, which are accepted on their merit and suitability rather than by their value.

Approximate costings late-1995 prices, unless otherwise stated, can be obtained from details given of previous projects by the chosen charity or others within the same category.

6 Price Guide to Memorials

Memorials for up to £50

Brookside Health Centre
The Donkey Sanctuary
Help the Hospices
National Memorial Arboretum
  Appeal
Royal Society for the
  Protection of Birds
Royal Star and Garter Home
  for Disabled Sailors, Soldiers
  and Airmen

Memorials for up to £100

Addenbrooke's Hospital NHS
  Trust
American Air Museum in
  Britain
Anthony Nolan Bone Marrow
  Trust
Brighstone Parish Council, Isle
  of Wight
British Red Cross
British Trust for Conservation
  Volunteers
Brookside Health Centre
The Compassionate Friends
Derbyshire County Council
The Donkey Sanctuary
Hastings Borough Council
Help the Hospices
Hove Borough Council
International Star Registry

Isle of Wight County Council
Isle of Wight Zoological
  Gardens, Tiger Sanctuary
  and World Health
  Venomous Snake Centre
Jersey Wildlife Preservation
  Trust
Jubilee Sailing Trust
Julia Margaret Cameron Trust
London Zoo
Marie Curie Cancer Care
Marwell Zoological Park
National Maritime Museum
National Trust for Scotland
Paintings in Hospitals, Scotland
Prinknash Abbey
Royal Society for the
  Protection of Birds
Royal Star and Garter Home
  for Disabled Sailors, Soldiers
  and Airmen
Scout Association
Sherwood Forest Initiative
University of Edinburgh
  Development Trust
Woodland Creations
Young Women's Christian
  Association of Great Britain

Memorials for up to £500

ActionAid, Sponsor a Child
Addenbrooke's Hospital NHS
  Trust

Anchor Housing Trust
Arthritis and Rheumatism
  Council for Research
Brighstone Parish Council, Isle
  of Wight
British Trust for Conservation
  Volunteers
Brookside Health Centre
Buckinghamshire County
  Council Library and
  Museum Service
Cats Protection League
Derbyshire County Council
Friends of the Lake District
Handicapped Children's
  Pilgrimage Trust and
  Hosanna House Trust
Hearing Research Trust
Help the Hospices
Hove Borough Council
Isle of Wight Zoological
  Gardens, Tiger Sanctuary
  and World Health
  Venomous Snake Centre
Jersey Wildlife Preservation
  Trust
Jubilee Sailing Trust
Julia Margaret Cameron Trust
Lewes District Council
Lewes District Council, Parks
  Department
Lincoln Cathedral
Liverpool City Libraries
London Zoo
Marwell Zoological Park
Moray Forest District
National Canine Defence
  League
National Library for the Blind
National Maritime Museum
National Tramway Museum
National Trust for Scotland
National Waterways Museum
  at Gloucester
Nuffield Hospitals

Royal Botanic Garden,
  Edinburgh
Royal National Institute for
  Deaf People
Royal National Lifeboat
  Institution
Royal Naval Benevolent Trust
Royal Society for the
  Protection of Brids
Scout Association
Sherwood Forest Initiative
Society of Authors
Starlight Foundation
Treloar Trust
University of Glasgow
University of Edinburgh
  Development Trust
Winchester Cathedral Trust
Worcester Cathedral Appeal
  Trust
Worcestershire County Cricket
  Club
Yarmouth Pier and Harbour
  Trust
Young Women's Christian
  Association of Great Britain

Memorials for up to £1,000

Anchor Housing Trust
Brookside Health Centre
Buckinghamshire County
  Council Library and
  Museum Service
Derbyshire County Council
Hearing Research Trust
Help the Hospices
Imperial Cancer Research
  Fund
Isle of Wight Zoological
  Gardens, Tiger Sanctuary
  and World Health
  Venomous Snake Centre

Jersey Wildlife Preservation Trust
Jubilee Sailing Trust
Julia Margaret Cameron Trust
Lincoln Cathedral
Liverpool City Libraries
London Zoo
Marie Curie Cancer Care
Marwell Zoological Park
National Canine Defence League
National Library for the Blind
National Maritime Museum
National Tramway Museum
National Trust for Scotland
Royal Botanic Garden, Edinburgh
Royal School of Church Music
Salisbury Cathedral
Scout Association
Society of Authors
Starlight Foundation
Treloar Trust
University of Edinburgh Development Trust
Winchester College of Art
Woodland Creations
Yarmouth Pier and Harbour Trust
Young Women's Christian Association of Great Britain

Memorials for up to £5,000

Anchor Housing Trust
Animal Welfare Foundation (British Veterinary Association)
Birmingham Museum of Science and Industry
British Limbless Ex-Service Men's Association
Brookside Health Centre
Cheshire County Council

Contemporary Art Society
CORDA (Heart Charity)
Dorset County Council
Fight for Sight
Friends of the Lake District
Guide Dogs for the Blind Association
Hearing Research Trust
Help the Hospices
Imperial Cancer Research Fund
Isle of Wight County Council
Isle of Wight Zoological Gardens, Tiger Sanctuary and World Health Venomous Snake Centre
Jersey Wildlife Preservation Trust
Leukaemia Busters
Lincoln Cathedral
Liverpool City Libraries
London Zoo
Marie Curie Cancer Care
Marwell Zoological Park
Musicians' Benevolent Fund
National Maritime Museum
National Playing Fields Association
National Tramway Museum
Paintings in Hospitals, Scotland
Pestalozzi Children's Village Trust
Royal Naval Benevolent Trust
Royal School of Church Music
Royal Shakespeare Company
Royal Society for the Prevention of Cruelty to Animals
Royal Star and Garter Home for Disabled Sailors, Soldiers and Airmen
Scottish Society for Psychical Research
Scout Association
Sherwood Forest Initiative

Society of Authors
Starlight Foundation
Winchester College of Art
Woodland Creations
Young Women's Christian
Association of Great Britain

Memorials for up to £10,000

Addenbrooke's Hospital NHS
Trust
Animal Welfare Foundation
(British Veterinary
Association)
Arthritis and Rheumatism
Council for Research
Colon Cancer Concern
CORDA (Heart Charity)
Friends of the Lake District
Hearing Research Trust
Help the Hospices
Isle of Wight County Council
Isle of Wight Zoological
Gardens, Tiger Sanctuary
and World Health
Venomous Snake Centre
Jersey Wildlife Preservation
Trust
Julia Margaret Cameron Trust
Lincoln Cathedral
Liverpool City Libraries
London Zoo
Marwell Zoological Park
National Playing Fields
Association
National Tramway Museum
Paintings in Hospitals, Scotland
Pestalozzi Children's Village
Trust
Royal National Lifeboat
Institution
Royal School of Church Music
Royal Shakespeare Company
Royal Society for the

Prevention of Cruelty to
Animals
Scout Association
Sherwood Forest Initiative
Society of Authors
St Andrew Animal Fund and
Advocates for Animals
Treloar Trust
University of Edinburgh
Development Trust
Winchester College of Art
World Jewish Relief
Yarmouth Pier and Harbour
Trust
Young Women's Christian
Association of Great Britain

Memorials for up to £50,000

AB Wildlife Trust Fund
Addenbrooke's Hospital NHS
Trust
American Air Museum in
Britain
Anchor Housing Trust
Animal Welfare Foundation
(British Veterinary
Association)
Arthritis and Rheumatism
Council for Research
Birmingham Museum of
Science and Industry
British Limbless Ex-Service
Men's Association
British Lung Foundation
Buckinghamshire County
Council Library and
Museum Service
Cathedral Church of St Peter in
Exeter
Children's Hospice Appeal
(Wessex)
Clinical Studies Trust Fund
Limited (British Small

Animal Veterinary
Association)
Colon Cancer Concern
CORDA (Heart Charity)
Fight for Sight
Friends of Friendless Churches
Friends of the Lake District
Hearing Research Trust
Help the Hospices
Isle of Wight Zoological
Gardens, Tiger Sanctuary
and World Health
Venomous Snake Centre
Jersey Wildlife Preservation
Trust
Jubilee Sailing Trust
Julia Margaret Cameron Trust
Lincoln Cathedral
Liverpool City Libraries
Marwell Zoological Park
Musicians' Benevolent Fund
National Kidney Research
Fund and Kidney
Foundation
National Maritime Museum
National Playing Fields
Association
National Tramway Museum
Nuffield Hospitals
Paintings in Hospitals, Scotland
Pestalozzi Children's Village
Trust
Royal Botanic Garden,
Edinburgh
Royal National Institute for
Deaf People
Royal Naval Benevolent Trust
Royal School of Church Music
Royal Shakespeare Company
Royal Society for the
Prevention of Cruelty to
Animals
Royal Star and Garter Home
for Disabled Sailors, Soldiers
and Airmen

Scout Association
Sherwood Forest Initiative
St Andrew Animal Fund and
Advocates for Animals
Treloar Trust
University Of Glasgow
University of Bath
Winchester College of Art
World Jewish Relief
Young Women's Christian
Association of Great Britain

Memorials for up to £100,000

AB Wildlife Trust Fund
Anchor Housing Trust
Arthritis and Rheumatism
Council for Research
Birmingham Museum of
Science and Industry
British Limbless Ex-Service
Men's Association
British Lung Foundation
Buckinghamshire County
Council Library and
Museum Service
Cancer Relief Macmillan Fund
Cathedral Church of
Canterbury
CORDA (Heart Charity)
Dorset County Council
Fight for Sight
Friends of Friendless Churches
Grail Centre
Hearing Research Trust
Help the Hospices
Hove Borough Council
Imperial Cancer Research
Fund
Isle of Wight Zoological
Gardens, Tiger Sanctuary
and World Health
Venomous Snake Centre
Jersey Wildlife Preservation
Trust

Jubilee Sailing Trust
Julia Margaret Cameron Trust
Liverpool City Libraries
Musicians' Benevolent Fund
National Canine Defence
  League
National Kidney Research
  Fund and Kidney
  Foundation
National Maritime Museum
National Tramway Museum
Paintings in Hospitals, Scotland
Pestalozzi Children's Village
  Trust
Royal Alexandra and Albert
  School
Royal National Institute for
  Deaf People
Royal National Lifeboat
  Institution
Royal Shakespeare Company
Royal Star and Garter Home
  for Disabled Sailors, Soldiers
  and Airmen
Scout Association
Society of Authors
Starlight Foundation
Tamar Protection Society
University of Bath
Winchester Cathedral Trust

Memorials for up to £250,000

Addenbrooke's Hospital NHS
  Trust
Anchor Housing Trust
Birmingham Museum of
  Science and Industry
Cathedral Church of
  Canterbury
Clinical Studies Trust Fund
  Limited (British Small
  Animal Veterinary
  Association)

Friends of Friendless Churches
Friends of the Lake District
Jersey Wildlife Preservation
  Trust
Julia Margaret Cameron Trust
Liverpool City Libraries
Marwell Zoological Park
National Canine Defence
  League
The National Tramway
  Museum
Nuffield Hospitals
Royal Shakespeare Company
Royal Star and Garter Home
  for Disabled Sailors, Soldiers
  and Airmen
Scottish Society for Psychical
  Research
Scout Association
Starlight Foundation
University of Edinburgh
  Development Trust
University of London

Memorials for up to £500,000

Anchor Housing Trust
Animal Welfare Foundation
  (British Veterinary
  Association)
Arthritis and Rheumatism
  Council for Research
Birmingham Museum of
  Science and Industry
British Heart Foundation
British Limbless Ex-Service
  Men's Association
Cathedral Church of
  Canterbury
CORDA (Heart Charity)
Fight for Sight
Help the Hospices
Imperial Cancer Research
  Fund

Jersey Wildlife Preservation
Trust
Julia Margaret Cameron Trust
National Kidney Research
Fund and Kidney
Foundation
National Maritime Museum
Nuffield Hospitals
Pestalozzi Children's Village
Trust
Royal Alexandra and Albert
School
Royal National Lifeboat
Institution
Royal School of Church Music
Royal Shakespeare Company
Scout Association
Sherwood Forest Initiative
Society of Authors
St Andrew Animal Fund and
Advocates for Animals
Treloar Trust
World Jewish Relief

**Memorials for up to £1 million
and more**

Addenbrooke's Hospital NHS
Trust
Age Concern
Anchor Housing Trust
Animal Welfare Foundation
(British Veterinary
Association)
Arthritis and Rheumatism
Council for Research
Birmingham Museum of
Science and Industry
British Heart Foundation
Cancer Relief Macmillan Fund
CORDA (Heart Charity)
Fight for Sight
Help the Hospices

Isle of Wight Zoological
Gardens, Tiger Sanctuary
and World Health
Venomous Snake Centre
Jersey Wildlife Preservation
Trust
Leukaemia Busters
Liverpool City Libraries
Marwell Zoological Park
National Tramway Museum
Royal National Lifeboat
Institution
Royal Shakespeare Company
Royal Society for the
Prevention of Cruelty to
Animals
Royal Society for the
Protection of Birds
Sherwood Forest Initiative
St Andrew Animal Fund and
Advocates for Animals
Thomas Coram Foundation for
Children
Treloar Trust
University of Bath
University of Edinburgh
Development Trust
University of London
Yarmouth Pier and Harbour
Trust

Memorials for unspecified prices

The Abbey, Caldey
Aberfoyle Forest District
Alister Hardy Trust
Apostleship of the Sea
Arthritis Care
Arts Council of England
Arts Council of Northern
Ireland
Arts Council, Ireland
Baptist Missionary Society
Ben Hardwick Memorial Fund

Birmingham Macmillan
Nurse Appeal
The Book of Oaks
British Film Institute
CAFOD
Chatham Historic Dockyard
Trust
Christian Aid
Church Army
Commonwealth Society for the
Deaf
Corrymeela Community
Council for the Protection of
Rural England
Distressed Gentlefolk's Aid
Association Homelife
Durham County Council
Duxford Aviation Museum
East Midlands Arts
Eastern Arts
Elizabeth Garrett Anderson
Hospital Appeal Trust
English Heritage
English Regional Arts Board
Ex-Service Fellowship Centres
Forestry Commission
Guide Association
Historic Churches Preservation
Trust
Imperial War Museum
Jewish Care
Karuna Trust
Lancaster University
London Arts Board
Malcolm Sargent Cancer Fund
for Children
National Army Museum
National Trust
North West Arts Board
Northern Arts
Oxfam, United Kingdom and
Ireland
Plymouth Hospitals NHS Trust
Rescue (Foundation for the
Brain-injured Infant)

Royal Berkshire and Battle
Hospitals NHS Trust
Royal College of Physicians
Royal National Institute for the
Blind
Royal Photographic Society
Saffron Walden Friends' School
Save the Children
Scottish Arts Council
Society of Mucopolysaccharide
Diseases
Somerville College, University
of Oxford
South East Arts
South West Arts
Southern Arts
St Thomas' Hospital, Florence
Nightingale Fund
University of Durham
Victoria and Albert Museum
Welsh Academy
Welsh Rugby Union (Undeb
Rygbi Cymru)
West Bromwich Albion
Football Club Limited
West Midlands Arts
Wester Ross Forest District
Woking Homes
Yorkshire and Humberside
Arts

**Organizations with memorial
books**

Addenbrooke's Hospital NHS
Trust
American Air Museum in
Britain
Apostleship of the Sea
Arthritis Care
The Book of Oaks
British Red Cross
Cathedral Church of
Canterbury

Catholic Children's Society
Christian Aid
Church Army
The Compassionate Friends
Council for the Protection of
  Rural England
Cystic Fibrosis Trust
Duxford Aviation Museum
Grail Centre
Help the Hospices
Imperial Cancer Research
  Fund
Jewish Care
Jubilee Sailing Trust
Marie Curie Cancer Care
National Trust
National Trust for Scotland
Oxfam, United Kingdom and
  Ireland
Plymouth Hospitals NHS Trust
Prinknash Abbey
Royal Berkshire and Battle

Hospitals NHS Trust
Royal National Institute for the
  Blind
Royal National Institute for
  Deaf People
Royal Society for the
  Prevention of Cruelty to
  Animals
Royal Star and Garter Home
  for Disabled Sailors, Soldiers
  and Airmen
Society for
  Mucopolysaccharide
  Diseases
Treloar Trust
University of Edinburgh
  Development Trust
Winchester Cathedral Trust
Woodland Creations
Yarmouth Pier and Harbour
  Trust

Part 2   Categories

The suggested categories are one way of dividing the organizations and charities into common areas of interest to potential benefactors. However, some charities could fit into more than one category, for example children's charities that have a medical bias. Rather than cross-referencing, I have entered each organization under the category in which its main area of concern lies.

The categories used here are more focused than many, more conventional charity listings and usually have no more than a dozen entries in each. Some entries are only samples, especially in the case of localized entries, and there are thousands of local organizations that can be contacted directly, although they will probably have similar price ranges.

7   Animals and Birds

The animal and bird charities listed provide a great deal of scope for tangible memorials from a modest sum to £1 million or more. Most of those listed have schemes whereby memorials can be offered within set price ranges. Animal charities generally are a good source of memorial schemes and there was a high positive response to my enquiries. Local wildlife trusts are also well worth contacting.

Animal Welfare Foundation
(British Veterinary Association)

The British Veterinary Association's Animal Welfare Foundation was established in 1984 to apply the knowledge, skill and compassion of veterinary surgeons in an effective way to all animals through a variety of projects and activities.

It believes that animal welfare problems often arise through ignorance rather than deliberate cruelty and so aims to educate those with responsibility for animals. The foundation has supported research projects in which improved welfare has been a primary aim and in 1986 the Colleen MacLeod Bequest was used to establish the world's first Chair in Animal Welfare, at the University of Cambridge. This was the beginning of a major commitment to the advancement of scientific study and education in relation to animal welfare matters. The Alice Stanley Jaye Bequest provided £10,000 a year to fund an annual scholarship to study animal welfare and an annual award to be given to a person or body that has worked towards the improvement of welfare for animals. The BVA Animal Welfare Foundation welcomes bequests and in memoriam gifts towards its work and there are a range of educational initiatives which need funding, such as lameness in farm animals, the problem of sheep scab and lamb welfare, and the transmission of the knowledge gained to farmers and stockmen. There are several commemorative opportunities in the research field which could be funded from about £5,000 upwards. For example, a studentship could be named for approximately £7,500 a year; £35,000 upwards for a research fellowship for a year; £500,000 to name a research project being undertaken by the foundation; and for £1,000,000 a new chair in an aspect of animal welfare could be named. Contact the foundation to discuss bequests, in memoriam gifts and suitable forms of commemoration.

Prices: Up to £5,000, up to £10,000, up to £50,000, up to £500,000, up to £1 million and beyond

Marie Reilly, 7 Mansfield Street, London W1M 0AT. Tel.: 0171 636 6541

Cats Protection League

The Cats Protection League, founded in 1927, is the oldest national charity devoted solely to the welfare of cats. Its chief aim is to rescue unwanted or injured cats and each year its 230 groups and branches are active in promoting the welfare of cats and supporting its thirteen shelters.

These shelters, based in London, the South East, East Anglia, Wales, Scotland, the West Country, the Midlands, the North of England and Belfast, place more than 70,000 cats in new homes. The league is also active in promoting the neutering of cats not required for breeding and the education of the general public in the care of cats and kittens. The Cats Protection League undertakes to become responsible for one or two cats, owned by a person at the time of his or her death. It does its best to comply with the wishes of the owner as to the cat's future welfare, although it prefers where possible to rehouse the cat in a family environment with a loving, carefully checked applicant. However, where a bequeathed cat or cats are elderly and infirm they will be given a home in one of the society's shelters. This scheme does provide a tangible memorial for those who leave money, although it will care for any cat in need whose owner has died. The service also operates in the case of illness and injury, to care for the cat temporarily if a person is incapacitated, and the league's headquarters in Horsham offers free emergency cards. The society suggests that one copy of the emergency card is kept in a prominent place in the home and one lodged with the will. The instruction that the Cats Protection League should care for any cats surviving after the legator's death can be incorporated in the will. A way of remembering a loved one is to sponsor a cat on his or her behalf. The sponsorship scheme exists mainly for cats who are unlikely to find a home mainly due to age or disability. The cost is £12 a month which helps to provide food and veterinary care. The family would be sent a photograph of the cat and would visit the cat at all reasonable times. Should the cat die or unexpectedly find a home, an alternative needy cat will be offered. £500 enables a sponsor to maintain a chalet or pen and the cats therein for a year. This can be done in memory of a loved one or a treasured cat, with a suitably worded plaque mounted on the wall for one year (or longer if sponsored for more than a year) and then displayed at the shelter. This charity is ideal for cat lovers who may have modest sums to bequeath but need to know that their own cats will be cared for after their deaths.

Prices: Up to £500 (per annum)
Brian L. Morris, Legacy Officer, 17 Kings Road, Horsham, W. Sussex RH13 5PN. Tel.: 01403 261947

Clinical Studies Trust Fund Limited (British Small Animal Veterinary Association)

The Clinical Studies Trust Fund (Petsavers) was set up in the 1970s with the prime intention of providing support for investigations into the diseases of dogs and cats. Because so few sources fund clinical studies in this area, the CSTF is very important in advancing the knowledge of pet diseases. Since 1975, it has given nearly £1 million towards numerous studies including breast cancer and blindness in dogs, and leukaemia and anaemia in cats. Clinical studies do not involve experimental animals nor would the CSTF support such research. The fund awards grants for clinical studies and supports residencies, studentships and scholarships at the UK veterinary schools. Some awards and studentships bear the name of a donor or a pet. Most awards granted by the fund are in the region of £50,000. Minor awards in the region of £5,000 are also made to top up an existing award. In these circumstances it would be impossible for a donor to specify an area in which he or she would like the award to be used. For the very large awards, however, it is possible to indicate appropriate areas for funding, e.g. cats, dogs, skin disease, lameness, etc. A donation of about £30,000 would be needed to fund one residency for a three-year period. A named residency continuing in perpetuity would be a very conspicuous memorial to a loved one and would cost about £150,000.

Prices: Up to £50,000, up to £250,000
Head of Administration, The Clinical Studies Trust Fund, (Petsavers), Kingsley House, Church Lane, Sturdington, Cheltenham, Glos. GL51 5TQ. Tel.: 01242 862994

The Donkey Sanctuary

The International Donkey Protection Trust is administered by the Donkey Sanctuary at Sidmouth. The sanctuary is open to the public every day of the year. Its aim is to help donkeys in trouble anywhere in the UK. More than 6,500 donkeys have been taken into the sanctuary where they will be guaranteed care and protection for the rest of their lives. For a minimum donation of £15, a name can be recorded on a plaque on the veterinary hospital wall. For a minimum donation of £50, a name can be recorded on a plaque under trees planted along the Memory Walk. For a legacy of any amount, an appropriate inscription is made on the Memory Wall. An annual memorial day is held on St Francis of Assisi Day (4 October) when all loved ones are remembered, and family and friends invited to attend a service and blessings. Contact Sandra Harrington for donations in memory and Brian Bagwell for legacies.

Prices:Memorial Wall, Walk and Day, up to £100

Dr Elizabeth Svendsen MBE, The Donkey Sanctuary, Sidmouth, Devon EX10 0NU. Tel.: 01395 578222

Guide Dogs for the Blind Association

This organization is responsible for the training and provision of all guide dogs in the UK. Applications for a guide dog are welcomed from anyone aged sixteen or over (there is no upper age limit) who finds mobility difficult because of visual impairment. A nominal 50p is charged for the dog and the association pays a substantial feeding allowance and also pays vets' bills.

The association has a scheme whereby a guide dog can be named and sponsored in memory of a deceased friend or relative (or even a loved former pet) or, of course, as a living memorial during one's own lifetime, with perhaps a future bequest to continue the work. For a minimum of £2,000, a donor can choose the name to be given to a guide dog puppy. The association suggests that the best names are two syllables long as these do not too closely resemble a command word, such as 'No' or 'Right'. The chosen name is submitted to the association's breeding manager for approval. Once this has been obtained, a puppy will be named as soon as possible. Litters are named by letter of the alphabet, with each puppy in the litter being given a name starting with the same letter. The association provides the donor or relation with details of the puppy's breed, colour and date of birth. At six weeks of age, the puppy is placed with one of the association's voluntary puppy walkers to gain experience and confidence in home and busy town conditions. When the named puppy is about twelve months of age, the dog will be brought back to one of the regional centres for assessment and, if all is well, he or she is accepted into the training programme. At this stage the donor or relative is informed that the puppy has successfully completed the puppy walking and gone on to the first part of its training as a young dog. When the dog has successfully completed the first phase, it is allocated to a qualified instructor for about two months or more of advanced training, after which a potential owner is selected with whom the dog is compatible. The final month's training is spent adapting to the needs of the new owner. Once a visually impaired owner has been trained to work with the new guide dog, a framed and inscribed photograph of the sponsored dog in harness is presented to the donor or the family. The scheme is a unique way of perpetuating the memory of a loved one every time the dog is called or greeted; it also provides the recipient with a pair of eyes.

Prices: Up to £5,000
A.T. Castleton, National Fund-raising Manager, Hillfields, Burghfield, Reading, Berks. RG7 3YG. Tel.: 01734 835555

Isle of Wight Zoological Gardens, Tiger Sanctuary and World Health Venomous Snake Centre

This family-run zoo on the sea-front near a famous fossil beach holds the world record for the most tiger cubs produced by a single breeding pair, Shere Khan and Tamyra; the latter has given birth to thirty cubs. The zoo works to preserve endangered species of big cats, especially tigers, including the rare Siberian tiger from which all other species are descended and whose blood-line has been pure for millions of years. There are only 300 Siberian tigers left in the wild. The director Jack Corney says that all tigers will be extinct in the wild within five to ten years and believes that only within a protected environment can the species survive. He sees education as the first priority of a zoo and he offers a varied programme for visitors to meet and learn about the animals, who are all in excellent condition and greet the zoo attendants with real affection. Jack believes that breeding of endangered species is another vital priority, but fears that to return them to the wild would end in their ultimate extinction, by both poachers and nature. In this he differs from other conservationists but argues his case powerfully, not least given the fine condition of the animals and their breeding record. Ninety-two per cent of animals in British zoos are born in Britain. Of Jack Corney's most famous tiger pair, Shere Khan is a Lancashire tiger and Jack argues that the temperate climate of Britain suits big cats. The average lifespan of a bird, reptile or animal in the wild is four months. Ninety per cent die before they are four months old and in the wild the biggest threat to the tiger cub is its father. Animals in the wild are also full of disease, Jack argues. This is partly caused by inbreeding but in a controlled situation like a breeding zoo, the blood-line can be varied. Tigers are also often malnourished in the wild since they are inefficient hunters and may only eat every ten days. They tend to have a single partner for life. The animals in the zoo are in large enclosures, approved by Ministry of Agriculture and zoo inspectors. Jack has bred sixty-nine big cats, forty-nine of whom were tigers.

The zoo is not registered as a charitable trust and therefore legacies do not benefit from exemption from inheritance tax. However, the zoo receives no government or council subsidies and desperately needs money to expand and improve facilities as well as to maintain current needs and breeding programmes. It costs £800 a day to keep the zoo running and the animals fed; initially £100,000 would ensure its future. Some of the world's deadliest snakes are also kept at the zoo and milked for their venom so that antidotes can be provided for victims all over the world through the World Health Organization and the Liverpool University School of Tropical Medicine.

Jack Corney is willing to allow any appropriate form of memorial for legacies and in memoriam gifts, and would welcome potential testators to visit the zoo, see the work that is being done and talk with Jack and his wife about projects and permanent memorials. Animal adoption can provide a low-cost source of giving for a living donor or as an in memoriam gift for a child, beloved grandparent, parent, friend or colleague who was an animal lover. Donors' names are displayed in the zoo entrance hall together with a photograph of the animal, while a photograph of the animal and the sponsor's name are sent to the donor or his or her family in the case of an in memoriam gift. The donor or in memoriam sponsor is invited to the zoo open day to meet director, staff and the sponsored animal. Because the zoo is quite small, the animals are easily identified and treated as family members. Annual sponsorship is based on the cost of an animal's food. Animals with a yearly food bill of more than £100 can be sponsored in shares of £20. For example: £5 – budgie; £10 – ducks, cockatiels, parakeets; £15 – spiders; £20 – sheep, goats; £25 – chipmunks; £30 – small snakes, owls, porcupines; £35 – squirrel-monkeys; £40 – coatis; £45 – ponies, iguanas, lizards; £50 – capuchin monkeys, pot-bellied pigs; £60 – large snakes, (rattlesnakes, pythons, etc.); £75 – lemurs, guanacos; £100 – leopard cats, jungle cats; £2,500 – leopards, pumas; £4,500 – tigers. A new breeding enclosure for tigers or other big cats would cost about £8,000. Jack would like to get rid of wire netting round cages and use water-filled trenches and electric wire to ensure safety for animal and visitor. This would cost about £50,000 for a large enclosure. He has acquired wooded and meadow land adjoining the zoo and hopes to use the meadow area for breeding. The enclosure could be named after the donor and/or have a plaque. The wooded area is to be used for breeding lemurs, also threatened with extinction in the wild and the special project of Judith Corney, who has successfully hand-reared several whose mother died or abandoned them. A lemur enclosure for a single species, utilizing the trees on the new land so that the creatures could climb freely, would cost from £5,000 and could be dedicated to a sponsor. A zoo attendant can be sponsored for a year for £7,800+ and again a suitable memorial could be arranged. A house for nocturnal lemurs would also be a welcome addition.

Jack Corney's ultimate dream is a big-cat sanctuary; at present none exists in Europe. This would provide the best of a zoo and breeding sanctuary, the best of entertainment for visitors and the best of a museum in offering educational facilities. The cost for the entire concept would be £5–£10 million, but the first £1 million would get the project started and ensure the benefactor's name on the project. For £2–£3 million, the present zoo could be enclosed and comfortable seating provided for lectures and displays so that the zoo would be an all-year, all-weather concept. Again it could be named after a donor of a substantial amount.

Prices: Up to £100 (per annum), up to £500 (per annum), up to £1,000 (per annum), up to £5,000 (also per annum), up to £10,000, up to £50,000, up to £100,000, up to £1 million and beyond

Jack and Judith Corney, The Zoo House, Yalverland, Sandown, Isle of Wight PO38 1BQ. Tel.: 01983 403883/405562

Jersey Wildlife Preservation Trust

Jersey Zoo was founded in 1959 by the late Gerald Durrell and the trust was formed in 1963 for the breeding of endangered animal species. Over the years, the Jersey Wildlife Preservation Trust has become the headquarters for breeding, teaching and research programmes for a network of worldwide survival centres.

It is at the forefront of projects to release captivity-bred animals into the wild. As natural habitats shrink and their animal populations shrink with them, the successful management and reproduction of small groups of endangered species is an essential component for global biodiversity. The trust finds it valuable to talk to any potential donor or legator about its current and future needs and to establish the kind of figure the donor is envisaging giving, so that a suitable project can be found to match the donor's own wishes with the needs of conservation and commemoration discussed. The zoo feels that the policy of adopting an animal can have the disadvantage of needing annual renewal. However, for an animal lover or to remember a young person, the idea offers a small, continuing memorial, beginning from only £10 to £15 a year. Plaques with the names of donors are mounted on the wall of the interpretation centre, the Princess Royal Pavilion. Examples for 1995 included the following: for £40 a year, a red-breasted goose or shelduck can be adopted; for £50, a Chilean flamingo or a Palwan peacock pheasant; for £60, a Mellers duck; for £100, a Rodrigues fruit bat; and for £150, a Livingstone's fruit bat. A bench with a plaque costs about £250. Benches get taken in for the winter so it can be difficult to guarantee that the bench will always be in a specific site. Enclosure construction costs from £50,000 and enclosure upgrading from £20,000. Dedicated species-education display boards have been erected but again, if a specific animal is chosen, there can occasionally be difficulties as enclosures are moved, changed or refashioned on a regular basis. On a few occasions, the boards do not get remounted. The Jersey Wildlife Trust is exceptionally forthcoming about these possible hazards and their overall attitude is very caring and responsible towards donors. Memorial trees have also been planted, in major planting schemes rather than individually. One sign with a map and a list of names is erected, rather than single plaques, which gives the impression of a memorial garden, rather than a grove. Landscape development costs from £10,000 to £75,000. The zoo welcomes books for the International Training Centre, some of which are on a short print-run and therefore can be quite expensive. A bookplate commemorates the named individual. Training centre books cost from £100. Training scholarships lasting for three months cost from £3,500. Graduates have returned to manage national parks, or reforest and protect natural habitats and to breed and release animals into the wild. For example the chief of the Royal Forest Department in Thailand, the chief of national parks and wildlife in Liberia and the curator of Jamaica's national zoo have all graduated from the school in Jersey, which aims to offer a high proportion of scholarships. A three-year research post costs £50,000 to finance. A training scholarship endowment for research costs from £75,000 in perpetuity. A research project costs from £1,000 to £3,000 in Jersey and from £3,000 to £9,000 overseas. Organic farm development costs £500,000. A research centre and endowment, including the conversion of the old Mammal House for £150,000, would involve £1–£1.5 million. This would build and name a centre for the research department, underwrite the future of the JWPT research programme and create an opportunity for the improvement and/or expansion of species recovery research. Such a sum, the trust says, would contribute in a very significant way to endangered species conservation at JWPT and worldwide.

The trust tries to match gifts in memory to specific items, ranging in value from a hundred pounds or so to seven figures. There are many examples: paintings by art students, for the training centre; equipment, such as a microscope for the laboratory; a new aviary or range of aviaries, or upgrading of those existing; library furniture; council-room chairs; a stand for the visitors' book; a building development; or one of the trust funds, for example the Gerald Durrell Memorial Fund which supports ex-trainees in their own countries with small grants. The Gerald Durrell Memorial Fund stood at the end of 1995 at over £1 million. The income from the fund provides largely for material needs, to offer help for graduates from the ITC. Small grants converted to local currency can have a profound effect, for example to the fieldworker without field glasses, a zoo without basic equipment, a breeding station without water. For smaller sums there is an appeal, SAFE (Saving Animals from Extinction), providing an opportunity to donate to one of the species recovery programmes, although this also welcomes larger sums, which can be recognized. For example, the lion tamarins of Brazil are under threat of extinction and donors can buy rain-forest by the acre to protect their habitat. The trust is purchasing a corridor of rain-forest linking the last two strongholds of the golden-headed lion tamarin in Brazil. Jersey-bred tamarins are now in the rain-forest. A breeding centre in the forest in Madagascar has been established for the rarest tortoise in the world, but a protected habitat must be found for the creatures. Projects can be based both in Jersey and in the natural habitat. A new habitat is being established for orang-utans in Jersey and a species survival plan established in Sumatra. Legacies received without any specific instruction are divided equally between the JWPT Overseas Fund and the JWPT Headquarters Fund. Although they are both capital funds, they play an essential and active role in breeding and conservation of endangered animal species.

Prices: Up to £100 (also per annum), up to £500, up to £1,000, up to £5,000, up to £10,000, up to £50,000, up to £100,000, up to £250,000, up to £500,000, up to £1 million and beyond
Simon Hicks, Trust Secretary, Les Augres Manor, Trinity, Jersey, Channel Islands JE3 5BP. Tel.: 01534 864666

London Zoo

Many animal species are becoming rare, endangered and finally extinct, through loss of habitat, persecution by exotic-pet traders, poaching and pollution. London Zoo campaigns to conserve endangered species. More than one hundred species, ranging in price from £20 a year for a dormouse to £6,000 a year for an Asian elephant, are available for sponsorship.

The money is used towards the specialist diet, ongoing veterinary care and upkeep of the zoo habitat of a chosen species. Although many people adopt animals in their own names, an animal can be adopted in memory of a loved relation or even as a living memory during one's own lifetime with perhaps money in a will to continue an in memoriam adoption. The best way to adopt an animal in memory is through a four-year renewable covenant. Bequests are obviously welcomed and can be for updated or new buildings or for equipment to any amount, with a suitable acknowledgement and commemoration if appropriate. When adopting an animal in memory of a relation, any amount over £20 a year ensures a plaque listing in that person's name. This is made of laminated plastic with metal surround. For a donation of over £300 a year an individual metal plaque can be engraved. For £20 or £30 a year, a small animal can be dedicated in memory. A part of any animal whose annual adoption cost is £60 or more can be adopted in £30 units. A small snake can be dedicated for £20 and a large one like a boa constrictor for £60. A chipmunk or a bat can be adopted for £60 a year. £90 a year buys a shark or flamingo. A lemur can be adopted for £150, a llama or penguin for £300, a wolf or lar gibbon for £500, a chimpanzee or crocodile for £750, a camel, reindeer or gorilla for £1,000 a year, a giraffe or Persian leopard for £1,500. An Asiatic lion, a Sumatran tiger or a black rhinoceros is £3,000 and an Asian elephant £6,000 a year. A lady, whose daughter was a veterinary student and died very young, donated money to adopt four of her daughter's favourite animals.

Prices: Up to £100 (per annum), up to £500 (per annum), up to £1,000 (per annum), up to £5,000 (per annum), up to £10,000 (per annum)

*Animal Adoption Manager, Regent's Park, London NW1 4RY.
Tel.: 0171 586 4443*

Marwell Zoological Park

Marwell is a preservation trust and charity for endangered species.
Current projects include the golden-headed lion tamarin, the snow
leopard and the scimitar-horned oryx.

The most common and durable form of memorial is a bench,
often sited near a favourite exhibit or certain animals. The cost of
a bench with a plaque is £120, with the benches made by the park's
own craftsmen. People have asked for their ashes to be scattered
in the zoo. A favoured spot is the very pleasant lawn behind
Marwell Hall. Plaques can also be erected on animal enclosures,
dedicated to a loved one in a general way. 'In memory of ... who
loved all animals' is one example. For this a donation would be
sought. In the above case, a one-off gift of £200 was made. An
animal adoption scheme enables relations to adopt animals in
memory of loved ones. Costs vary according to the choice of
animal, from £50 to £900 a year. A breeding or conservation
programme can be supported from £50 a year. A plaque is placed
in the relevant animal enclosure. Relatives receive news of the
animal as well as general information on the zoo. A natterjack
toad costs £25 a year, a grey-lag goose £30; a parrot £40; a share in
a zebra or a kookaburra £50; a goat £75; a kangaroo or rhea £100;
a golden-headed lion tamarin £150; an otter or ostrich £150; a
lemur or lynx £200; a maned wolf £250; a cheetah £300; a pygmy
hippo £500; a giraffe £800; and a white rhinoceros £900. All costs
are per annum.

Trees can be planted as a memorial. One small oak tree was
taken from the garden of a zoo supporter who worked as
gate-keeper during his retirement years. It was planted on the
zoo's Macaque Island with a plaque. When a visitor died at the zoo
a commemorative tree was planted on the spot. On a larger scale
bequests are invited as testimonials to a person's life and it is
suggested that a legator could state interest in specific projects.
The director is willing to discuss this. However, the zoo maintains
the right to the final decision since the endangered status of
different animals may change: what was once necessary may no
longer be so. Alternatively urgent accommodation may be needed
for a species whose conservation may be imperative. Running
costs of £3,000–£5,000 a year are necessary for heating,
maintenance, etc. of some animal houses even after initial
funding. A current project, Penguin World, set up to create a

suitable environment for the species, will cost £400,000. However donors who provide more than £250 will be permanently acknowledged on a plaque in Penguin World. The trust needs funding for a new educational centre and research scholarships could be instituted in a donor's name; £5,000 to £10,000 would fund a full-time researcher for three to six months.

Prices: Up to £100 (also per annum), up to £500 (also per annum), up to £1,000 (also per annum), up to £5,000 (also per annum), up to £10,000 (also per annum), up to £50,000, up to £250,000, up to £500,000, up to £1 million and beyond

John Knowles OBE, Director, Colden Common, Winchester, Hants SO21 1JH. Tel.: 01962 777407

National Canine Defence League

The league operates a scheme whereby a friend or relative can be remembered by a permanent plaque on a kennel at one of the rescue centres. It costs £400 to place.

The league is looking at a legacy promotion strategy which, it says, may well involve some form of recognition to those kind enough to bequeath money. In the meantime it points out the pitfalls of bequeathing money on the condition that a rescue centre is built in the legator's area. Centres involve indefinite running costs and therefore tend to be sited in areas of particular need which may not correspond with the chosen area. For this reason, the society asks for bequests to be left for general purposes. The cost of building and maintaining rescue centres varies according to the size and location of the facility. An approximate figure for a centre with a capacity for 120 dogs is £750,000. This would include education facilities, vet's room, isolation blocks, administration buildings, land purchase, etc. Annual running costs are approximately £130,000 for a rescue centre of the above size. £100 would support a dog at a rescue centre for a whole month including food, vet bills, heating, staffing, etc. £50 is the average veterinary bill for a dog in the care of the NCDL.

If specifically requested in a will, the NCDL will look after dogs after the owner has died. Many people choose to do this as they are comforted by the fact that the NCDL never destroys a dog except for humane reasons. There is a sponsor-a-dog scheme that, while not an official memorial, could provide a living memorial for a deceased dog lover by family or close friends. In return for a donation amounting to at least £1 a week, sponsors receive a certificate and regular updates on a dog's progress. Sponsored dogs can be visited at rescue centres.

Prices: Up to £500, up to £1,000 (per annum), up to £250,000 (per annum), up to £1 million
Adrian Burder, Head of Fund-raising, 17 Wakley Street, London EC1V 7LT. Tel.: 0171 837 0006

Royal Society for the Prevention of Cruelty to Animals

The RSPCA saves thousands of animals every year from cruelty, neglect and abandonment. Every thirty seconds someone in the British Isles contacts the RSPCA about an animal in need.

There are 350 inspectors who monitor animal welfare standards in boarding kennels and catteries, pet shops, race-courses, markets and ports, riding stables, slaughterhouses and zoos. In addition, they rescue animals they find in jeopardy, ranging from sheep trapped on ledges to beached porpoises. As well as gathering evidence for prosecutions, inspectors are in the forefront of animal welfare education. The running of animal centres is one of the services carried out by RSPCA branches. There are forty-one branch-run animal centres and thirty-five branch-run clinics. The animal centres offer refuge to abandoned or unwanted animals and every year rehouse about 80,000 animals. There are also three animal hospitals serving the whole of England and Wales, providing assisted veterinary care for animals whose owners cannot afford ordinary veterinary fees. Three wildlife hospitals give specialized care to over 10,000 injured wild animals throughout the country every year.

The manner in which the RSPCA most frequently acknowledges the kindness and generosity of testators is by entering their details in the society's Gold Book of Remembrance, housed in a glass display case in the reception area of the headquarters in Horsham. This book is updated monthly and available for inspection by any interested persons. All bequests are entered into the book regardless of their value. If specifically requested, the RSPCA will arrange for a plaque in memory of the testator at one of its homes, catteries, clinics or hospitals. However, the society does not encourage bequests specifically for this purpose or for any more expensive form of memorial because the RSPCA's prime concern is for the welfare of the animals themselves; it is preferable that as much income as possible is spent on this. The RSPCA therefore prefers bequests to be expressed as being for general charitable purposes so that they can be used at the relevant time wherever the need is greatest. The RSPCA asks that testators and/or their advisers contact the society before drafting any provisions that may place restrictions on the use of bequests.

Stapeley Grange, near Nantwich in Cheshire, the former country home of Mrs Cynthia Zur Nedden, was bequeathed to the RSPCA as part of a £750,000 legacy for conversion to an animal home and refuge with a clinic. The gross cost of setting up the hospital (see chapter 2 for more details and the problems of setting up a restricted bequest) was around £1.7 million and the annual running costs based on the 1996 budget were approximately £424,000. The RSPCA offered to name the centre after the testatrix whose bequest represented about a third of the total costs, but the executors preferred it to remain as Stapeley Grange; it is now a wildlife hospital and cattery. Stapeley Grange is the only wildlife hospital of its kind in the North West and deals with casualties from a fifty-mile radius, including care of twenty-five swans who were badly affected by an oil spill in the autumn of 1995 in the River Mersey.

Costs for building a new animal centre of medium size would be approximately £1.5 million at 1995 prices, plus a further £50,000 for equipping costs and an annual running cost of £180,000. RSPCA centres often incur additional costs with abandoned animals, as they may require significant veterinary attention and treatment, neutering, etc. These costs would normally be passed directly to the animal's owner. Any donation of £1 million or more would be welcomed as it would permit the regional animal centre development programme to proceed. In 1995, the RSPCA was working on two sites, Quainton in Buckinghamshire and Leybourne in Kent. Work on a further seven is awaiting funds. Smaller donations would also be welcomed as partial contributions towards procuring, equipping and running centres. Similarly, those individual RSPCA branches which own and administer centres or wish to do so would also welcome donations.

However, costs rise constantly. For this reason, the RSPCA is anxious to avoid a situation whereby a person might bequeath a legacy of perhaps £10,000, specifying that it could be used only to purchase an RSPCA inspector's van. By the time that the legacy was realized the sum would be nowhere near sufficient and so the society would have to turn down the legacy. Annual running costs are also (as with the case of Stapeley Grange) a consideration in leaving even a large bequest specifically to set up a rescue centre. Typical 1995 costs were as follows: cat basket £16; dog module £60; set of animal catching equipment £90; interview recording equipment (for prosecutions) £500; set of walkie-talkies (for surveillance and rescues) £1,000; rescue boat and trailer £5,000; inspector's van £10,000; minibus for inspectorate training £20,000; sponsorship of one inspector for seven months' training, including all equipment and operational costs £30,000.

Prices: Memorial Book, up to £5,000, up to £10,000, up to £50,000, up to £250,000 (also per annum), up to £1 million and beyond

Linda Norgrove, Head of Legacy Department, Causeway, Horsham, W. Sussex RH12 1HG. Tel.: 01403 264181

Royal Society for the Protection of Birds

The society is concerned with the conservation of wild birds in their natural surroundings and provides an environment which helps to create a habitat also beneficial to other forms of wildlife and plants. Because many British wild birds migrate during the winter, the society is also closely involved with international campaigns of bird conservation.

In Britain many important wildlife sites are threatened by development and the society not only represents natural interests on public inquiries but also buys important tracts of land to manage as nature reserves for birds and people. Education, through the Young Ornithologists' Club, the RSPB junior membership, as well as leaflets to every school in Britain, is another important role of the society, which relies heavily on in memoriam donations and takes no administrative costs out of bequests. Donations of £50 and above to the RSPB are inscribed in the name of the testator or a loved relative in the memorial book which is on permanent display at the headquarters in Sandy, Bedfordshire. There is a flower-filled memorial garden there to honour members who have left money in their wills or living members who make a donation of £500+ in memory of loved ones. The tranquil garden is popular with birds as well as visitors. A plaque, engraved according to the wishes of relations or decided before death by the testator during his or her lifetime, is placed in the garden. The plaque itself is provided by the society free of charge (it costs the society £25 including engraving), with members of the RSPB or members of the public making a donation; the society is very flexible and caring towards those who wish to be remembered in the garden but have only modest income. Recently a lady asked for a plaque as her daughter had died young, but she could not afford a big donation. As she had been a lifelong member, the RSPB gave her a plaque in return for a small donation.

At the other end of the scale, it is possible to buy a bird reserve. The smallest owned by the RSPB, Chapel Wood in Devon which covers about fourteen acres, has been created on land donated in a will. It is quite possible to have a reserve named after a person or a

In Loving Memory

memorial within a reserve, subject to any local regulations. However, it is important to talk to the society before bequeathing the land as it would need to be not only of conservation value but also in tune with current or future needs. In September 1995, the RSPB launched a £1 million appeal to create Britain's largest fenland bird reserve. The Little Ouse will be allowed to flood, creating marshes and expanses of open water. Lakenheath Fen will become a haven for bitterns, some of Britain's rarest birds, bearded tits, marsh-harriers and water-rails. The RSPB wants to create the reserve in memory of Ian Prestt, its former president and director-general, who died in early 1995. Money for the project will come from the RSPB's Land for Life, East Anglia Appeal which will run for several years to aid conservation work elsewhere in the region, including the Broads and Breckland, and the Essex coastal grazing marshes, reed-beds and salt-marshes. Projects throughout Britain are aided by bequests.

Mrs Ivy Bates who lived in Powys in Wales left a residuary legacy that included her jewellery to benefit birds and wildlife in Wales, a bequest worth over £150,000. The RSPB was seeking to buy Ramsey Island at the time of Mrs Bates's death, where the chough and peregrine falcon, puffin and guillemot breed. Her endowment was used to help complete the purchase. Roy Philips retired to Dorset and made his garden there a haven for birds. He left a pecuniary legacy of £2,000 for the RSPB to continue vital habitat management at the RSPB Arne Nature Reserve, a remnant of Dorset's former vast heathlands. Arne Reserve is famed for its nightjars and Dartford warblers.

The work of these benefactors is commemorated in the current booklet on bequests produced by the RSPB, *Who Will Look after the Birds?*. Pulborough Brooks Nature Reserve in West Sussex, which welcomes over 84,000 visitors annually, was bought with the help of a bequest by Winifred Smith Wright, who lived much of her life overlooking the river valley. She wanted the brooks restored as she had remembered them in her childhood, full of birds, and she left over £350,000 to make this possible. Within two years of the reserve being bought, according to warden Tim Callaway, lapwing and snipe, wintering widgeon and teal returned in great numbers. A bequest from Mrs Annie Jane Green provided £3,000 which was used to help develop the visitors' centre, where children can learn more about birds and wildlife. For smaller donations, it is quite possible to leave money to the restricted fund for the purpose of buying into a larger conservation project. A bequest for £350 was used to extend part of the West Sedgemoor development. Suitable memorials, whether naming areas of land or something more tangible, can be arranged in advance with the society.

A plantation of trees, if available, could be named after a donor if so requested. Consultation prior to making a bequest is important to avoid problems. If, for example, £1,000 was donated for bird boxes, it would buy quite a number but it would not be feasible to label them. However, such donations can be acknowledged in the in memoriam book. The trust is concerned with balancing the needs and wishes of donors with the needs of conservation, but will always try to respect any requests or wishes for a specific memorial. Sometimes donors specify a reserve in a particular area and this can tie up the money if legal and personal restrictions are too specific. For example, the RSPB has been left money for a reserve in Surrey but, at the moment, there is little suitable land available in the county. The RSPB is a charitable cause that might appeal not only to bird lovers but also to all who enjoy wildlife and the countryside. Because of its flexible and caring approach to those who give money, it provides not only a living memorial in its bird reserves but also a real interest in those bequeathing money.

Prices: Memorial Book, up to £100, up to £500, up to £1 million
Legacy Marketing Co-ordinator, The Lodge, Sandy, Beds. SG19 2DL. Tel.: 01767 680551

St Andrew Animal Fund
and Advocates for Animals

St Andrew Animal Fund and its sister organization, Advocates for Animals, provide financial and other means of support for the welfare of animals and wildlife, including grants made for the development by scientists of humane methods of research.

St Andrew Animal Fund was formed in 1969 to carry out the purely charitable activities formerly carried out by Advocates for Animals, concerning the protection of animals from cruelty or suffering throughout Scotland and elsewhere. Advocates for Animals does not have charitable status as such, because, under the present law, its anti-vivisection stance excludes it. Among the aims of both organizations are encouraging humane methods of study and research for the advancement of knowledge in natural and medical sciences, and organizing educational activities to create a proper understanding and appreciation of animals and wildlife. They make many grants and awards, including those for the protection of wildlife, to societies caring for domestic animals and for the benefit of farm animals. Legacies are commemorated in the annual Advocates Pictorial Review and there have been a few examples of benefactors who have been remembered in tangible ways. For example, the Oakley Clinic, the first low-cost spay/neuter clinic in Britain, was opened in December 1995 in Glasgow. It was named after Miss A.D.M. Oakley, a former member who made it possible by her legacy of £27,000. She left the money to the society requesting that some aspect of its work was named in her memory. The clinic has been established at the Glasgow Dog and Cat Home and will treat unwanted strays prior to rehoming. It also offers a low-cost service to the public to encourage more owners to have their pets neutered.

Janice Sheldon was a life member of Advocates for Animals and worked as a veterinary assistant in the town of Castle Cary. After her death in 1991, those who knew her and had benefited from her kindness to their animals had a special stone engraved with her name and dates that had on the front a bowl from which dogs can drink. The stone and bowl have been placed outside the local pet shop. St Andrew Animal Fund and Advocates for Animals are both willing to discuss commemoration for bequests of any amount, although obviously tangible commemoration is more difficult for small amounts. However, they express a real desire to help both legators and their families positively. For £10,000 or more it would be possible to take out an advertisement in a major newspaper about one of their projects and this advertisement could be dedicated to the donor. £50,000 could be used to buy video equipment and fund a project for uncovering animal cruelty, such as that recently undertaken investigating the condition of livestock in some Scottish markets. For £500,000 research studies, perhaps into alternative humane methods of study, could be funded and named in memory of the donor. For £1 million a university chair on some aspect of animal welfare or humane studies could be named after the donor. Contact St Andrew Animal Fund or Advocates for Animals at the same address to discuss possible legacies or in memoriam gifts and appropriate commemoration.

Prices: Up to £10,000, up to £50,000, up to £500,000, up to £1 million

Les Ward, Secretary, 10 Queensferry Street, Edinburgh EH2 4PG. Tel.: 0131 225 2116

8   Children

The children's charities listed offer a wide range of tangible memorials in most price ranges, although Save the Children has more difficulty because of the fact that much of its work is overseas. Similar organizations do not necessarily follow a pattern. The Starlight Foundation offers a very imaginative scheme. There was a high response to my enquiries.

Anthony Nolan Bone Marrow Trust

The trust manages the world's first and largest fully independent register of bone marrow donors with more than a quarter of a million volunteers on the donor register at the end of 1995.

It was set up in 1974 by Shirley Nolan in an attempt to save the life of her son Anthony, by establishing a register of un-related bone marrow donors. Anthony died at the age of seven in 1979 of an immune deficiency disease without a matching donor being found (see chapter 4). However, the trust continued as a memorial to him. Each year thousands of people with bone marrow diseases such as leukaemia, aplastic anaemia and inborn metabolic and immune deficiency conditions reach a stage when only a bone marrow transplant can save them. However, only approximately thirty per cent of these cases have a suitable family donor. Each day the trust receives ten requests for help and it can take at least 300 tests to find a matching donor to save one life. To fully sample tissue type, one blood sample alone costs £50 and this task is performed hundreds of times a week. It costs £5,000 every time a volunteer donates bone marrow to a British patient. A lamp for a microscope costs £140 and the trust has twelve. Each year at least £6 million is needed to further the work. Legacies and in memoriam gifts will be used either to expand the register, which needs many more members of ethnic minorities, or for research into making bone marrow transplants more successful.

Although the trust does not offer a formal scheme of

commemoration, it is possible to purchase a tree for £10 and this is frequently used as an in memoriam gift. A memorial book is to be kept at the trust headquarters at the Royal Free Hospital, listing those who have dedicated a tree or the person in whose name it is purchased. A certificate is also issued and visits to the wood where a tree has been dedicated are very welcome. Through the Woodland Project, the trust is creating a series of Anthony Nolan Memorial Woods. The trust is also working with local councils in the development of new community forests on unused and often derelict land. Anthony Nolan Memorial Woods are at Shaw Ridge, where 5,000 broad-leaf trees are being planted on reclaimed land as part of the Great Western Community Forest in Wiltshire, and the new Forest of Arden, where three memorial sites are being developed by the trust's project partners, Warwickshire County Council. There is a possibility of other memorial woods in Bedfordshire and the South of England. The first dedicated tree was planted in the Community Wood in Swindon in April 1994 by David Bellamy. The cost of setting up and maintaining the memorial woods is covered by the project partners and so the money donated goes to leukaemia research. For enquiries or orders, which may be by credit card or cheque, contact Jenny Hincks, Anthony Nolan Bone Marrow Appeal, Woodland Project, 43 Burge Court, Cirencester, Glos. GL7 1JY (Tel.: 01865 875758). Alternatively, contact the Anthony Nolan Bone Marrow Trust, Woodland Project, 51–53 High Street, Wheatley, Oxon (telephone as for Jenny Hincks).
Prices: Up to £100
Robin Dobson, Appeals Manager, The Royal Free Hospital, Pond Street, Hampstead, London NW3 2QG. Tel.: 0171 284 1234

Ben Hardwick Memorial Fund

Ben Hardwick was the first small child to receive a liver transplant in Britain and the fund, set up in his memory, is dedicated to saving the lives of other children (see chapter 4 for details). The money raised in Ben's name was used to staff and equip the Ben Hardwick Room, an intensive care room in Addenbrooke's Hospital, and to pay for a special doctor's post, called the Matthew Fewkes Fellowship after the little boy whose liver was used to try to save Ben. This post was created specifically to work with children who suffer from liver disease. The fund now concentrates on helping low-income families with children who have primary liver disease and makes small cash grants to help with the cost of travelling to specialist hospitals for treatment and the subsistence

costs of the relative who lives in hospital with the very sick child.
Prices: Unspecified
Anne Auber, Co-ordinator, 12 Nassau Road, London SW13 9QE.
Tel.: 0181 741 8499

Catholic Children's Society

The Catholic Children's Society (Westminster) was set up in 1859, and for more than one hundred years the basis of its work was adoption, fostering and the care of children in residential homes. This work was aimed at the Catholic community.

Since the sale of the children's homes in the late 1970s and early 1980s and after a change of name from the Crusade of Rescue to the Catholic Children's Society (Westminster), it continues to focus on adoption and fostering. However, the work has broadened to help children and families in need and includes three family centres, school counselling, child psychotherapy, a homelessness team and community work in areas of need. The largest part of the society's income has come from legacies. While names of deceased supporters have been published in annual reports, there were until recently no formal occasions to pay tribute to legators. However, in 1994, the first ever benefactors' mass was held for supporters. On 1 October 1995, the annual benefactors' mass was held at St Etheldreda's, the oldest Catholic Church in Britain. At present the invitation is limited to people connected with the society, to adopters, street-level collectors, high-level donors and other specific guests. The purpose of the mass is to draw supporters together to celebrate what the society has been able to achieve with the help of supporters living and dead. An in memoriam book was set up in October 1995 where the names of supporters and more particularly the names of legators will be permanently inscribed.
Prices: Unspecified for Memorial Book and Mass
Patricia Gallagher, Appeals Manager, 73 St Charles Square, London W10 6EJ. Tel.: 0181 969 5305

The Compassionate Friends

The Compassionate Friends, founded in 1969, is a nationwide organization of bereaved parents offering friendship and understanding to other bereaved parents with links around the world. Help and support are offered to all parents, including those of an adult child, whose son or daughter has died from any cause, whether accident, illness, murder or suicide.

The Compassionate Friends offer three ways to commemorate a loved child. Families can sponsor reprints of existing TCF leaflets and booklets or the first print of a new title. Prices vary according to the number of pages and the print run. Parents may choose which leaflet they wish to sponsor, which price bracket and the phrasing of the text of the printed memorial. An approximate price would be £50–£200.

A memorial book scheme also exists. The organization has a postal library carrying more than 700 titles, covering all aspects of bereavement. Parents can donate a book to the library. Commemorative wording is placed in the front of the book. The memorial book scheme offers parents the choice of either donating their own book or asking for suggestions from the TCF librarian. Apart from the commemorative wording they can also have a small photograph of the child placed in the book. Costs would be in the region of £1–£15 with a £2 administration charge. The Compassionate Friends' rose was launched in 1994 as part of the commemorative activities to mark the twenty-fifth anniversary. Parents can buy this fragrant pink floribunda bush rose direct from the growers, R. Harkness and Co. Ltd., The Rose Gardens, Cambridge Road, Hitchin, Herts. SG4 OHT. It costs £5.50 and a proportion of each rose sold benefits TCF. Initially, the growers offered a special price for bulk orders but any such offers would need to be negotiated direct.

Prices: Memorial Book, up to £100, up to £500
Pat Neil, 53 North Street, Bristol BS3 1EN. Tel.: 0117 966 5202

Leukaemia Busters

Leukaemia Busters, a charity for children's leukaemia research, funds the development and implementation of new antibody-based therapies for the treatment of patients with currently incurable forms of leukaemia (see chapter 4 for details of the charity's history).

It aims to ensure an improvement above that found with today's existing treatment and ultimately to contribute towards finding a cure for all. The charity has no paid fund-raisers, almost negligible overheads and relies on the initiative of ordinary people who have since 1990 made the work possible. The charity has a heavy commitment from parents of children undergoing treatment for leukaemia and lymphoma and was brought into existence by such parents. With money raised by Leukaemia Busters between 1990 and 1992, the Simon Flavell Leukaemia Research Laboratory was built and equipped within the medical faculty at Southampton General Hospital. It was necessary to build and equip the new facility in order to carry out studies which would lead to the implementation of clinical trials for leukaemia patients with antibody-based therapeutics.

The new laboratories also act as the centre of manufacture of the new immunotoxin drugs, currently requiring a staff of five. The first trial of one of several immunotoxins developed in the Simon Flavell Research Laboratory is underway with patients with B-cell lymphoma in the Royal South Hampshire Hospital in Southampton. If this first trial proves successful, agreement has been reached with the appropriate authorities to expand the trials to include other children's cancer units around Britain. In addition research work continues, always with the specific aim of developing even better therapeutics for further clincial trials a number of years ahead. It costs £120,000 per annum to run the laboratory facility and manufacture clinical-grade immunotoxin for use in clinical trial. The more successful the trials are and the more patients that can be treated, the higher the expense; it costs £200,000 per annum to achieve the long-term goals. The best way to provide this income would be to set up an endowment for the laboratory which would guarantee an annual income and allow the research team to concentrate on the task of undertaking its work without the worries and distractions of fund-raising.

Dr Flavell is very aware of the importance of commemoration and says that the existing unit contains many plaques to children who have died. For even a relatively small donation, perhaps £5,000 or even less, it would be possible to have a memorial plaque in the unit and for larger amounts a personal form of commemoration could be negotiated. £1 million would enable a new laboratory to be opened to help the work and this could be named as wished. It is stressed that every donation, however small, is valued.

Prices: Up to £5,000, up to £1 million
Dr David J. Flavell, Honorary Scientific Director, Children's Leukaemia Research, Southampton General Hospital, Southampton SO16 6YD. Tel.: 01703 796528.

Malcolm Sargent Cancer Fund for Children

The fund was set up in 1967 as a lasting and practical memorial to Sir Malcolm Sargent, the much-loved conductor who died that year from Hodgkin's Disease, a form of cancer.

For the first decade, only children under fifteen received

financial help. Now the fund provides support and practical help to children and young people under twenty-one and their families, suffering from any form of cancer, including leukaemia and Hodgkin's Disease. It distributes more than £1 million each year in grants. In 1976, the Malcolm Sargent social workers were established to work only with children with cancer and their families. They are paid by the Malcolm Sargent Fund, are managed by hospital social-work departments on the fund's behalf and are part of the paediatric oncology teams who treat and care for the children. In some centres, the fund also provides specialist Malcolm Sargent play therapists, Malcolm Sargent occupational therapists and a Malcolm Sargent nurse. In return for a substantial in memoriam gift or bequest to the fund, a memorial could be set up. This could range from sponsoring a Malcolm Sargent social worker in the field right up to naming a holiday home. Money could also be directed towards a particular area of the country or area of work. Contact Diane Yeo for a discussion of potential donations, in memoriam gifts and bequests and possible commemorations. The fund also runs two sea-front holiday homes, one at Jaywick Sands in Essex and the other in Ayrshire, which are fully staffed and accommodate two or three families at a time.

Prices: Unspecified
Diane Yeo, Chief Executive, 14 Abingdon Road, London W8 6AF. Tel.: 0171 937 4548

Pestalozzi Children's Village Trust

The trust is named after the eighteenth-century Swiss humanitarian, Johann Pestalozzi, who helped to restore the broken lives of children orphaned by the Napoleonic Wars. It aims to provide educational opportunities in the UK for some of the most able people from the poorest areas of the world to give them the education and knowledge they need to improve the quality of life in their home communities. Since the foundation of the Pestalozzi Children's Village in Sedlescombe, East Sussex, in 1950, more than 300 children have lived there and been educated at surrounding schools and colleges. The trust is taking care of more than seventy young people in the UK at any one time. This responsibility will extend into the next century, so it is vital that individual sponsorship and other fund-raising activities support these young people and future students. It costs just over £750,000 each year to maintain the village.

In the past, secondary and further education was not available to children from remote areas or from poor families in developing countries. Such children left their country and came to the Pestalozzi Village at the age of nine or ten. Although better secondary education has now been developed in many of these poorer countries, many people still cannot afford to pay for it. Therefore, former Pestalozzi students who have returned home now organize secondary education. Other sponsorship for such children *in situ* is also available through the Pestalozzi Overseas Children's Trust. When the children are fifteen or sixteen, they are then offered scholarships in the UK for a further two or three years. On their return home, the students have the qualifications for their chosen career or to go to university, taking with them the latest technological skills, learned while at the Pestalozzi Children's Village, to help their own communities. They then in turn participate in the work of the Pestalozzi Foundation in their own countries to sponsor the next generation of poor but able children.

While in East Sussex, the young people live in multi-cultural, mixed-nationality houses. The charity has, in the past, encouraged major donors to contribute to a named building as a tangible way of commemorating a loved one. The village has the Louise Centre, which commemorates the mother of a donor. This is a prefabricated building which the trust wished to upgrade and a contribution of £25,000 was made by her son. The Sainsbury Building, erected in 1962, celebrated the considerable contribution made by Lord Alan Sainsbury over a long period. The Pestalozzi Children's Village hopes to rebuild three of its main buildings and would like each of them to bear the name of a major donor. Each of the renewed buildings will cost about £450,000 and were the money available, the trust would also wish to build a sports hall. The trust also hopes that individual donors will fund the furniture, fittings and equipment for each house, either on a single room basis or for a whole building. Specific costings are not yet available but would range from about £5,000 to £100,000.

Prices: Up to £5,000, up to £10,000, up to £50,000, up to £100,000, up to £500,000

Maurice Phillips, Director, Sedlescombe, Battle, E. Sussex TN33 0RR. Tel.: 01424 870444

Rescue (Foundation for the Brain-injured Infant)

Rescue was initially established in 1991 by the parents of a brain-injured boy called Max because of the trauma they experienced in obtaining answers and gaining help. An original photograph of Max is used on the logo.

As many as twenty-five per cent of children start life with neurological problems and the foundation's aim is the prevention of brain injury and development of proven therapy and brain repair. The foundation funds research projects into why babies are born with brain damage, and how to prevent and ultimately end its occurrence. Research projects have been carried out at universities and university hospitals, including the universities of Warwick, Loughborough, Greenwich and Swansea, St Mary's Hospital, Manchester, St Michael's Hospital, Bristol, and the Gloucester Royal Infirmary. Other projects include the infant massage video and manual, auditory training therapy clinical trial, hyperbaric oxygen therapy and deficit-hyperactivity research. There are opportunities to fund and name research projects and perhaps contribute to the library and international bibliography that is being developed at head office, along with a database of the latest treatment, therapy and diagnosis methods and centres which provide information on any topic free of charge for parents. Parent research projects are also funded. The director would welcome any legacies and in memoriam gifts and would be very willing to discuss suitable commemoration in any area of particular interest.

Prices: Unspecified

Miriam Lewis, Director, Operations Centre, Kingsgate House, Church Road, Kingswood, Bristol BS15 4NN. Tel.: 0117 940 5860

Save the Children

Save the Children operates in more than fifty countries, including the UK, and aims to meet the basic needs of children in need and poverty in a way that can eventually be taken over by the community.

Those who want to make an in memoriam donation have the opportunity to select the project which their donation will support so that they can respect the wishes of the deceased relative or friend. Remembrance giving is especially welcomed and project giving of £90 yearly may be a way of keeping alive the memory of a loved relation, friend or colleague. Specific project areas that may be chosen include: teaching children to read and write in Laos and other countries, helping to stop children dying from killer diseases such as malaria in Zanzibar and other countries, helping orphaned children in Uganda and other countries or in the area of current greatest need. Supporters receive an annual report on the progress of the chosen project. Over the years the project areas may change, but there is always a new area of need to be sponsored. Up-to-date details can be obtained from the society. In addition the society will send to the family a list of all the people who made donations in memory of their loved one together with a total amount of the donation made.

The fund may in future produce an in memoriam book but at present this is not done. As far as legacies are concerned, the fund cannot allocate money to specific projects automatically. The money from legacies may well be received twenty years or more from the will being made and work may no longer be required in the country chosen by the legator. However, if someone does want to specify a project area, for example, health, this is possible.

In all cases, potential benefactors should contact Save the Children to discuss their wishes as the fund administrators are always happy to discuss suitable projects. Save the Children does not produce plaques or memorial stones because all the money raised is spent directly on helping children in the UK and around the world.

Prices: Unspecified
Yagnesh Patel, Head Office, 17 Grove Lane, London SE5 8RD. Tel.: 0171 703 5400

Society for Mucopolysaccharide Diseases

The society was established to help children and the families of those affected and to help research into effective treatment and ultimately a cure. Mucopolysaccharide diseases are a group of rare metabolic diseases that affect the way the body produces enzymes, which replace used materials and break them down for disposal. Children who are born with one of these diseases may initially show no sign, but the conditions are progressive and sufferers have short life expectancy. Some sufferers may be mildly affected, but for many there are severe disabilities. In most cases growth is restricted and some of the diseases cause progressive mental as well as physical handicap. Those conditions causing severe mental handicap can also lead to death in childhood. Sometimes more than one child in the family can be affected. The society supports about 800 families in the UK, of whom more than one hundred have two, three or even four children affected. Over the past ten years the society has funded £300,000 of research into treatment and clinical management. The society supports two specialist MPS clinics at the Royal Manchester Children's Hospital and at the Hospital for Sick Children at Great Ormond Street, London. It also funds three biochemists, one at Manchester Children's Hospital, one at the Christie Hospital, Manchester, and one at the Institute of Child Health, London. Gene therapy for Hurler Disease costs £16,000 for three years at the Christie Hospital. Mutation analysis of MPS at the Institute of Child Health costs £15,635 for one year. The annual conference cost £40,000 to fund, and when family contributions were deducted, £19,000. Holidays in 1994 cost the society almost £16,000 (£11,500 when family contributions were taken into account).

There are many areas in which memorials could be given to a loved one or as part of a bequest, such as named fellowships or research projects, named bursaries for holidays or an endowment towards the education of children afflicted with the diseases. An alternative might be to sponsor an adventure holiday for a group of teenagers and young adults with the disease or a family day for members of the society, a speaker or facilities at the annual conference or a specialist bursary, perhaps for music therapy. An endowment could be named after the donor or a loved one. The society is open to any suggestions for in memoriam gifts or legacies and will gladly discuss suitable commemoration in its research or care fields. All donations and sponsorships are acknowledged in the society's newsletter.

The society has a childhood memorial wood in Sherwood Pines in Nottinghamshire, planted and named in memory of the children who have died from mucopolysaccharide diseases. An inaugural planting of 141 saplings took place on 26 February 1993, attended by over a hundred MPS families. In the annual report are listed those children who died in the current year and who are remembered in the wood.

Prices: Memorial Wood, Unspecified
Christine Lavery, Director, 55 Hill Avenue, Amersham, Bucks. HP6 5BX. Tel.: 01494 434156

Starlight Foundation

This is a registered charity that grants wishes every year to hundreds of children between the ages of four and eighteen who are critically, chronically or terminally ill. It was started by the actress Emma Samms and her cousin Peter Samuelson in 1982, when they flew a boy who was suffering from a brain tumour to California, as his greatest wish was to visit Disneyland.

Starlight now has branches in the USA, Canada, Australia and the UK. Children are asked to choose three wishes in order of importance and Starlight endeavours to grant their first wish.

Every wish involves the child's parents, and brothers and sisters under the age of eighteen. The wishes fall into four categories: celebrity wishes for meeting famous people; experience wishes, for example riding in a racing car or hot air balloon; gift wishes, such as a computer or mountain bike; and travel wishes, perhaps visiting theme parks abroad, like Disneyland Paris. Each wish is organized and paid for by Starlight. It is possible to sponsor a specific wish in the name of a loved one. Details of the 'special child' and his or her wish, plus feedback on the experience, would be sent to the family.

There are three categories of sponsorship: Diamond Wishes for £1,000, Gold Wishes for £700 and Silver Wishes for £400. Another project suitable for in memoriam gifts is to buy a fun centre. There are currently thirty in the country and at late 1995 prices cost £3,000+ each. A fun centre provides video and Nintendo computer games on a stable, coloured bedside trolley for children who are temporarily or permanently bedridden. The first Starlight Express Room in a British hospital is being built at Llandough Hospital in South Wales. It will contain TV, video, computer games, educational and entertainment software, as well as more conventional toys and games. A second and third are being planned in Cambridgeshire and Essex. A room, similar to the one at Llandough Hospital, costs from £100,000 and could be dedicated in someone's name. Legacies, donations and in memoriam gifts are very welcome and can be discussed with Cheryl Nelson.

Prices: Up to £500, up to £1,000, up to £5,000 up to £100,000, up to £250,000

Cheryl Nelson, Director of Children's Services, 8A Bloomsbury Square, London WC1A 2LP. Tel.: 0171 430 1642

Thomas Coram Foundation for Children

The foundation is London's oldest children's charity. It has been working continuously with deprived and disadvantaged children since 1739, when Thomas Coram established the foundling hospital to provide care for the homeless children he found living and dying on the streets of London. With the support of distinguished figures in the world of the arts, including William Hogarth and George Frideric Handel, the new hospital became a centre of eighteenth-century philanthropy. One consequence of this is the foundation's remarkable collection of treasures, now housed at 40 Brunswick Square, London, on the site of the original hospital. Coram is a charity working with the most needy children and young people, and runs three important projects, partially funds others and offers space on the Mecklenburgh site, which is to be developed to offer services to children, particularly those with special needs, and their families.

The adoption service, one of the existing projects, is a specialist agency, finding families for the most hard-to-place children, those with Down's Syndrome or Aids or who have suffered physical and emotional abuse. The second project, Coram Leaving Care, provides supported accommodation for teenagers who have lived most of their lives in care. In Coram's houses they are encouraged to develop the skills to live independently so that they do not join the population of homeless young people on the streets of London, sixty per cent of whom have been in care.

The third project, Coram Meeting Place, provides the most comprehensive package of contact arrangements for children and their families in the Greater London area, providing a safe, comfortable venue for supervised and unsupervised contact between parents and their children where there has been separation because of past abuse, mental illness or neglect. In the next few years Coram will be developing the Mecklenburgh site for the use of London's children and their families, and turning 40 Brunswick Square into a museum and art gallery. Fund-raising will be crucial in supporting and expanding the existing work and for funding new projects, redeveloping the site and creating the museum. The conversion of the museum into a dedicated art gallery and museum will need a capital injection of at least £1 million. Anyone with ten times that sum would be most welcome to fund the capital cost of the proposed children's centre. Coram would also welcome possible bequests into childcare work.

Although the foundation does not yet have any formal schemes for remembering legators, in the past many were commemorated by memorials in the foundling hospital chapel, now part of Ashlyns School, Berkhamsted. The only instance of a substantial memorial donation in recent years was made by Sidney Levene in memory of his wife, to meet part of the cost of establishing the Coram Children's Centre in 1974. Roger Hickling, the fund-raising adviser, points out that this is not an unwillingness on the part of the Coram but reluctance by some former Coram children to acknowledge the connection. My own brother was a Coram boy and I remember the place with great affection. Financial support was also given in the 1950s for the building of Coram's Gregory House in memory of two members of the Gregory family, both of whom were treasurers of the foundling hospital. Contact the finance director to discuss bequests, in memoriam gifts and suitable areas for commemoration.

Prices: Up to £1 million and beyond
Richard Wyber, Finance Director, 40 Brunswick Square, London WC1N 1AZ. Tel.: 0171 837 8084.

9   Cultural and Scientific

This is a very fruitful area for tangible commemoration in most price ranges. Some unusual forms of commemoration are offered, for example with the Star Registry and Internet Memorial Garden, for quite modest sums.

Alister Hardy Trust

The Alister Hardy Trust at Westminster College, Oxford, is committed to supporting research into the nature and varieties of religious experience, in whichever ways those phenomena are understood. The trust, set up to recognize and extend the thought of Sir Alister Hardy FRS, who died in 1985, supports the Religious Experience Research Centre. The centre has assembled over the last twenty-five years an archive of around 6,000 accounts of religious experience and it continues to explore the meanings they carry and the ways in which these experiences are expressed. To continue this research it depends on grants and benefactions.

Benefactions are recorded in a legacy book. Such benefactions support the general purpose of the trust. These might include, for example, the endowment of a prize for a competitive essay relating to religious and spiritual experience or in support of a specific research project. Contact the director to discuss legacies and suitable commemoration.

Prices: Memorial Book, Unspecified
Robert Waite, Administrator, The Religious Experience Research Centre and Alister Hardy Society, Westminster College, Oxford, OX2 9AT. Tel.: 01865 243006

British Film Institute

The institute exists to promote the appreciation, enjoyment, protection and development of moving image culture in and throughout the UK. It runs the National Film and Television Archive, the National Film Theatre, the London Film Festival and the Museum of the Moving Image, and assists the production and distribution of film and video, and the funding and support of regional activities.

The National Film and Television Archive is always pleased to receive in memoriam gifts or bequests of films or film collections of any kind, especially with film rights, and even old home movies, although not home videos. It will mark any films that are accepted with a leader or credit acknowledging the donor or deceased owner. If a bequest suggests an area or even specific films in the archive that can be copied for preservation this request will be followed and, again, a leader or credit placed on the film. For example, someone might mention twenty or so films in the Film and Television Archive that he or she adores and these could be copied with money given in memory or bequeathed. Both small and large bequests, even up to £1 million, would, if given for general purposes, be used for the urgent task of preserving old films by copying them.

Occasionally people leave a collection of films and these are most welcome. For example the widow of Horace Shepherd, a minor film-maker, left her husband's collection to the archive on her death. Among them were his series of short animated chess films that were shown on Granada Television. Since all the material came with rights, the collection was of special value. The curator says that old films have little monetary value but are of immense worth to posterity and so could be offered to the archive as an in memoriam gift, bequest or even a lifetime gift.

Prices: Up to £1 million
Clive Jeavons, Curator, National Film and Television Archive, 21 Stephen Street, London W1P 2LN. Tel.: 0171 255 1444.

Contemporary Art Society

The society promotes the development of contemporary art and acquires works by living artists to give or loan to member galleries and museums. Some of these works are acquired by gift or bequest and a donor may ask the society to give the work to a specific museum to be displayed 'In memory of ...'. The society is especially committed to young artists and regional museums. Examples of bequests include a self-portrait by David Bomberg, presented in his memory by his family. *Villa Ariana à la memoire d'Antinoue*, by Anne and Patrick Poirier, was presented anonymously in memory of Mrs Amy Colls. The Contemporary

Art Society accepts works of art 'of museum quality'. Donations of any sum over £50 are added to the purchase fund and are acknowledged in the annual report. Donations of £1,000 and over would be used to purchase specific works of art and could carry a memorial. Although the society does not purchase or present work on demand, it is always willing to meet donors' wishes where possible. The society also manages commissions for the whole range of visual arts, from land art to applied art and all the traditional media in between. It would therefore be possible to enter into discussions about memorials in private or public sites.

Prices: Up to £5,000
Gill Hedley, Director, Tate Gallery, 20 John Islip Street, London SW1P 4LL. Tel.: 0171 821 5323.

International Star Registry

In spite of a highly commercialized leaflet, the International Star Registry provides an unusual way of remembering a loved one or ensuring one's own special star as a lasting memorial.

Choosing a star for a loved one has been practised informally in many cultures. In another of my books, *Families are Forever*, Maura, a Mexican mother, described a personal ceremony she and her husband devised for her two young sons after the death of their baby brother: 'The four of us went into the yard and I told my sons to pick the star they liked best and that the star was their little brother. Omar picked a tiny star just below Orion's belt and that became the infant's special star.'

The International Star Registry was founded in 1979 and is the twenty-seventh star listing made. The previous twenty-six, which span the centuries, were devised by astronomers in the Middle and Far East, Europe, the USA and the former Soviet Union. They were numerical and used coordinates for all except major stars such as Polaris and Vega. The International Star Registry uses names, the stars being listed according to personal and historical significance. The registry regards this as symbolic rather than scientific. Half a million stars have been registered so far by celebrities and the general public. The registry offers a certificate of registration in a chosen name, the date of its registration and the star's telescopic coordinates. This information is hand-inscribed by a calligrapher. A plan of the constellations and a large astronomical chart showing the exact position of the chosen star are also provided. The new names are registered with their telescopic coordinates in Switzerland and the USA. The names are copyrighted in the book *Your Place in the Cosmos*, which is published every few years, deposited with the British Library and registered with the Library of Congress in the US. The fee is £47.50, to include postage, plus an additional £5 for airmail postage if the donor lives outside the European Community.

Prices: Up to £100
Freepost, 24 Highbury Grove, London N5 2BR. Freephone 0800 212 493

The Internet Virtual Memorial Garden

Although there are currently three electronic memorial gardens on the Internet, Dr Lindsey Marshall's Virtual Memorial Garden network is the only one that is free (see chapter 1 for more details).

Organizations such as Demon Internet offer subscription to the many newsgroups and information on the Internet for about £10+ a month. To join the 'information superhighway' you would also need a computer, modem and software. Phone charges are those for a local call. If you lack the equipment or technical ability to log into the Internet yourself, it is relatively easy to find a young computer wizard who will be only too pleased to demonstrate his or her technical skill by making an entry for you and helping you to visit the site. The garden offers reasonably simple instructions for making an entry and accessing the entries. Often public libraries offer access to the Internet network, plus expert help, so even if a person does not have a suitable computer or knowledge of computers, entries can be made. There is a visitors' book on the memorial garden for comments.

The Virtual Memorial Garden was set up in 1995 by Dr Marshall, a lecturer in the computing department of Newcastle University, and by August 1995 had 300 names from all over the world. Up to six new names a day were being added. The bereaved can include a photograph or lines of verse. Dr Marshall has pledged that as long as the facilities remain, the garden will operate twenty-four hours a day. Entries from all over the world are stored in alphabetical order in the way chosen by family or friends. Some entries resemble conventional headstones in content but others lead to another computer where a full life story, poems and even photographs may be included. The Internet Memorial Garden places no restrictions on the wording used.

Prices: Memorial Book, Unspecified
You can log into the Virtual Memorial Garden on the World Wide Web at HTTP://catless.ncl.ac.uk/VMG.

Musicians' Benevolent Fund

In 1994 the Musicians' Benevolent Fund distributed almost £900,000 to 7,140 beneficiaries across a wide spectrum of the music profession. The fund takes care of retired and elderly musicians, increasingly within their own homes. Help is also given to musicians in illness or difficulty and to help them return to their chosen career on recovery.

Since the majority of the work of the MBF is ongoing and may involve the care of individual beneficiaries for many years, money bequeathed to the general fund is immensely valuable. The awards programme offers £80,000 in a variety of musical disciplines such as the Leggett Award for young brass players. In 1994, the awards and trusts department offered an extra £56,000 in new awards. For example, the Miriam Licette Scholarship offered £5,000 to students of French song, the Guillermina Suggia Gift provided £1,500 to cellists under twenty-one and the Sybil Tutton Awards gave £20,000 to opera students.

The committee has also decided to help fund genuine performance opportunities for young professional instrumentalists by making a contribution from the Ludgate Trust to the London Symphony Orchestra String Experience and Live Music Now schemes. Similar help was given to young professional singers from the Henry and Lily Davis Fund by underwriting the cost of both an ensemble member and a young principal in Kent Opera's performances of Britten's *The Prodigal Son*. It would require an endowment of £50,000 or more to produce enough income to fund an effective musical award. The cost of endowing an annual concert would depend on the proposed venue and scope of the concert but would need to be very substantial. The costs of single performers in specific productions could be much more manageable and need not be the product of an endowment, but could be one-off donations channelled through one of the existing associated trusts. Any sum from £1,000 upwards would be a useful addition to the funds used for this type of award.

As the fund has only one residential home that is very well equipped, it tends not to seek too specific a restriction on donations to it, but it is always possible to designate funds for outings or entertainment for the residents. Those considering an in memoriam donation or legacy are asked to contact Helen Faulkner so that she can work together with potential donors in satisfying their wishes and identifying an area of real need.

Prices: Up to £5,000, up to £50,000, up to £100,000

Helen Faulkner, Secretary to the Fund, 16 Ogle Street, London W1P 8JB. Tel.: 0171 636 4481

Royal Botanic Garden, Edinburgh

The Royal Botanic Garden is a direct descendant of the Physic Garden established near the Palace of Holyroodhouse in 1670. It has been on its present seventy-two-acre site since 1820. As a charitable organization, it welcomes a whole range of memorial donations, bequests and legacies. In addition to four beautiful gardens, the Royal Botanic Garden is an internationally renowned centre for plant-science research, for conservation initiatives and for formal and public educational provision.

As well as research into plant groups and the plant life of particular areas such as South-east Asia, Brazil, Bhutan, Middle East, China and Scotland, the Royal Botanic Garden is involved in plant conservation programmes worldwide. Specific projects include the World Conifer Conservation Programme. Researchers work on the cultivation, propagation and in some cases reintroduction of endangered plants. At the heart of the garden's research programme are the herbarium, an internationally important resource of more than two million preserved plants, and the library, the largest collection of botanical work in northern Britain.

The other three gardens are the Younger Botanic Garden at Benmore in Argyll, famous for its extensive range of flowering trees and shrubs, the Logan Botanic Garden in Wigtownshire, a sub-tropical garden where a range of southern hemisphere plants are grown outdoors, and Dawyk Botanic Garden in Peebleshire, situated in a Borders glen, a historic arboretum that is full of wildlife. The most common memorials are garden furniture and benches, tables and chairs that are fitted with commemorative plaques.

Because the garden is a botanic garden and research institution, it is unable to plant memorial trees. However, it has a book of remembrance which contains specially commissioned memorial paintings created by botanical artists. There is a wheelchair fund to enhance the provision of wheelchairs and electric buggies for disabled visitors, and also equipment, such as microscopes, is needed. There are always projects, large and small, which urgently require support and cover the whole range of the garden's activities. Individuals with a particular interest in an area can be directed to a suitable project or an element of it, which would be delighted to have their help.

The costs involved change from year to year. However, prices for late 1995 included a page in the book of remembrance for a minimum donation of £400, while garden furniture ranged from £500 upwards. An example of a legacy made towards a specific project was the Ferguson Bequest of around £231,000 to be used specifically for projects which would give pleasure to people with a love of plants, particularly plants from certain parts of Africa. Potential donors can discuss their ideas and preferences with the administrators and receive information about the garden's current priorities. In this way a fitting memorial can be decided upon. If donors prefer to make a general donation, funds will be allocated to a relevant project at the trustees' discretion. At the time of writing, work is urgently needed on the glasshouses, particularly the restoration of the historic palm houses. Supporting a research project would cost around £30,000.

Prices: Up to £500, up to £1,000, up to £50,000 (per annum)
Elaine Carmichael, Department of Public Services, Inverleith Row, Edinburgh EH3 5LR. Tel.: 0131 552 7171

Royal Photographic Society

The society exists to promote the general advancement of photography and its applications, and is open to beginners, enthusiastic amateurs and professionals. At its headquarters is a nationally recognized centre of photography and photographic history and it has a vast collection of rare photographs, books, equipment and periodicals. It organizes lectures, workshops, exhibitions, master classes, conferences, field trips and makes annual awards to both members and non-members.

The society receives many donations, mainly from members, living and deceased, in the forms of money, books, photographic equipment and photographs. For possible bequests and in memoriam gifts of artefacts, contact Mrs Pamela Roberts, the curator, to see whether an item is suitable. Sponsorship is welcomed from any source since the society operates as an educational charity, runs continual exhibitions and houses one of the most famous collections of photographs in the world.

Named awards, prizes and medals have been made and exhibitions are another possible area for commemoration, the cost depending on the number of items to be displayed, whether framing is needed and the time an exhibition would run. Named awards during 1995 included the Fenton Medal, established in 1980 and named after one of the society's founders. It is open to members and non-members for outstanding contributions to the work of the Royal Society; the Berg Medal, introduced in 1993 and sponsored by the society's Imaging Science and Technology Group in memory of Professor W.S. Berg, an eminent photographic scientist who was the recipient of the society's Silver

Progress Medal in 1970 and the Williamson Research Award in 1943. In view of Professor Berg's contribution to the teaching of photographic science, the award is intended for those under the age of thirty-five who, in the opinion of the council, have conducted research leading to the solution of one or more technical problems connected with imaging in general. The Bertram Cox Bequest was left to the society to provide sufficient money to enable a paper to be prepared and presented as an original contribution to the aesthetic side of creative photography.

Prices: Unspecified

Stuart Blake, Company Secretary and Finance Officer, The Octagon, Milsom Street, Bath BA1 1DN. Tel.: 01225 462841

Royal School of Church Music

The school was founded in 1927 by Sir Sydney Nicholson, Organist of Westminster Abbey, to aid all engaged in church music to appreciate its spiritual basis, discover its glories and achieve higher standards of music making.

From the beginning, work with children was a high priority and today the RSCM represents the largest youth movement in the church throughout many parts of the world. The RSCM has over 7,000 affiliated churches and schools in the UK and the English-speaking world as well as 4,000 personal members. The RSCM trains church musicians, singers, organists and instrumentalists. It also offers specialist help to those wishing to start groups of musicians, whether young or old, large or small. One priority is offering training to more members near their homes.

The school also needs a new base, since Addington Palace can no longer accommodate it. Cleveland Lodge, a house near Dorking, has been given by the late Susi Jeans and her family, but this needs extensive repair and renovation. Once the house is adapted, maintenance and running costs will be low, releasing more money for expansion in the regions, with new regional training centres, involvement in clergy training and initiatives for smaller churches and those without musical resources. £1.5 million is needed to move to Cleveland Lodge and to continue and expand the work for the whole church. The refurbishments will cost at least £400,000.

The Royal School of Church Music is particularly looking for donors to support its work in its regional centres: Huddersfield, Portsmouth, Buckfast Abbey in Devon, Cardiff and Liverpool. Memorials in the new developments are possible in many ways, for example plaques in rooms, over fireplaces or on furniture at the new headquarters or regional offices. There are several examples in the present school's premises. Contact Charles King, who is very willing to discuss individual ideas of commemoration. Good second-hand pianos for training would cost £1,000 each. Overhead projectors would cost £600 each and multi-media composition software from £800. A wish list at a recent dinner concert at Cleveland Lodge suggested the following: redecoration and new lighting in large music room £9,000; restoration of Lady Jeans's music room and historic organ £7,500; second car park £6,000; gates £5,000; lawn £4,000; external lighting £5,000; new courtyard £3,000; new RSCM sign £2,000.

Prices: Up to £1,000, up to £5,000, up to £10,000, up to £50,000, up to £500,000

Charles King, Chief Executive, Addington Palace, Croydon CR9 5AD. Tel.: 0181 654 7676

Royal Shakespeare Company

The RSC is the largest and most productive classical theatre company in the world, performing to a total of more than 1.1 million people annually. The 650-member company travels throughout Great Britain and abroad as well as presenting performances at its three home bases at Stratford-upon-Avon, London and Newcastle upon Tyne. As well as offering Shakespearean plays and classical drama, the RSC also encourages new writing.

It is always interested to discuss ways of commemorating friends and relatives. In the past, the RSC has acknowledged memorial gifts through placing seat plaques on designated seats in the Royal Shakespeare Theatre, the Swan Theatre and the Barbican Theatre. The typical cost of a theatre seat named in perpetuity is currently £5,000, although the figure is to be reviewed. Such a memorial should be discussed with the development director at Stratford-upon-Avon. In the case of people with very close associations with the RSC, such as leading actors, it has very occasionally been possible to plant trees with memorial plaques in the theatre gardens.

The RSC is considering other potential memorial schemes, such as a single commemorative performance or an annual performance named for someone on a personal anniversary date, together with ticket entitlements. The minimum figure for a single memorial performance would be £10,000. A multi-million-pound international fund-raising campaign is underway to generate an endowment fund for the RSC and to undertake very substantial capital and refurbishment projects to the theatre buildings in Stratford.

There are many opportunities for donations from £1,000 to several million pounds. For gifts in excess of £1 million, the RSC offers to be imaginative in tailoring acknowledgements to suit the interests of a particular person. Within the endowment fund, for example, named bursaries for specific positions within the RSC, such as directors, actors and designers, are being considered, which could recognize an important gift. On the capital side, there are many areas of the theatre and buildings which would lend themselves to being named in acknowledgement of an appropriately large gift.

The RSC is also very pleased to hear from potential donors who may wish to make gifts in kind. The company is especially grateful for gifts of residential accommodation in the Stratford-upon-Avon area, which is used to house artists working for the RSC. Also of interest are gifts of quality works of art or rare books on the theme of Shakespeare or the theatre generally, ideal for inscription as memorials, which are added to the RSC Collections, its permanent archive and library.

Prices: Up to £5,000, up to £10,000, up to £50,000, up to £100,000, up to £250,000, up to £500,000, up to £1 million and beyond
Jonathan Pope, Development Director, Royal Shakespeare Theatre, Stratford-upon-Avon, Warwicks. CV37 6BB. Tel.: 01789 296655

Scottish Society for Psychical Research

The society, a recognized Scottish charity, was founded in 1987 by its president, Professor Archie Roy. Its objectives are to investigate all types of those phenomena known as paranormal or parapsychological, and to collect, classify and study reports of such phenomena. It has a helpline for members of the public who have problems and experiences of a paranormal nature. It also has a group which investigates cases of haunted houses, poltergeist activity, etc. and it is always willing to help anyone with such a problem, in complete confidence. Monthly lectures are held in the Boyd Orr Building at the University of Glasgow, and prestigious speakers talk about their research and particular interests and expertise. Members of the public are always welcomed to these lectures and also to the smaller discussion group meetings which take place each month. There is a small but lively Edinburgh branch which also has a full programme of talks and activities. It is hoped that eventually branches will be formed in other major

Scottish cities. The society is almost entirely funded by the members' annual subscriptions.

The society is seeking premises to house its book and tape libraries and to provide office and meeting facilities. A sum of upwards of £150,000 would need to be invested to provide the annual rent, council tax and expenses required. The society hopes to establish several well-equipped teams of investigators to meet the needs of the public. Each team would require funds of between £1,500 and £2,000 for camcorders, ambient temperature meters, audio-recording equipment, etc. Bequests of books and relevant archive material would be considered, depending on the storage space available. It is suggested that interested parties contact the secretary to discuss mutually suitable memorials such as special memorial lectures, bookplates, plaques, etc.

Prices: Up to £5,000, up to £250,000
Daphne Plowman, Secretary, 131 Stirling Drive, Bishopbriggs, Glasgow G64 3AX. Tel.: 0141 772 4588

Society of Authors

A literary prize, grant or memorial prize can offer a prestigious form of remembrance. Some people like to negotiate a memorial prize in their lifetime, which can be set up for a few hundred pounds in legal costs, plus a nominal amount to start the fund. A literary award can be quite modest. For example, the cost of getting two or three nominated writers together once a year to decide on a suitable author to sponsor for a project would be about £10,000. The income from the investment would provide an annual award of a few hundred pounds in perpetuity. For £100,000, a testator could endow an annual prize of several thousand pounds. However, your prize might be helped by another sponsor or organization. People should not be deterred if they only have a small sum to give.

Various charities, such as the Authors' Foundation, administered by the Society of Authors, offer annual grants to writers whose publisher's advance does not cover research costs. A total of £35,000 is available annually. For £250–£500, a testator could make a one-off grant in his or her name. For £5,000 given to the fund, a grant of about £250 a year could be provided in a chosen name in perpetuity. The advantage is that the fund is already set up and so does not involve initial legal costs or separate administration charges. Leaving a bequest to one of the charitable funds is fairly straightforward, but in all cases a meeting is suggested to discuss the society's requirements and suitable projects.

Prices: Up to £500, up to £1,000, up to £5,000, up to £10,000, up to £100,000, up to £500,000

Mark Le Fanu, General Secretary, 84 Drayton Gardens, London SW10 9SB. Tel.: 0171 373 6642

10   Educational

During my survey, the amount of detail provided was quite varied. Bath, Edinburgh and Glasgow universities gave very precise and detailed memorial guides in all price ranges while other universities wanted to negotiate individually. I had quite a low response from schools; however, those listed are enthusiastic and versatile in the schemes they offer.

Lancaster University

The university commemorates people in a variety of ways. It is setting up a memorial volume to include all the people closely associated with the university who have died during the thirty-one years of its existence. Gifts have been received to set up prizes and scholarships or to donate such items as an outdoor bench with a plaque. No predetermined structure of cost exists, nor does the university consider one appropriate. For example, at present, the parents and friends of a deceased undergraduate or the close colleagues of a member of staff either collect what they can and the university makes the best use of the money in accordance with their wishes, or sometimes the university is asked how much would be needed to offer, perhaps, a prize within a certain price range for the foreseeable future; it then advises accordingly.
Prices: Memorial Book, Unspecified
Mrs Marion McClintock, Academic Registrar, Lancaster LA1 4YW. Tel.: 01524 65201

Royal Alexandra and Albert School

The Alexandra and Albert School dates from 1758, when a group of city businessmen under Dr Pickard raised money for an orphanage school for twenty boys at Hoxton in east London. This became the Royal Alexandra School in Hampstead. The Royal

Albert School was formerly an orphan school founded in
Camberley in Surrey; the two schools combined in 1948. The
present voluntary-aided junior and secondary school with 400
pupils, almost all of whom are boarders, takes many service and
expatriate families. The school has a wide spectrum of memorials
including the school chapel, the Joseph Rank Memorial Chapel.
Boarding-houses can be named after donors. Sunley House was
named after the builder Bernard Sunley, and Weston House after
Garfield Weston of Associated British Foods.

Memorial trees have been planted on the estate and garden
seats placed around the grounds. The school riding stables were
provided by a bequest and money for school prizes donated. The
current appeal to raise more than £2 million centres around several
projects; the bursary fund (£1 million), which provides help with
boarding fees for families who have financial difficulties; £300,000
will provide sixth-form bursaries; £300,000 will also modernize
three more boarding-houses; £400,000 will upgrade science and
technology laboratories and build a new library and a further
£400,000 will build sports facilities and a centre for the performing
arts.

Prices: Up to £100,000, up to £500,000
*Nicholas Wright, Foundation Secretary, Foundation Office, Gatton
Park, Reigate, Surrey RH2 0TW. Tel.: 01737 642576*

Saffron Walden Friends' School

This boarding-school, run on Quaker principles, will do its utmost
to ensure that if a donor requires a specific memorial it will be
provided. For example, if money was provided for a new television
for one of the boarding-houses, the school would be happy to add
a small commemorative plaque.

If a substantial bequest refurbished a boarding-block, the school
would be happy to name the rooms after a family name. There is a
new teaching-block of five classrooms given in memory of a former
pupil. One bequest provided prizes for pupils in CDT, music and
art. The bursar is always happy to talk to potential legators so that
they can see where their wishes might coincide with current needs.
Specific bequests can be restrictive; if, for example, a former pupil
of forty or fifty years ago remembered the dining-room chairs as
desperately uncomfortable, he might leave money for their
replacement at a time when the school had just purchased new ones.

Prices: Unspecified
*The Bursar, Friends' School, Saffron Walden, Essex CB11 3EB.
Tel.: 01799 525351*

Somerville College, University of Oxford

The college's development has been assisted considerably by bequests and in memoriam gifts. Perhaps the noteworthy feature is the strong tradition, since the college's foundation, of legacies to support the library. In consequence, Somerville now has one of the strongest college libraries in Oxford. Not only have book purchase funds been established by legacy, but in many instances these have been augmented by further gifts in memory of the deceased. On other occasions, a fund has resulted solely from in memoriam gifts of friends and admirers of the deceased. These funds cover a range of subjects and bear the name of the person commemorated, and appropriate commemorative bookplates are placed in the volumes they acquire. Contact the development director to discuss possible bequests and in memoriam gifts and appropriate commemoration.

Prices: Unspecified
David Rutherford, Development Director, Somerville College, Oxford OX2 6HD. Tel.: 01865 270635

Treloar Trust

All donations and legacies, whether £3, £300,000 or £3 million are acknowledged and accepted with gratitude by the Treloar Trust, which incorporates the Lord Mayor Treloar School and Lord Mayor Treloar National Specialist College of Further Education, and offers education, independence and care to young people with disabilities.

The Lord Mayor School and College are two of Britain's largest non-maintained or independent residential establishments for young people with severe disabilities. These disabilities include cerebral palsy, muscular dystrophy (a progressive weakening of all muscles), spina bifida, ataxia, haemophilia, brittle bones, epilepsy and those resulting from serious sporting or traffic accidents. The school takes pupils from eight to sixteen. Younger children are occasionally accepted. The National Specialist College of Further Education, at a separate site at Holybourne, accepts students between seventeen and twenty-five. In the past, the school has named houses at the school and college after individuals. It is happy to put up memorial plaques and there are a few photographs, prominently displayed, of people who have given legacies. The trust is willing to consider all proposals and does not put a set price on a particular memorial.

One way of recording a donor's generosity is by putting a simple plaque on wheelchairs and on computers used by students who cannot hold a pen, although such plaques are not normally in memory of someone. A computer would cost about £1,000. Wheelchairs cost from a few hundred pounds to £3,000 or £4,000 for an electric one. Part of the trust is Impact, the Independent Mobility Project, which normally provides one third of the cost of a wheelchair – about £700 – while the student raises the rest where possible. Students keep the chairs when they leave Treloar School. For about £2,000 a liberator, a special keyboard, can be fitted on the wheelchair, to help students with communication difficulties. A mini-bus can be provided from about £25,000 upwards.

In 1982 a lady from St Anne's left her entire estate of £700,000, which enabled a new hostel for sixth formers to be built. Plaques can be put on beds, in study bedrooms, sitting-rooms or to commemorate the refurbishment of a house. There are beautifully designed memorial boards around the school recording the generosity of individual and corporate donors for all major projects. On completion of a project a donors' day is held at the school.

As an example of the costs, a new single-storey boarding-house for the youngest children at Lord Mayor Treloar School is priced at £2.6 million, but the trust has already raised £500,000. Forty-eight bed spaces will cost £280,500. Curtains and blinds for an individual bed space will cost £300; £1,250 will provide furniture and fittings for a bed space; six bathroom units will cost £80,000; £5,000 will provide an external play space, £42,000 will provide an internal play area with ball pools etc.; hoists and access equipment for the forty-eight beds will cost £45,000. New projects are constantly arising while the cost of maintaining and refurbishing existing facilities remains.

Prices: Memorial Boards and Day, up to £500, up to £1,000, up to £5,000, up to £10,000, up to £50,000, up to £500,000, up to £1 million and beyond

Colonel O.J.M. Lindsay CBE, Trust Director and Secretary to the Trustees, Upper Froyle, Alton, Hants GU34 4JX. Tel.: 01420 22442/23248

University of Bath

The university produces a booklet for potential benefactors, suggesting approximate costs in a variety of areas. It suggests projects are 'an ideal setting for a living memorial and an investment in our future'. It is suggested that future legacies are not too closely tied to a specific research project as the issue may have run its course by the time the legacy comes into effect. But a laboratory can be named after a donor in a chosen research area. A first-class researcher costs £60,000 for three years, with more modest contributions funding a vital piece of equipment. Medical research areas covered by the university include inflammatory bowel disease, multiple sclerosis, asthma, kidney rejection, thrombosis and rheumatoid arthritis.

The School of Material Sciences is exploring the reasons why joint diseases occur and why artificial replacements are occasionally not wholly successful. Research into the teaching and development of lip-reading skills for those with impaired hearing is another project being undertaken. The Centre for Advanced Studies in Architecture provides a research base for decision makers in Bath to study new building proposals in architecturally sensitive areas of the city, combining the skills of the architectural historian with the computer expert. Scholarship endowment could be linked to a particular academic school or to students from a chosen region, either at undergraduate or postgraduate level.

A bequest of £40,000 would provide a capital endowment which could maintain a £1,000 scholarship at its present value in perpetuity. The administrators are happy to discuss with potential benefactors the conditions for an endowed academic post. For posts to be truly *in perpetuo*, the capital endowed must produce sufficient investment income not only to meet annual outgoings but also for reinvestment against inflation. This therefore requires capital of between £1.2 and £1.7 million, although lesser amounts can also be used to provide a variation on the idea. Support for students with disabilities is seen as a potential area for bequests. The university suggests money could be directed as a memorial to a person who has triumphed over a disability in his or her lifetime.

Property is another welcome bequest. Houses could be left for student accommodation or sold as an asset to be used for providing student housing in Bath. They can also be bequeathed, 'subject to life interest', for example the lifetime of a surviving spouse. The university also encourages the setting up and management of a charitable trust in the donor's lifetime. The trust could be a residual beneficiary (after all debts, charges and other bequests have been paid from the estate). The university points out the advantages of bringing forward part of the eventual gift, namely the personal involvement in defining the object of the trust, the satisfaction as a trustee of setting up the trust, watching its beneficial effects, further reducing tax liabilities within overall tax planning and participating in the life of the university community. The last is seen as creating new and unexpected interests and friendships (see chapter 2 for more details of endowing charities

during one's lifetime).
Prices: Up to £50,000, up to £100,000, up to £1 million and beyond
*A.J. Leighton MA, Director of Development, Bath BA2 7AY.
Tel.: 01225 82685.*

University of Durham

The university is pleased to accept bequests for approved university purposes. These range from named prizes, available in particular subjects, to named rooms, buildings and posts. There are many other forms of donation that could involve commemoration, for example the donation of a book or the cost of a book that can be acknowledged by a special bookplate as well as being mentioned in the librarian's annual report. The university would wish to discuss possible bequests in advance to make sure that the purpose is acceptable to the university and that any conditions stipulated in the will could be met.
Prices: Unspecified
I.M. Stewart, Deputy Registrar and Secretary, Old Shire Hall, Durham DH1 3HP. Tel.: 0191 374 2000

University of Edinburgh Development Trust

The university of Edinburgh has for more than four centuries received gifts and bequests from its alumni and friends. In the ninteenth century, the governing bodies began actively to seek private funds for support. One of the most celebrated bequests of this era was made by General John Reid, a graduate of the university and a general in the army of George III, who bequeathed the residue of his estate to the university, instructing that the bulk should be used to establish a professorship of music and an annual concert on his birthday. In due course, the Faculty of Music was set up and the Reid Hall hosts the annual Reid Memorial Concert each year on the Tuesday nearest the general's birthday. The development trust aims to ensure the university is well-equipped to respond to the challenges of the future and is obliged to observe the wishes of donors.

The breadth of the university's work allows the recognition of many particular interests, for example medicine, the arts, music, languages, books and sport. In addition, the university is always eager to discuss new ideas. It is difficult to state with any precision the level of legacy which would be required to support various types of projects. Costs of scholarships, fellowships and studentships are always changing. It is therefore suggested that the university be contacted by any potential donors (see chapter 2 for more information on Edinburgh University's approximate investment figures).

Many postgraduate students find it difficult to secure funding for their studies. A scholarship endowed by funds donated or bequeathed by an individual can be named after that person or a nominee. The financial level of these scholarships will vary from year to year in line with inflation, fees and the cost of living generally. An undergraduate scholarship would be based on fees but would also have to include an element for maintenance. Fees for medical courses range from £2,800 to £14,840 per annum and for other faculties from £750 to £8,160 per annum. Travelling scholarships provide a sum of money to help finance research trips abroad.

For example, the Dr Margaret Enid Crichton Stewart Fund was established when John Anderson Stewart left £50,000 to constitute a fund in memory of his wife to provide travelling grants to archaeology students researching European Beaker pottery or similar work. The Gwen Clutterbuck Scholarship was set up by Mrs Clutterbuck through a £6,000 lifetime donation and by varying the terms of her husband's will. This resulted in a total of some £56,000 coming to the university. The fund has enabled music graduates to undertake further study. A gift can establish and fund the post of a lecturer or research fellow named after a benefactor. The fund would have to cover not only the salary of the post but also the expense of any extra clerical and back-up staff and perhaps an element of accommodation. At least £25,000 per annum would be needed for up to five years.

Endowing an academic chair in perpetuity would require funds in excess of £1 million. The chair can be named according to the wishes of a benefactor if he or she has contributed at least a third of its funding. A fund could be established to which other donors could then contribute for the purpose of, for example, medical research. This could then provide a source of funding for medical equipment and other research tools. Again, it would be possible for such a fund to bear the name of a donor. The McGhie Fund for Research was established because in 1956, Mrs Amy McGhie left half of the residue of her estate to the university, 'the income to be applied in consultation with the Professor of Psychiatry in the University for the time being for research into and the study of medical nervous disorders and the prevention and treatment thereof'. Grants have been made from the fund for the purchase of equipment, the employment of temporary staff and the provision of training in specialized techniques. A donation or legacy can form a fund to provide an annual, biennial or other prize for academic achievement or otherwise, which can be named after a donor or his or her nominee.

The Colin Gilbert Dunnan Prize came about when Mr Dunnan left £2,000 to the development trust. As he had been a graduate in Business Studies, the prize is awarded each year to the best overall student in the Business Studies course in Strategy and General Management to purchase media materials. A donation or legacy of £1,000 or more ensures the inscription of the donor's name on the board located within the law library in Old College. The Development Trust Annual Giving (Small Projects) Campaign takes a different form each year. In 1994, a scheme was initiated to place book plates bearing the names of donors in books purchased for the library from donations of £25 and more. More than 1,400 books were purchased and the scheme is still being operated. In 1995, the campaign was to raise money for student sport. Donations of £25, £100 and £250, corresponding to bronze, silver and gold medals, are donated to a chosen club from the forty-nine individual sports' clubs within the university. Donors' names are recorded on a board within the university's sports complex at the Pleasance. Every donation and legacy to the University of Edinburgh Development Trust is recorded in the memorial books held by the university.

Prices: Memorial Book, up to £100, up to £500, up to £1,000 (also per annum), up to £5,000 (also per annum), up to £10,000 (also per annum) up to £250,000, up to £1 million and beyond

Frances M. Shepherd, Legacy Manager, Old College, South Bridge, Edinburgh EH8 9YL. Tel.: 0131 650 2240

University of Glasgow

The university is happy to acknowledge a donor and can provide detailed costings especially for small donations. Gifts are automatically acknowledged in the newsletter which is circulated to all graduates. For several major fund-raising projects, small gifts of £300 or more allow a brick in a wall or seat in a department to be named after the donor. Larger donations can be used to name a room or other identifiable unit if they come near to meeting the cost, for example £20,000–£30,000. Chairs and academic departments can be endowed or sponsored. Endowments need to be sufficient to produce income to meet an academic salary, possibly with an element for suitable support staff. Sponsorship pays for a salary for a limited number of years. In either case, the post will be named after a sponsor or donor. The sponsorship is named only for the period of sponsorship.

Prizes and scholarships are named after donors. The sum invested must be sufficient to produce an appropriate annual sum. The Gifted Scheme was originally set up for the funding of bedrooms in student halls of residence. The scheme has been expanded to provide naming opportunities, particularly for two of the university's current capital projects: the development of a centre for the study of theatre, film and television and the Weiper's Centre for Equine Welfare. Either a gifted seat in the Gilmorehill Halls development, which will house the Centre for the Study of Theatre, Film and Television, or a brick in the donors' wall at the Weiper's Centre can be purchased for £300. Smaller or larger gifts are welcome and donors can name more than one brick or seat. In addition, the campaign centre has details of areas which require a range of funding to which names can be attached.

Prices: Up to £500, up to £50,000

Jean Hewitt, Assistant Director, Development Campaign Office, 3 The Square, Glasgow G12 8QQ. Tel.: 0141 330 4951

University of London

Benefactors have been commemorated through having buildings or parts of buildings named after them. Two of the ceremonial halls in Senate House are named after Lord Beveridge and Lord Macmillan, two very distinguished servants of the university in the first half of this century. The building occupied by the Institute of Advanced Legal Studies is called Charles Clore House after the donor, who provided the bulk of the construction cost.

Donors often leave money to individual colleges rather than the university itself and it is then for the college to decide whether the bequest is sufficient for the purpose the donor has in mind. Similarly, while the university welcomes contributions towards its building projects, these have to be considered on merit after the examination of all factors. In particular, the question of running costs of the proposed building is of great importance since these costs may not be covered by the offered gift or bequest. It is suggested that a prospective donor should discuss in advance with the university or college any proposals for the use of their donation; this generally removes any potential difficulties.

Examples of benefactions made between 1992 and 1994 illustrate previous costings and/or the naming of projects either in memory of or for living donors. They include, for 1992: the Denton Hall Chair of Environmental Law at the Imperial College of Science, Technology and Medicine, funded through five annual payments of £50,000 from Denton, Hall, Burgin and Warrens; the British Postgraduate Medical Federation Institute of Child Health Chair of Developmental Biology, funded by an endowment of £1.3 million, obtained as part of the Wishing Well Appeal, which was launched on behalf of the Great Ormond Street Hospital for Sick Children some five years previously. The institute intended to use the income from the invested sum to provide the salary of the professor, a non-clinical lecturer/senior lecturer, secretarial support and some running expenses; the Dickinson Chair of Craniofacial Biology at the United Medical and Dental Schools of Guy's and St Thomas' Hospital funded from the Dickinson Trust through an initial payment of £50,000 on the establishment of the chair, together with annual amounts; at the University Marine Biological Station, Millport, bequests under the will of Miss Dorothy Marshall, amounting to about £300,000, provided the Sheina Marshall Scholarships for workers in marine biology. Dr Sheina Marshall FRS was the donor's sister and a distinguished figure in marine biology at Millport.

In 1993, Birkbeck College instituted the Cable and Wireless Chair in Business Information Systems, funded by Cable and Wireless PLC for five years from September 1993. The cost (to include additional library and software costs of £12,000) was estimated at £352,500 over five years at an average of £70,500 per annum. At the Institute of Classical Studies, the Winnington-Ingram Memorial Appeal was launched to commemorate Professor Reginald Winnington-Ingram, an eminent classical scholar and director of the institute from 1964 to 67. It funds a trainee librarian appointment at the institute. At the Imperial College of Science, Technology and Medicine, the Chair of Earth Observation in the college's Department of Physics was funded by sponsorship of up to £150,000 over three years from the Science and Engineering Research Council. After the first three years the college will assume responsibility for long-term funding. At the British Postgraduate Medical Federation Institute of Ophthalmology, the Glaxo Chair of Ophthalmic Epidemiology was funded by an endowment of £1.45 million from Glaxo UK. This will support the chair and establish a new Department of Ophthalmic Epidemiology.

Prices: Up to £250,000, up to £1 million and beyond
Jane Howard, Estates and Legal Affairs Division, Senate House, Malet Street, London WC1E 7HU. Tel.: 0171 636 8000

Winchester School of Art

The college has several trust funds commemorating its donors. The Alley Award produces an annual prize of £60 for a fine art student aiming to study at the Royal College of Art, while the Bateson Mason and E. Bendall awards provide annual prizes of £200 and £50 respectively, to be awarded to a fine art student. The Lina Garnade Memorial Awards provide an annual sum of £1,500 in prizes distributed at the discretion of an internal panel for fine art students in support of degree exhibition expenses.

The college would welcome bequests or named scholarships or fellowships and would much appreciate proposals for an annual memorial lecture, which would cost between £750 and £1,000 per annum. A junior fellowship would cost from £15,000 a year to fund and a more senior fellowship in the region of £25,000 per annum. A named scholarship for students from the UK or European Community would involve £2,500 per annum for fees, with perhaps an element towards accommodation costs of £2,250 per annum. A named scholarship for a student from overseas would entail £6,500 per annum in fees, plus any element towards accommodation costs.

Prices: Up to £1,000 (per annum), up to £5,000 (per annum), up to £10,000 (per annum), up to £50,000 (per annum)

Professor Ian Hunter, Head of the Department of Fine Art, Park Avenue, Winchester, Hants SO23 8DL. Tel.: 01962 842500

11 Heritage and Conservation

Because of the nature of the work of these organizations, tangible commemoration is quite common in this field, especially in the higher price bands. Although most listed prefer to discuss gifts and commemoration individually, there was a general willingness, especially with the smaller organizations, to be accommodating wherever possible to a donor's wishes. Of the larger organizations, the National Trust in Scotland offered several commemoration schemes for modest sums and the National Trust in England, Wales and Ireland has memorial books at its properties to record donations.

Council for the Protection of Rural England

The council has protected England's countryside for seventy years and is active in every county in England. A local branch can be made a beneficiary of a bequest. It is the only independent environmental group working for the whole countryside, as a place of work and farming as well as for pleasure.

The CPRE campaigns for firm planning laws, green belts, national parks, stronger woodland and hedgerow protection and more benign agricultural, forestry and water policies. In 1994, issues that it tackled included opposition both to a major new settlement around York as unnecessary and environmentally damaging, and to the threat to the green belt around Newcastle. It also opposed plans to build a reservoir in the Higher Buckland Valley in South Devon and stands against wider motorways because of the destruction this can cause to the countryside and wildlife habitats. The CPRE has formed relationships with all the main environmental organizations in the country and many others in Europe, as well as entering into dialogue with all concerned on local issues to find the best solution to development that will not harm the countryside or its dwellers and visitors. Legacies, a vital part of the CPRE's income, are commemorated in a variety of ways. All legacies are inscribed in an in memoriam book on public display at the CPRE's national office in London. All legacies are also listed in the annual report, regardless of value. The council also offers relatives the option of having the legator's name linked to a particular project, if they so wish. The council is appointing a legacy officer to whom enquiries about making a will can be directed.

Prices: Memorial Book

Catherine Miles, Fund-raising Assistant, Warwick House, 25 Buckingham Palace Road, London SW1W 0PP. Tel.: 0171 976 6433

English Heritage

English Heritage sees as its role the conservation of historic buildings and sites in England, Wales, Scotland and the Isle of Man and the promotion of the public's understanding and enjoyment of its heritage.

Founded in 1984, it owns heritage sites such as Stonehenge and Hadrian's Wall, Old Sarum (Salisbury), which was first an Iron Age fort, and Osborne House, Queen Victoria's holiday home on the Isle of Wight, Avebury stone circle in Wiltshire, the Avebury Museum and West Kennet long barrow, one of the largest Neolithic tombed chambers of its type. It also owns properties and sites throughout the UK, including Melrose Abbey and Dunfermline Abbey in Scotland, Caernarfon Castle and Harlech Castle in Wales and Laxey waterwheel, the largest working watermill in the world, on the Isle of Man. Bequests to English Heritage are not usually linked to any specific property or project. However, testators' wishes are adhered to when possible. Recent examples have included a bequest of over £100,000 for the Kenwood Landscape Appeal and a small donation of under £500 to be used for the maintenance or other benefit of St Mary's Church, Kemley, in Gloucestershire.

English Heritage does not operate any formal scheme for bequests but, in the case of significant amounts of money, it is possible that the expenditure could be dedicated to the memory of the donor. At any one time, English Heritage has a large number of major projects in progress, such as the restoration of the Albert Memorial, and it also undertakes a sizeable programme of repair and restoration every year at a large number of the 406 sites it manages.

As far as historic property is concerned, English Heritage is an acquirer of last resort and only would take into its care a property which was outstanding and at risk. Consequently, it is extremely rare for English Heritage to acquire properties but when it does do so, they tend to be large, high-quality sites such as Brodsworth Hall in Yorkshire, Danson House, Bexley, and Eltham Palace or ruins such as Wigmore Castle. Where property or artefacts are to be donated, different considerations apply. English Heritage, whose formal title is the Historic Buildings and Monuments Commission for England, was established by the National Heritage Act of 1983 for specific statutory purposes. Consequently, any legacy or bequest would have to be consistent with its statutory powers and there are occasions when a gift must be declined. For this reason it is important that anyone who does intend to leave either property or artefacts to English Heritage should contact the legal director Michael Brainsby to discuss the bequest.

English Heritage enjoys some of the tax benefits of charitable bodies. In particular, under Section 25 of the Inheritance Tax Act, 1984, a transfer of value to English Heritage is exempt. Projects for 1994 included a grant of £400,000 for roof repairs to St Walburge's Roman Catholic Church in Preston, Lancashire, that was designed by Joseph Hansom, inventor of the Hansom cab and builder of Birmingham town hall. The first phase of the stabilization of the quayside area close to the walls of Berwick was aided by a grant of £201,400. Because the peat soil of wetlands acts as a preservative of bodies and artefacts, English Heritage has agreed to fund a seven-year archaeological field survey in the Humber wetlands at a cost of £995,000. Some of the most important discoveries about early man of Britain and Ireland have been made in peat bogs and marshes.

English Heritage is the largest funder or archaeology in Britain and in December 1993 Boxgrove Man was found on a quarry site near Chichester in Sussex, in a project costing over £750,000, funded for over ten years. These were the earliest remains ever found in Europe, and stone-cutting tools and the bones of elephants, rhinoceroses, bears and mink were found near the leg of the 500,000-year-old hominid. The gymnasium at Prior Park, a Palladian house overlooking Bath that is designed in the form of a Doric Temple, is being saved from ruin by a grant of £275,000 towards repair work on the understanding that it will become a venue for concerts and cultural events.

The disused round chapel of Clapton Park United Reformed Church in Hackney, which is Grade II listed, is to become a performing arts centre, aided by repair grants of £400,000 from English Heritage. £1 million was offered to fund the excavation of

a Romano-British town near Heybridge, Essex, the largest ever made by English Heritage for a single archaeological project.
Prices: Unspecified
Michael Brainsby, Legal Director, 23 Savile Row, London W1X 1AB. Tel.: 0171 973 3000

Friends of Friendless Churches

This small charity owns twenty historic but redundant churches in England and Wales, either on freehold or long lease. It was founded in 1957 by Iver Bulmer Thomas as a nationwide, ecumenical and voluntary organization to save from demolition historic places of worship that had passed out of pastoral use. The majority of redundant churches in the society's care are Anglican. Although the Church of England can give these buildings to the society for nothing (along with the repair bills), nonconformist chapels etc. have to be sold to the highest bidder. Eighty Anglican churches alone close each year. The society is asked to help many buildings, but it has to refuse many cases because of lack of funds. All bequests and donations go to the churches in its care. These tend to be buildings that may be Grade I listed but are not adopted by such heritage trusts as the Historic Churches Preservation Trust, which take only those of high quality. These really are the friendless churches.

An area where help is needed is in the preservation of private chapels, when a convent or hospital closes and the chapel is left redundant. Large private houses too can have historic chapels, often Anglican ones, that are not wanted when the house is sold. Without help, these chapels and churches will be demolished. One church in Cambridgeshire alone needs £98,000 for internal repairs. It has been badly vandalized, like so many of these abandoned churches and chapels. A small medieval church would cost about £30,000–£50,000 to put into good repair. Dry rot and other major problems could double the cost. £100,000 would save three churches of modest size and in a modest state of repair. A large Victorian church with a spire in reasonable condition could cost £200,000 or more to restore to its former glory.

If the society were left £1 million, it would be able to take on fifty buildings instead of the current twenty and employ paid help instead of relying on volunteers. The society could accept money relating to a particular church if the person to be commemorated was buried there, had been married or christened there, had lived in the parish, had his or her ancestors buried in the churchyard or indeed had any plausible connection. It is often very easy to identify a particular operation where the donor could know that there was an exact correlation between his or her gift and the execution of the work, whether this was repair to a memorial, stained-glass window or exposed or suspected wall paintings, or the taming of a churchyard which had become overgrown. Each church has its own fabric fund that cannot be used for any other church.

The friends' churches include the Bargees' Church at Boveney on the banks of the Thames, the ruined churches of Eastwell in Kent and South Huish in Devon, the seventeenth-century chapel of the former castle at Urishay in Herefordshire, and the Welsh chapels at Llantrisant on Anglesey and Llanfair Kileddin in Gwent.

Prices: Up to £50,000, up to £100,000, up to £250,000, up to £1 million

Matthew Saunders, Honorary Director, St Ann's Vestry Hall, 2 Church Entry, London EC4V 5HB. Tel.: 0171 236 3934

Friends of the Lake District

The organization was first formed more than sixty years ago to campaign for a national park in the Lake District. When the park was founded in 1951 the friends continued their work to protect the area.

They purchased Hobcarton Crag, Baskett Fell and Little Langdale Tarn, all of which were transferred to the National Trust. Now their concerns include the whole of Cumbria. They work in liaison with other bodies, such as local villages and civic societies, to improve local amenities in schemes that include tree planting, cleaning of village becks, clearing bridleways and footpaths and providing footbridges. In 1985, an American benefactor established the substantial Kirby Bequest. Projects under this have included the inauguration of an annual Kirby Lecture and the establishment of bursaries for students in higher education for research projects on subjects related to the Lake District environment. It also finances the annual walling and hedge-laying competitions, arranged by the friends to keep alive the old skills and maintain the traditional appearance of the agricultural landscape.

The fund has enabled the friends to formalize the amenity grant scheme to offer help to village communities in Cumbria. Since 1986, more than eighty schemes have been established and, of the £50,000 already made available from the Kirby Fund, more than half has been allocated to environmental improvement. Projects include contributions to the appeal fund for the Geoffrey Berry Memorial Bridge, Eskdale, in 1990 and the Peggy Webb Jones Memorial Bridge at Buttermere in 1991, a grant for the creation of a nature garden at the Montreal Infant School at Cleator Moor and, also in 1991, replacement of a sundial in St Mary's Churchyard, Kirkby Lonsdale, and a contribution towards the purchase of and cost of footpath management at Quarrybeck Wood, Brampton, near Lanercost.

Most bequests are not tied to a specific project and usually go towards the running of and the pro-active work of the society. In other cases, the society has been able to channel money to other bodies to undertake valued conservation or access work. Sometimes the work is directly requested in the bequest, for example a new footbridge. It is difficult to suggest definite prices because the society can often add its own money to the bequest or use its money in conjunction with other organizations' resources. In suitable cases, a small plaque is attached to the work.

Memorial schemes should be in keeping with the environment but also serve a useful purpose, for example, if a cairn was requested, a wooden seat might be attached as an amenity. Repairs to a small bridge or a stone pack-horse bridge would cost £250–£500. An average bridge would cost £2,000–£10,000 and up to £20,000 for a sizeable bridge. A large stone bridge over a major river would cost from £200,000. In all these cases, a plaque can be put on a part of the bridge, commemorating the donor. Contact should be made through the secretary at the office to discuss individual bequests and suitable memorials.

Prices: Up to £500, up to £5,000, up to £10,000, up to £50,000, up to £250,000

Ian O. Brodie, Secretary, No. 3 Yard, 77, Highgate, Kendal, Cumbria LA9 4ED. Tel.: 01539 720788

Historic Churches Preservation Trust

The trust was founded in 1953, following a report entitled *The Preservation of our Churches*, commissioned after the enforced neglect of churches during the Second World War. It found that the fall in church attendance, high repair costs and taxation, urban migration and air pollution were causing a general decline in churches' maintenance and repair. Although the report was commissioned by the Church of England, the problem was not confined to the established church and so the trust was conceived as a national, non-denominational registered charity to help finance church repairs in England and Wales. Several million pounds, raised by voluntary giving, have been passed on in grants and interest-free loans to over 6,000 churches and chapels with daunting repair bills. On average the trust helps over 400 churches a year, many in small rural communities.

The trust's committee of honorary consulting architects ensures that assistance goes towards repairs that meet acceptable conservation standards. Limited resources mean that the trust can assist only towards fabric repairs. Over the years, the trust has been left a number of bequests to be administered in a specific way and these commemorate the name of the benefactors when they are used. For example, some years ago the trust was left a legacy by Mr Norman Tarbolton for the specific use of Lincolnshire churches. The money is held with the trust's main investment funds and when awards are made to Lincolnshire churches, a specific amount is given from the Tarbolton Legacy. The Llewellyn Jones Fund is reserved for Catholic churches. The Wilson Fund is reserved for churches in the Bristol diocese. The recipients of grants so awarded are always informed of the source and so the people who leave money to the trust have a practical and lasting memorial. Legacies are acknowledged in the annual report, listing the name and amount received, and in the year 1993/4 these ranged from £50 to £71,500 in individual value.

Prices: Unspecified
Wing Commander Michael Tippen, Fulham Palace, London SW6 6EA. Tel.: 0171 736 3054

Julia Margaret Cameron Trust

Dimbola Lodge at Freshwater Bay on the Isle of Wight is the nineteenth-century home of Julia Margaret Cameron, the pioneering Victorian photographer. Until recently the property was divided into holiday flats and a private residence, Cameron House, which was unoccupied and under threat of demolition. The trust was set up to save the house as a memorial to Cameron and her work and received assistance from the Foundation for the Sports and Arts, Olympus Cameras, the Esme Fairbairn Trust and other organizations and individuals around the world (see chapter 4 for full details of the campaign).

Dimbola Lodge, restored to much of its former beauty, is now open to the public and houses a photographic museum, the Cameron Gallery, a tea-shop and rare book shop. The trust is setting up a museum and gallery dedicated to Julia Margaret Cameron, together with a study and workshop centre, to promote interest in the history of photography and the preservation of photographic artefacts. There is a permanent display of Cameron images, and between April and July 1995 an exhibition of eighty contemporary photographs by some of the world's leading photographers was held at Dimbola. There is still a great deal of restoration work to be done, especially to the former Cameron House, where the original staircase was moved twenty or thirty years ago when the house was divided. A grant from the Rural Development Commission will help to restore the staircase to the front of the house, in its original location, and it is this part that, when opened to the public, will house a photographic study centre with lecture room, studio and darkroom facilities. Already the centre holds seminars and musical evenings. £1 million would buy up the properties around Dimbola Lodge and restore the original garden, on which the new dwellings have encroached. Already one has been purchased and the unsightly former yard of Dimbola is being transformed into a garden. £250,000 would clean the outside of the house and strip back to the original red and yellow brickwork and restore the original roofing to slates.

The property needs reslating and new roof timbers. Any surplus money would be used to re-lay the original quarry tiles outside and provide matching tiles for those missing. £100,000 would make and fit out a contemporary art gallery within the existing building. £50,000 would fit out a library room and buy some more books about Julia Margaret Cameron. £10,000–£25,000 would locate and restore the wells surrounding the property. Two have already been located and one, featured in a Rejlander's photograph of 1864 showing Julia and one of her maids drawing water, has been partially excavated. There are believed to be seven. £1,000–£10,000 could restore the stained glass in the two remaining doors and the porch. £100–£1,000 could be used to refurbish the museum. The trust has several display cabinets from the Natural History Museum. In all these cases, a notice or plaque commemorating the donor would be arranged as required, but all bequests and in memoriam gifts are welcome and could be commemorated in some way.

The trust accepts any suitable photographs or photographic equipment and especially welcomes those connected with Julia Margaret Cameron. Indeed, during 1995, the trust acquired two Cameron originals, one of Herschel and the other of Tennyson. One of these was presented by an anonymous donor. Life membership for the immediate family would be given to those who bequeath or donate more than £250. The trust is willing to discuss any projects close to the donor's heart, as there is much scope for imaginative remembrance.

Prices: Up to £100, up to £500, up to £1,000, up to £10,000, up to £50,000, up to £100,000, up to £250,000, up to £500,000, up to £1 million

Ron Smith, Chairman of Council of Management, Dimbola Lodge, Terrace Lane, Freshwater Bay, Isle of Wight PO40 9QE. Tel.: 01983 756814

National Trust

The National Trust in England, Wales and Northern Ireland has been described as the most important conservation society in the world. Its great houses and their contents and gardens, as well as places of national historical interest such as woodlands and areas of unspoilt coastline and countryside, are held in trust for the nation in perpetuity. All legacies are used either for capital expenditure at existing properties or for purchase or endowment of new ones. The trust does not spend the bequests on administration, except for the costs associated with legacies. It is not supported by government subsidies and so gifts and legacies are vital.

Legacies to the trust fall into three main categories: devises of property for permanent endowment together with any endowment fund that may be necessary for their upkeep; bequests for a specific purpose, usually for the purchase of land or upkeep of properties; and most helpful of all, according to the trust, money for general works to support its work of preservation.

The National Trust has a variety of permanent appeals: Enterprise Neptune, a campaign to save the coastline, the National Trust Parks and Woodlands Fund, the National Trust Gardens Fund, the Lake District Appeal, the Snowdonia Appeal, the Peak District Appeal, the Yorkshire Moors and Dales Appeal, the South Downs Appeal and the Mourne Mountains Appeal. In addition there are the Acorn Camp Scheme, which provides accommodation for young volunteers, the Foundation of Art (work by contemporary artists), nature conservation work, textile conservation, sculpture or metalwork, and the purchase of works of art or furniture that may interest the testator.

It does not usually put up plaques; its policy is to keep its properties as near to the original as possible and too many plaques could be obtrusive. However, it has a memorial book at each of its properties, in which the names of donors and the artefacts bought with their donations are recorded.These books are on open display. A list of legacies received during a year appears in each annual report and accounts, although bequests under £1,000 are not entered by name. A list of those who have bequeathed chattels is also included, as well as a list of investment properties, i.e. houses or land which have been vested in the trust's name pending their sale.

Where new properties have been acquired using funds from a bequest, these are mentioned in the annual report, itself in a small way a memorial to the generosity of the testators. For several hundred thousand pounds, commemoration can be flexible. A very large bequest which purchased an old foundry for the trust was commemorated by linking the name of the family involved in the bequest with the foundry. The trust may also accept old furniture if it is in good condition. In some cases this could be used in the growing number of holiday cottages it now owns.

The trust advises that anyone thinking of donating furniture or properties should contact its legacies department so that a representative can look at the property being offered and discuss its later use. Even if a property is not considered to be of national importance, it may still be of value to the trust, either to accommodate someone appropriate who needs to work locally or to be tenanted. If it is of national importance, it would need to be considered first by regional staff and then by the executive committee. Equally the trust says it views the contents of a home not merely as saleable assets but in their own right. As well as taking legal advice and consulting the trust's solicitor if in doubt, potential donors are also advised to talk to trust officers to ensure that potential bequests are useable. A trust spokeswoman recalled one unfortunate case where a woman left her property to the trust and another charity; there were so many stipulations in the will (for example, that there should be no changes to certain parts of the property, that no children should be allowed in the gardens, that any new windows could not be west facing and had to be in a certain kind of glass) that neither the trust nor the other charity felt the legacy could be accepted. The woman had not contacted them beforehand and there was no way of changing the will after her death. So, by default, the propery went to the treasury and it is almost certain that none of the stipulations in the will were met.

Legacies to the trust do not have to be expensive or extraordinary. In the case of William Straw, his terraced house is being preserved as a 'time capsule'. Neither he nor his brother, who shared the home in Staffordshire, saw it that way. It was the house in which they had lived since their parents died in the 1930s but they had not changed a single detail. The trust saw it as a perfect relic of its time, a unique record.

Examples of commemorative legacies include the base camp built in the name of the late Mr E. Howard at Little Scotney on the

Scotney Estate in Kent, which provides accommodation for young
volunteers working on the estate.
Prices: Memorial Book, Unspecified
*Michael Beaumont, Head of Legacies, 36 St Anne's Gate, London
SW1H 9AS. Tel.: 0171 222 9251*

National Trust for Scotland

This charity, supported by membership of a quarter of a million, is
Scotland's leading conservation organization. It was founded by a
small group of Scots in 1931 who were concerned at the growing
threat to their heritage. It now owns more than one hundred
properties and 100,000 acres of countryside, including Culloden
Moor and Glencoe. Its remit, set out in various acts of parliament,
is to promote the care and conservation of Scotland's landscape
and historic buildings while providing access to the public.

The National Trust in Scotland has a very flexible policy
concerning memorials. For £50–£80, a tree or group of shrubs can
be planted at a great many trust properties. For £250–£750, a seat
can be accepted at certain properties. Location is a consideration
to avoid a surfeit of seats at certain popular locations to the
detriment of less popular locations. For £250–£750, flower-beds
can be replanted at certain locations. In all cases, a memorial is
recorded in the benefactors' book at the relevant property. Larger
projects can be arranged by mutual agreement.

Julian Birchall, the controller of external funding, has requested
ideas for memorials from all interested parties, not just potential
donors. The trust has such a wide variety of properties, castles,
cottages, coastlines, islands, battlefields and bird reserves as well
as gardens, that almost any reasonable request can be
accommodated. Larger bequests have included that of Myles
Morrison, a member of the trust and keen hill-walker, who left the
trust £320,000 in 1992 'to help maintain the hills of Wester Ross in
their wild and natural state'. The money was used to extend the
trust's property at Kintail by the purchase of 9,300 acres of wild
hill-country.

Enid MacDonald, widow of a Glasgow Sheriff, who retired to
Galloway, left £300,000 to the trust. Her executors suggested that
the money be allocated to the restoration and refurbishment of
Threave House at Castle Douglas. Walter Scott Davidson left just
over £1 million to the trust in 1990, which has been used for the
maintenance and restoration of the trust's castles and historical
buildings. All these are given credit in the trust's magazine and

annual report and, where appropriate, in benefactors' books at each property.

Prices: Memorial Book, up to £100, up to £500, up to £1,000

Julian Birchall, Controller of External Funding, 5 Charlotte Square, Edinburgh EH2 4DU. Tel.: 0131 226 5922

Tamar Protection Society

This registered charity was formed in 1967 to stop the development of a particularly beautiful promontory in the River Tamar. The action succeeded and now the society's membership extends not only along the Tamar Valley but as far away as Surrey and London.

The next project was to rescue from demolition a fifteenth-century cottage in Saltash, Cornwall, on the grounds that it had been the home of Mary Newman, the wife of Sir Francis Drake. The house and cottage garden have been restored and now are open to the public. A granite sundial was erected in the garden in the memory of a society benefactor. The most recent endeavour involves the complete restoration of Elliot's grocery store, also in Saltash (mentioned in chapter 1), as a museum, preserving the store's old-fashioned charm.

The society is aware of many buildings in desperate straits, such as the oldest windmill in Cornwall which needs a roof and renewed sails and working parts. A Grade I listed farmhouse which dates back to Norman times is in danger of collapse. £100,000 would save this unadulterated set of original buildings. A strong supporting team of skilled professionals ensures that any conservation work is carried out in a manner which is sympathetic to the type of building, with the minimum of intrusion into the character of the building and its environment. The ultimate aim is to preserve the current use of a building, and the society does not sell restored buildings because it does not want to lose control of them.

The trust is also keen to acquire fifteenth-century furniture for Mary Newman's Cottage and would welcome suitable artefacts (contact Keith Johnston for discussion on this). The society is happy to erect memorial plaques on restored buildings for any substantial donation towards a restoration project and to discuss any appropriate form of memorial for bequests and in memoriam gifts, to combine the donor's or family's wishes with a suitable project.

Prices: Up to £100,000

C.K. Johnston, Chairman [Mrs J. Slater, Honorary Secretary], 26 Cowlin Gardens, Menheniot, Liskeard, Cornwall PL14 3QJ. Tel.: 01579 347993 (evenings)

Yarmouth Pier and Harbour Trust

Yarmouth Pier on the Isle of Wight is the last wooden pier in operation in the British Isles. It was originally built in 1876 as the deep-water terminal for the London and South Western Railway Company paddle-steamers from Lymington Town and was used by Alfred Lord Tennyson (one crossing inspired him to write the poem 'Crossing the Bar'). It is now used by pleasure-boats, as a tourist amenity and for fishermen.

By 1991, the pier was considered dangerous and so an appeal was launched for its restoration, which produced a novel method of commemoration. A wooden plank on the pier could be bought for £35 and named for whoever the donor chose. As tourists, fishermen and local people walk along the pier, the names of the donors unfold beneath their feet like a roll of honour. Initially, about 200 planks were named either in memory or by local firms and families. These are to be maintained in perpetuity. If there is sufficient demand, planks could be named at the end of the pier, although these tend to vary considerably in length and breadth.

Whether £1 or £5,000 is donated towards the upkeep of the pier, the donor is remembered in the Round House, a shelter at the end of the pier where a laminated plastic and metal gold plaque, mounted on a plinth, lists and thanks those who have contributed to the rebuilding of the pier. The harbour-masters are planning to build an amenity for visiting yachtsmen on the quay (yachts visit from all over the world). The amenity, made of Purbeck stone, will include shower and toilet blocks, facilities for the disabled and a fuel berth. While donations for the project, costing around £810,000, are not actively being sought, were a legator to pay for the building it could be named after him or her. Other large bequests would also be recognized in a major way. Gifts from about £500 to £10,000 towards projects could be commemorated with an appropriate brass plaque.

Memorial benches are always welcome and a local firm, Honnor and Jeffrey, of Afton Garden Centre, Afton Road, Freshwater (Tel.: 01983 752870), can provide a suitable bench and brass plaque for between £400 and £500 (this includes concreting the bench in the appropriate setting). Engraving (see chapter 3 for details) can be carried out by Sula Products of Cowes. However, the harbour-masters are willing to arrange for the bench and engraving, and donors need provide only the dedication they require. Very occasionally, an existing undedicated bench can be fitted with a memorial plaque for the cost of the plaque only, if a family has strong connections with the town or harbour. This would cost about £100 for the brass plaque. The benches are maintained by the harbour commissioners and can often be sited at a favourite spot.

The harbour trust is self-funding and uses any profits to maintain and improve amenities. It is run on commercial lines and as such does not qualify for relief of inheritance tax or capital gains tax.

Prices: Memorial Board, up to £500, up to £1,000, up to £10,000, up to £1 million

Nick Ward, Harbour Master and Clerk to the Commissioners, Yarmouth Harbour Commissioners, Yarmouth, Isle of Wight PO41 0NT. Tel.: 01983 760321

12   Hospitals and Medical Centres

There are opportunities for tangible commemoration, especially in the higher price ranges, such as endowing research projects. However, several organizations, such as Nuffield Hospitals and hospices, can offer commemoration for quite a modest sum.

There was a low response to my enquiries and out of fifty local surgeries I contacted throughout Britain, only one replied – my local surgery. It may be that, as several entries show, gifts to hospitals and surgeries are an area best made by personal negotiation and approach. However, with the demand on hospital trusts for money, commemorative schemes may be the way forward, to supply those facilities that have suffered from budget cuts.

Addenbrooke's Hospital NHS Trust

The Addenbrooke's Endowment Funds are always pleased to receive benefactions, whether as memorials or in general. The nature of the memorial would depend on the nature of the gift, but the hospital has many ways of recognizing memorials.

For example, generous donations of equipment have been marked with plaques. Rosie Maternity Unit, completed in 1984 at a cost of approximately £6 million, was named after the mother of Mr Robinson who provided half the cost (he also founded Robinson College in Cambridge). The gift was given with the proviso that the building was planned and constructed within a timescale specified by Mr Robinson. Pemberton House provides eight double bedrooms and one single bedroom to accommodate the families of transplant patients who live a long way from Addenbrooke's. The building was completed in 1990 and the costs of £150,000 were met by trust funds. In 1995 the orthopaedic clinic was extended and completely refurbished at a cost of £250,000.

Medical equipment is always required and there is a vast range of needs in a large complex hospital such as Addenbrooke's. Examples include: rise and fall couch, £2,000; mobile X-ray unit, £30,000; CT body scanner, £50,000; MRI scanner, £1 million. The costs of other items can be provided on request.

Memorial trees cost between £20 and £50 for a sapling and up to £500 for a semi-mature tree, marked with plaques. Space for trees is somewhat limited within the trust's estate. However, landscape considerations are very important in the context of new developments. Benches made of teak (from managed forests) cost from £300 upwards and high-quality engraved plaques cost around £50. Wherever possible the estate's staff will position benches in accordance with relatives' wishes. Books, videos and games would be welcome on the wards and could be marked or inscribed as appropriate. The trust has a memorial book for relatives of all patients who have died.

Prices: Memorial Book, up to £100, up to £500, up to £10,000, up to £50,000, up to £250,000, up to £1 million and beyond

Rachel Wheeler, Trust Board Support Manager, Administrative Directorate, Box 146, Hills Road, Cambridge CB2 2QQ. Tel.: 01223 217983

Brookside Health Centre

The fund-holding centre on the Isle of Wight, administered by the doctors, has purchased many items for use by all the health workers in the community. It is suggested that potential donors contact the health centre to discuss current needs and how memorial gifts can be commemorated.

The district nurses need very expensive items (such as Nimbus mattresses which cost £3,000 each) that are of special benefit to cancer sufferers. Seat cushions are also much needed at a cost of £100 each. Syringe drivers, for the use of terminally ill patients, are £700–£800 each. The nurses have two but would welcome more. The physiotherapy department has bought TENS (pain relieving) machines at £50 each, many advice books and a laser machine, which cost £1,500. New curtains have been purchased for the physiotherapy department at the local residential care and convalescent home for the elderly. The doctors purchased a new ECG machine for £2,000 and resuscitation equipment to carry in their cars. The centre hopes to fund another ECG machine. The chiropody department was given a new magnifying lamp for £150. The practice nurses now have more ear syringing equipment and always need more nebulizers to help asthmatic patients, which cost about £80 each. The midwives have had scales, advice books and videos for the clinic. Brookside Health Centre attracts donations mainly from local people but, as the main health centre in West Wight, has helped many holidaymakers.

Other non-medical expenditure from April 1994 to March 1995 included £190 for new signs for the doctors' rooms and extension, £1,280 for new telephone systems for the Brookside and Yarmouth surgeries, £2,850 for a new carpet in the Brookside waiting area and £2,250 for replacement windows at the Yarmouth surgery. There is scope for bequests and donations from just a few pounds, perhaps for a book which could be inscribed, to large amounts for a major piece of equipment or even an extension. As with all surgeries and health centres, there are always new demands for funds as technology improves and old equipment wears out or is superseded. Therefore a personal approach is recommended either by a potential donor or a family wanting to remember a loved one who perhaps was helped by Brookside Health Centre while on holiday.

Prices: Up to £50, up to £100, up to £500, up to £1,000, up to £5,000
Christine Johnson, Practice Manager, West Wight Community Fund, Brookside Health Centre, Freshwater, Isle of Wight PO40 9DT. Tel.: 01983 753433

Children's Hospice Appeal (Wessex)

The appeal is raising £5 million to build, equip and help run the first children's hospice in central southern England. There are fund-raising committees in towns and cities across the central south, as far as the Isle of Wight. However, even when the hospice opens, funds will be needed indefinitely to keep it running. The appeal managers are encouraging donors to support staff, particularly nurses, at a cost of approximately £20,000 per year for each nurse. Marks & Spencer has already pledged to provide one nurse for the first three years. There will also be a constant need for expenditure and additional items of equipment for the staff and for the children that, in some cases, could perhaps lend themselves to dedication. Rooms are also available for sponsorship. A Tree of Life mural will be displayed as a testament to donors.

Prices: Up to £50,000
Brian Walker, Director of Fund-raising, Wessex Children's Hospice Trust, The Police House, Micheldever, Winchester, Hants SO21 3DF. Tel.: 01962 774895

Elizabeth Garrett Anderson
Hospital Appeal Trust

Elizabeth Garrett Anderson pioneered the way for women doctors in the UK, although to obtain her MD she had to go to the University of Paris. In 1866, she opened the St Mary's Dispensary for Sick Women in Marylebone in London, to give particularly the very poor women from the nearby slums their first chance to be treated by women. At the same time she gave women the opportunity to work in a hospital. The hospital was renamed the New Hospital for Women when it moved to larger premises in Marylebone Road in 1876, remaining there until the new hospital on its present site in Euston Road was completed. Elizabeth Garrett Anderson's greatest achievement came in 1892 with the admission of women to the British Medical Association.

The Elizabeth Garrett Anderson Hospital, which is still run for women by women, has recently been renovated. Many services are provided by volunteers. An appeal trust was founded in September 1980 with the original purpose of running the £500,000 national appeal and to administer the fund. The reason for the appeal was that in 1974, the government announced that the hospital was to be closed, a decision confirmed in 1978. A major campaign was launched and Margaret Thatcher promised that if she came into power, she would save the hospital. As a result, a £2.4-million inflation-proof grant was made to cover the cost of renovation and construction work. The money was given on the understanding that the EGA trust should raise the money needed to equip and refurnish the newly restored hospital. The result of the appeal, which exceeded its target, was that ninety per cent of the equipment and furniture in the hospital has been bought by the trustees and is on loan to the health authority.

The appeal continues to purchase modern equipment and other items which it is felt are essential for the efficient operation of the EGA. There have been a number of memorial gifts. For example, when Elizabeth Garrett Anderson was raising funds to build the present hospital in the late 1880s, Mrs Gertrude Lorillard of New York City made a donation to purchase the freehold of the land. A plaque on the ground floor was placed 'in grateful and abiding memory' of the 'munificent bequest'. There are sixty-four stained-glass windows which record how in the late 1890s and early 1900s donors endowed beds in memory of an individual. The windows also recorded organizations who had made gifts. In recent years, where appropriate and if a donor so wishes, a small plaque has been placed in the hospital.

In the early 1980s, Dr Sachs, whose wife Muriel Elsie Landau had been a gynaecologist at the hospital, gave a considerable sum as a memorial donation. There is a plaque commemorating her in one of the four in-patient single rooms paid for by Dr Sachs and also a memorial bench in the garden. More than £1 million was bequeathed by Dr Joan Haram, a pathologist who had worked at the hospital. In recognition of her generosity the Well Woman Centre is named after her. Donations and bequests are especially welcome to fund equipment in the Well Woman Centre, where although the Elizabeth Garrett Anderson is an NHS hospital, women can make their own appointments without a GP referral. The EGA trust has also funded a urology research project and a laser project, the latter in co-operation with the National Medical Laser Centre at University College, London. Cancer treatment is another area where funding is especially welcome. Contact the trust administrator to discuss possible bequests and in memoriam gifts and suitable commemoration.

Prices: Unspecified

Elizabeth Ellett, Trust Administrator, Euston Road, London NW1 1YA. Tel.: 0171 387 2501

Help the Hospices

This is a national organization, dedicated to all aspects of hospice and palliative care, whether under the NHS or under charitable arrangements. It also funds research, study and education of the public for better care of the terminally ill.

Help the Hospices is pleased to create memorials in return for donations and will make necessary arrangements with the hospice of the benefactor's choice. Some newly bereaved families may find this easier than negotiating directly with the hospice where a loved one died. Of course, they would always be welcome to see the memorial. The hospice movement offers many forms of tangible memorials and so this entry represents only a sample list. The hospice or section of a hospice built with the aid of a benefactor's donation can be named after the donor or the donor's family for £50,000 upwards. For £25,000–£50,000, a specific area of the hospice benefiting from the donation can carry an inscribed plaque; for £1,000–£25,000, a part or whole of the hospice garden can be named after the donor. A stained-glass window can often be paid for by a donor and either be named after the donor or have an inscribed plate fitted below. £250–£1,000 could purchase shrubs, a pond, fountain or pergola, all of which may carry inscribed plates. £25–£250 would record the donor's name in the hospice book of remembrance.

Prices: Memorial Book, up to £50, up to £100, up to £500, up to £1,000, up to £5,000, up to £10,000, up to £50,000, up to £100,000, up to £500,000, up to £1 million
Terry Taylor, Chief Executive, 33–44 Britannia Street, London WC1X 5JG. Tel.: 0171 278 5668

Nuffield Hospitals

A legator can have his or her name on the plaque or any item or room purchased. Hospital equipment is quite expensive so the minimum donation would be about £100 for a plaque. For example, a pain-control machine was purchased for £200. A bed could be bought and named for £500. For £15,000 a legator can name a room and have his or her name on the door. A wing could be refurbished or added for £200,000 upwards. Potential legators and those wishing to make in memoriam gifts are encouraged to discuss the kind of gift they would wish to purchase and its location with the head of fund-raising.

Prices: Up to £500, up to £50,000, up to £250,000, up to £500,000
Bob Russell, Head of Fund-raising, Nuffield Private Hospitals, Nuffield House, 1–4 The Crescent, Surbiton, Surrey KT6 4BN. Tel: 0181 390 1200

Paintings in Hospitals, Scotland

Paintings in Hospitals is a registered charity which provides original works of art to be hung in Scottish hospitals and health-care units. The trust mainly supports young professional artists, although the collection also represents work by leading Scottish contemporary artists. The collection is steadily growing and increased in the year 1994/5 to 676 pictures. Work is on loan in hospitals as far afield as Aberdeen in the Grampians and Melrose in the Borders.

The trust operates a picture purchasing scheme under which benefactors are asked to donate a sum to buy a painting which will bear the name of the donor or that of a loved one. It is also possible to specify a picture that is suitable for a certain place, a children's ward for example. The cost of an individual work can be £50 for a print or many thousands for an original painting. Benefactors are also listed in the annual report of trustees. The trust does not normally accept paintings as a gift unless they fulfil its criterion but the director Sybelle Medcalf is always happy to discuss bequests of collections.

Prices: Up to £100, up to £5,000, up to £10,000, up to £50,000, up to £100,000
Sybelle Medcalf, Director, 10 Forth Street, Edinburgh EH1 3LD. Tel.: 0131 557 3490

Plymouth Hospitals National Health Trust

Julian Evans, the corporate business manager, will route any enquiries to the appropriate manager. If a baby dies at birth or within three months of birth, there is a memorial book in which parents are invited to write (this is free of charge). Each ward has its own trust fund and the relations of patients or former patients tend to bequeath money to their own particular ward or the nurses there. Occasionally, there are plaques and memorial chairs around the hospital, but the trust is entirely open to a patient's requests as to how money is to be spent and what form, if any, a memorial would take. The hospital would consider any reasonable requests and place a plaque even for a relatively small amount. If a donor is buying equipment, then a plaque could be mounted on it if requested.

Prices: Memorial Book, Unspecified
Julian Evans, Corporate Business Manager, Derriford Hospital, Plymouth PL6 8DH. Tel.: 01752 792811

Royal Berkshire and Battle Hospitals NHS Trust

The hospital has a memorial book in which the names of babies who have died may be recorded. This is offered free of charge with no suggestion that any donation is expected. This is part of the hospital service in helping parents to come to terms with the tragedy of the death of a baby.

In the past, memorial plaques have been erected and cots and beds endowed in memory of loved ones, especially victims of the First World War. The hospital administration has no specific way of acknowledging donations in the form of a memorial but the charity is prepared to consider ways of permanently recording donations. This has been done with two specific units and may occur with wards, rooms, laboratories or simply as a wall plaque or a memorial book entry. The hospital administration must agree to the concept and wording of, for example, the name of a ward, and the size and design of any commemorative display; it would also want the staff within that area to be happy with these. The trustees believe that each case should be treated individually and made as personal as possible. They should be contacted to discuss any possible in memoriam gifts or legacies and an appropriate memorial.

Prices: Memorial Book, Unspecified
Dr A. Marshall Barr, The Trustees, Appeals Office, Royal Berkshire Hospital, London Road, Reading RG1 5AN. Tel.: 01734 875111

St Thomas' Hospital, The Florence Nightingale Fund

In the days before the NHS was created in 1948, individual memorials on behalf of benefactors were the order of the day, with even individual beds being named. The hospital still receives bequests and legacies and is occasionally left property which the hospital either uses or sells.

Often today, individual bequests and legacies go into special-purpose funds for a particular activity, especially in the research field. Recently, a very substantial bequest set up a special fund in the name of the family concerned for a particular research activity with the emphasis on nursing and midwifery. Within the hospital, many departments raise funds and in these cases donors are recognized. Potential donors or those giving in memory of loved ones can negotiate with the relevant department as to the nature of a memorial. There are oil paintings naming the donor, rooms, wards and buildings named after a benefactor, and rolls of honour.

Wards and departments tend today to be named after prominent past individual members of either the board of management or staff who have made outstanding contributions to the life of the hospital. A centre within the hospital for post-intensive-care respiratory cases is called the Lane Fox Unit after a patient and principal benefactress, Baroness Lane Fox. Her portrait hangs in the centre and there is a very nice leather-bound book in which all those who donated have had their names entered. Plaques all over the hospital acknowledge donations of amounts varying from a few to many hundreds of thousand pounds. In the main hall, there is a very large Victorian brass plate acknowledging a gift of £10,000 in 1860 from the Worshipful Company of Grocers. Families who have suffered a loss frequently donate something to the hospital, such as paintings, sculptures and park benches. Many others raise money for the hospital.

Medical equipment is expensive. The Positron Emission Tomography scanner and the rooms needed to house it cost £5 million. Donations ranged from £1 million at the top of the scale to a few pounds. The naming of rooms, suites and other areas does not necessarily equate with the cost of the room or area. The Florence Nightingale Fund is quite new. Although Florence Nightingale was a St Thomas' nurse and all St Thomas' nurses are today known as Nightingales, the name was not originally associated with any of the hospital's many fund-raising activities. In the early 1990s it was decided to have one central hospital and medical school fund which raised money for the hospital as a whole rather than for a particular department, and so the name Florence Nightingale was chosen, itself a memorial.

Prices: Unspecified

Nicholas Ridley, Appeals Director, First Floor North Wing, St Thomas' Hospital, Lambeth Palace Road, London SE1 7EH. Tel.: 0171 928 9292

13   Local Authorities

The main forms of commemoration offered tend to be memorial benches and trees, but prices and, more importantly, responsibility for the maintenance and replacement of the donated items over time, can vary quite considerably from authority to authority. The response was lower than I expected, as I contacted every local authority in England and Wales, although those that did respond were very helpful and Dorset was unusually imaginative. If in doubt, contact the press officer, who may steer you through the minefield of bureaucracy. The library and museums departments were exceptions, in that their enthusiasm was great, and Liverpool have instituted a formal commemoration scheme in the libraries during the writing of this book.

Brighstone Parish Council, Isle of Wight

Brighstone is just a small village in the south of this picturesque island but it boasts seventeen public benches, with memorial inscriptions, donated by members of the public. If legators or families pay the council for the bench, they can then order it free of VAT. A bench costs upwards of £250, plus a small extra sum for setting it in place in concrete. A carved wooden plaque would be an extra £30, or there are local firms doing brass plaques for about £50. Alternative memorials might be a notice-board which would cost about £200, plus engraving. A tree would be £30–£50, according to the size, plus a plaque for about £30. The tree could be placed along an avenue or in an open space. Brighstone has several donated oak and beech trees.
Prices: Up to £100, up to £500
Clerk to Brighstone Parish Council, Brighstone, Isle of Wight. Tel.: 01983 740843

Buckinghamshire County Council Library and Museum Service

The new county museum cost more than £3.5 million, of which over £1 million was raised through sponsorship and gifts. The biggest bequest was £75,000 from the family of the late Roald Dahl. This seeded a project to create the Roald Dahl Children's Gallery, a hands-on children's museum at Buckinghamshire County Museum in Aylesbury.

The museum service can always produce a wish list of items suitable as memorials. For example, gates for the courtyard would cost £20,000 to be designed and built; £100,000 or more could be spent on new storage facilities for larger items; £50,000 would fit out an art store. The museums officer is eager to commission contemporary furniture or works of art to adorn the museum and these would start at £2,000. A showcase could be named for £5,000, £25,000 would name a room, and even a building could be named after a donor. Items of furniture, such as garden seats and other features, are popular as memorials and cost from £500. Cash donations could be put to a variety of uses, including the purchase of items for the museum collection, equipment and all or part of a display. The museum would always try to match the use of the funds to the donor and would discuss it with the family of the deceased. Displays as memorials are a little difficult since they have a limited lifespan. One donation of £1,000 to the art gallery appeal was made specifically so that the name on the plaque would be on permanent display and remembered in Aylesbury.

Donations for collections are particularly welcome. The museum has a major collection of British studio ceramics, particularly from the 1950s to the 1990s. The museum also welcomes any items relating to the county, especially works by Buckinghamshire-based artists of national importance such as John Nash, John Piper and Eric Gill. It is suggested that potential donors contact Colin Dawes to suggest possible future projects.

Prices: Up to £500, up to £1,000, up to £5,000, up to £50,000, up to £100,000

Colin V. Dawes. County Museums Officer, Buckinghamshire County Museum, Church Street, Aylesbury, Bucks. HP20 2QP. Tel.: 01296 331441

Cheshire County Council

A common memorial that can be provided through a county council is a dedicated bus shelter. Bus shelters in Cheshire tend to be in key locations, outside railway stations, schools, colleges and hospitals. As such, they get a great deal of wear and tear, although the council makes every attempt to maintain them to a high standard. A county council bus shelter would cost £2,500. A contribution of fifty per cent of the cost would ensure a memorial was included within the timetable information frame. Rural bus shelters are often constructed with the assistance of county council funding, using local builders to provide a design and material which best fits in with local needs.

Prices: Up to £5,000

Neil R. Archibald, County Transport Co-ordinator, Rivacre Business Centre, Mill Lane, Ellesmere Port, Ches. L66 3TL. Tel.: 01244 603407

Association of Cheshire Parish Councils, 96 Lower Bridge Street, Chester CH1 1RU. Tel.: 01244 32218

Derbyshire County Council

This council has a tree-planting scheme as part of the development of commemorative woods. It also sets up commemorative benches. Photographic collections and historical materials have been bequeathed to museums under the Countryside Service's control.

The Countryside Service is looking into other schemes, including the development of a memorial heritage woodland in which an area of the wood is bought, a tree or trees planted and the wood maintained in perpetuity; a memorial book for donations which would go to managing the historic gardens under the Countryside Service's control; and the development of a memorial bird-box or bat-box project. The costs for memorial seats and tree plantings vary considerably. Trees range from saplings to standard sizes, and costs, including assistance in planting in one of the county council's country parks and future management, vary from £20 to £50. Often people do not want a plaque as these can be stolen or vandalized but one can be supplied at extra cost. Commemorative benches range from £50 for a basic wooden bench, £250 for a rustic wooden bench, £250–£300 for a traditional hardwood bench with routed wording and £1,000 for a carved stone bench. Routing is recommended rather than a plaque, as plaques can go missing. Benches are sited within a country park or on a country trail and have a life of up to twenty years. Trails and country parks include: Shipley Country Park, Slack Lane, Heanor, Derby. DE7 7GX (Contact by phone: 01773 719961); Middleton Top, Middleton by Wirkworth, Derby. DE4 4LS (Contact by phone: 01629 823204); Hayfield Information Centre, Station

Road, Hayfield, Stockport, Ches. SK12 5ES (Contact by phone: 01663 746222).
Prices: Up to £100, up to £500, up to £1,000
Peter Clark, Chief Planning and Highways Officer, County Offices, Matlock, Derby. DE4 3AG. Tel.: 01629 580000

Dorset County Council

The county planning office has no specific arrangements for erecting memorials but it is a leading participant in two organizations that might be more able to commemorate a person. These are the Dorset Building Preservation Trust and the Dorchester Heritage Committee.

In one instance where a building was offered to the Dorset Building Preservation Trust, a plaque was erected bearing the benefactor's name. The trust would consider any reasonable proposal by a benefactor, but as its buildings are usually sold, the opportunities for such memorials are limited. The Dorchester Heritage Committee has been involved in carrying out a number of works that could have lent themselves to memorials, such as tree planting, installing tree guards, bollards, benches, erecting plaques describing the history of a particular historic building, and paving schemes. Any reasonable proposal would be considered on its merits. The county council faces restrictions on planting memorial trees as this can be done only on council-owned land and opportunities are limited.

Parish and town councils look after memorial seats on roads and land under their control, and they are able to include such seats on their insurance policy. Memorial stones have been erected by the roadside at a spot where someone was killed. One example is that for Owen Clarke, a roadman who was killed in a hit-and-run accident while on duty in May 1989. His memorial is looked after by former colleagues. Sometimes, where a person has been killed in a road accident a less permanent memorial appears, when flowers are placed on the spot and perhaps renewed on anniversaries. There is a stone cross on the highway verge in Wareham Forest, dating back to 1936. Memorials along the highways should be useful or ornamental, preferably both. They should not be a burden on the council-tax payer and should be vested in, maintained and insured by a statutory body, usually the appropriate parish council. The highway authority should have a veto to ensure public safety.

The rights-of-way department would be happy to accept bridges built to DCC specification in someone's memory. Such a bridge would cost about £1,000 including installation, depending on the length of the bridge and the relative difficulty of building it. Salkeld Bridge was erected in memory of Philip Salkeld, who died a hero in the Indian Mutiny. In the Purbecks, some decorative milestones in the form of sculptures were put along the coastal footpath. They were commissioned by the landowner, the Weld Estate, about ten years ago in conjunction with a body called Common Ground. They take the form of stone snails and stylized ears of corn created in hardwood. Close by is a massive stone bearing the name of the local poet, Llewellyn Powys. More recently a wayside sculpture has been built on the bridleway near Godmanstone. Such wayside structures could be suitable memorials. Anyone wishing to erect standing stones or sculptures should first consult the landowner. Planning consent may also need to be considered.

Chalk figures and markings have gone out of fashion, but those that exist within Dorset are cherished. There are two chalk hill figures in Dorset: one is the Cerne Abbas Giant and the other the White Horse at Weymouth. Any proposals for similar figures should be tasteful. There was a scheme some years ago to create a chalk figure on the hill facing the Cerne Abbas Giant in memory of the late Marilyn Monroe, based on the photograph of her attempting to control an unruly dress. This did provoke some opposition, as it was thought to be inappropriate in an area of outstanding beauty and the plan was never carried out. Over the border in Wiltshire there is a chalk hill upon which successive regiments in the nearby military camp carved their badges. The panda motif of the Worldwide Fund for Nature was added some years later. The consent and co-operation of the landowner and the county council are both needed.

Prices: Up to £5,000, up to £100,000

David Hutchinson, County Surveyor, Transportation and Engineering Department, and John Lowe, Principal Planning Officer for Historic Buildings, County Hall, Colliton Park, Dorchester DT1 1XJ. Tel.: 01305 251000

Durham County Council

At present, Durham County Council has no formal scheme enabling relatives to commemorate a loved one. However, it is very willing to consider any individual proposals, such as planting a memorial tree or placing a memorial bench in one of the picnic areas in the parks or open spaces. For more substantial bequests or in memoriam gifts, any proposals for a memorial would be looked at in their entirety, the criteria being that the memorial/project is suitable and appropriate, and will not incur any extra expense that would have to be met out of community charges. All enquiries should be routed initially through Fraser Davie, who can then direct them to the appropriate department.

Prices: Unspecified

Fraser Davie, Press and Information Officer, County Hall, Durham DH1 5UF. Tel.: 0191 386 4411

Hastings Borough Council

The department of tourism and leisure accepts both memorial seats and donations for planting memorial trees. The department has standardized the type of seat to be used throughout the parks and accepts donations from relatives of deceased persons for its purchase. An engraved inscription on the back rail of the seat is allowed. The donation covers the cost of the inscription and the purchase of the seat with the authority bearing the cost of installation. Regarding memorial trees, donations in multiples of £30 are accepted, this being the cost of supplying and planting a tree. Memorial plaques are not positioned near trees because they have been targets for vandalism. However, the location of the tree, together with the name of the donor, is recorded on a plan within the office. A commemorative poster, signed by the Mayor of Hastings and recording the date, type of tree and location, is given to the donor.

Prices: Up to £100

R.C. Dawson, Assistant Director, Tourism and Leisure, 5 Robertson Terrace, Hastings, E. Sussex TN34 1JE. Tel. 01424 781066

Hove Borough Council

For many years, the borough has offered sponsored memorial seats in parks, on the promenade or at strategic highway locations.

Sponsorship relates to the cost of the seat and plaque, plus installation to a ground fitting, for a one-off payment. For a further one-off payment, the council will also maintain the bench and replace the plaque if stolen. The seat's design depends upon its location but is to some degree flexible, depending on the amount of money available. A bench of the recommended style and design costs between £300 and £350. There are two main types: a basic wooden park bench and a more vandal-proof design of cast iron and recycled plastic, supplied by the council with a plaque. Sponsorship of an existing seat would be considered at a cost of £70–£100. Some Victorian benches were recently refurbished in recycled plastic in front of the town hall in keeping with the original design. The council is very open to all forms of memorials and sponsorship. For the more practically minded, a litter bin could be dedicated for £130, although it is not as long-lasting as a bench. Additionally, two kinds of bus shelters are available, the basic open-type shelter could be dedicated with a plaque for £300–£400. A dedicated public toilet would cost from about £100,000 to build. Sponsorship of trees can be arranged through the leisure services department. The council will also consider other forms of memorials. Criteria for acceptance would include a project appropriate to the provision of public amenities and in keeping with the setting.

Prices: Up to £100, up to £500, up to £100,000

The Chief Executive, Hove Town Hall, Norton Road, Hove, E. Sussex BN3 4AH. Tel.: 01273 775400

Isle of Wight County Council

This local authority does not have specific bequest or covenant schemes, as it does not actively seek donations. However, any bequests are gratefully received and the council officers will try to comply with the donor's wishes. Contact should be made beforehand to ascertain the viability of the project and discuss alternatives if necessary.

A tree in a park or designated open space could be provided for about £20 plus the same amount for a plaque. A bus shelter (apply to the highways department) costs between £1,350 and £8,000 for a ready-made kind, more for an individualized one. An appropriate plaque would be erected and the shelter maintained by the local authority. There is no limit to the kind of gifts made in legacies or as memorials. For example, the Ward family donated Northwood House in Cowes on the Isle of Wight to the local authority. In the case of property, discussion should be made before the will is written. Within the Isle of Wight, parish councils can also offer memorial schemes, perhaps in a well-loved holiday location.

Prices: Up to £100, up to £5,000, up to £10,000

The Chief Executive, High Street, Newport, Isle of Wight PO30 1UD. Tel.: 01983 82100

Lewes District Council

The majority of memorial donation requests are either for a public bench seat or for provision of a specimen tree or shrub. Benches can also be placed at certain points along the coastline of the district, most notably along the esplanade at Seaford, a pedestrian walkway adjacent to the beach and extending for about two miles. These are administered by the amenities section of the council.

The council accepts the cost price of the item as a donation towards public amenities. This avoids the need to recharge VAT and any disputes of ownership. If a member of the public wishes to endow a memorial seat, he or she should write to the administration and amenities officer. The council will send a map upon which the preferred location can be marked and the directorate will try to site the bench as close to the chosen site as possible. The directorate can arrange for an inscription, in the form of deep 'V' cut carved on to the back of the seat that has proved more appropriate than mounted plaques, in view of the area's exposure to severe weather at certain times during the year. The cost of one five-foot long 'Allington' bench is around £252.25 without armrests or £292.25 with armrests, payable after installation. The charge for carving inscriptions is approximately £1.50 per character and this service is subject to VAT. The wood from which the seats are constructed is a softwood obtained from recognized, managed, sustainable forestry sources.

Prices: Up to £500
S. Brigden, Administration and Amenities Officer, Leisure and Community Services, 32 High Street, Lewes, E. Sussex BN7 2LX. Tel.: 01273 471600, ext. 4157

Lewes District Council, Parks Department

The parks section administers requests for placement of plant specimens and benches in parks or gardens. A memorial tree in a park can cost from £30 to £300, depending on the type and maturity chosen, to include planting by the council which then incorporates it within the maintenance programme.

The parks department can put potential purchasers in touch with reliable firm to erect a brass plaque, burn the inscription into a wooden plaque or engrave a memorial stone at the foot of the tree. A brass plaque would cost £70+. Seats can be provided from £250 to £400, depending on the kind, and again an inscription can be burned into the wood or a brass plaque placed on the bench. The parks department can also suggest contacts to carry out this work. The seat will be maintained and repaired if necessary. Memorial herbaceous borders in parks would need to be negotiated as to suitable size and location.

Prices: Up to £500

Ms S. Maclaren, Lewes House, 32 High Street, Lewes, E. Sussex BN7 2LX. Tel.: 01273 471600

Liverpool City Libraries

Liverpool Libraries and Information Services have a long tradition of accepting and commemorating gifts. The Central Library consists of various buildings named after the donors – the William Brown Library, the Hornby Library, the Picton Library and Christopher Rawdon Library. In these cases, the benefactor gave the entire cost of the building, the equivalent of several million pounds today. There are also a number of subsidiary collections, such as the Shipley Collection, which have been donated to the library.

A formal structure of commemoration, partly inspired by this book, was approved in October 1995, and Liverpool Libraries are actively seeking donations to fund aspects of the service. Such items might include park benches for library grounds or the conservation of items in the fine books collection. £100+ will be recorded in a ceremonial book of gifts and reported to the library and arts sub-committee. Bequests or gifts of £1,000+ will be acknowledged with a special commemorative bookplate while those of £10,000 and more will be recorded on a commemorative plaque. A room can be named for £100,000 and a library can be named after a benefactor who gives £1–£5 million. Benches outside the library or particular pieces of display equipment could have a commemorative plaque. In the case of substantial gifts, the condition is imposed, if possible, that they are an absolute gift to the library and that there is no intention on the part of the donor to create any form of memorial trust. The library service also receives gifts and bequests in the form of books. These are accepted with gratitude on condition they are used or disposed of as seen fit by the library committee.

Prices: Up to £500, up to £1,000, up to £5,000, up to £10,000, up to £50,000, up to £100,000, up to £250,000, up to £500,000, up to £1 million and beyond

Paul Catcheside, Head of Libraries and Information Services, 3rd Floor, Steers House, Canning Place, Liverpool L1 8HN. Tel.: 0151 225 6346

14 Medical Research and Welfare

Medical research provides a good source of tangible commemoration in the higher price brackets, especially where research projects can be named. However, even in the lower price ranges, the charities listed were anxious to emphasize that all donations were gratefully received. The Imperial Cancer Research Fund, to name but one, has a memorial book for legacies. The Anthony Nolan Bone Marrow Trust has a memorial wood where trees can be purchased from £10. There was a high response rate in this category and an overall willingness to help, although most do prefer an individual approach to the question of commemoration.

Medical care organizations sometimes find it more difficult to offer tangible commemoration for lower amounts because of the sheer logistics involved, as are funds often spent on individual grants and smaller pieces of equipment. However, there are ways round the problem, such as the RNID Book of Friends. The Marie Curie daffodil bulb scheme also offers very reasonable commemorative opportunities. Larger amounts again are less problematic, as rooms or buildings can be dedicated or nurses sponsored.

Anthony Nolan Bone Marrow Trust

The trust manages the world's first and largest fully independent register of bone marrow donors. More than a quarter of a million volunteers were on the donor register at the end of 1995. It has a number of methods of commemoration (see chapter 8 for more details).

Arthritis Care

Arthritis Care is concerned with the welfare and rehabilitation of arthritis sufferers, providing information, advice and financial help. It runs specially equipped holiday hotels and self-catering units. There is also a residential home for the severely disabled. It receives about forty per cent of its income from legacies. There is a wall in the rose garden in one of the holiday hotels in Dorset, on which the names of legators are inscribed, unless they ask for anonymity. There is no differentiation between the amounts given; indeed, the amount is not mentioned at all. The only example of a specific legacy is the society's residential home, Patterson House, named after a donor who left a legacy to build it.
Prices: Memorial Wall, Unspecified
Patrick Hannah, Direct Marketing Director, 18 Stephenson Way, London NW1 2HD. Tel.: 0171 916 1500

Arthritis and Rheumatism Council for Research

The Arthritis and Rheumatism Council for Research in Britain and the Commonwealth is the only charity financing medical research into all forms of the disease. Two out of three people in Britain who are over sixty-five suffer from the disease. However, it also attacks millions of younger people, including 15,000 children, and is the greatest single cause of disability in Britain today.

Research has brought about significant advances in diagnosis, treatment and replacement surgery, through a research programme that costs more than £6 million annually. At present, 200 projects are being funded to discover the causes and a cure. There are several ways in which an in memoriam gift or legacy can benefit research and offer a tangible commemoration. Endowment of an ARC Chair of Rheumatology at a British university, named after the donor, would cost between £500,000 and £750,000. A named clinical research fellowship would cost £90,000. A named travelling research fellowship would be £25,000 and a plaque on equipment for research projects could be placed for donations from £100 to £25,000. To discuss possible legacies and in memoriam gifts with memorials along the above lines, potential benefactors should contact the chief executive, who will be pleased to help and advise.
Prices: Up to £500, up to £5,000, up to £10,000, up to £50,000, up to £100,000, up to £500,000, up to £1 million

Chief Executive, Copeman House, St Mary's Court, Chesterfield, Derby. S41 2TD. Tel.: 01246 558033

Birmingham Macmillan Nurse Appeal

The Birmingham appeal is part of a three-year national Macmillan appeal aimed at improving services substantially and developing new ones. Even beyond the three-year-period, money is always needed to train new nurses and improve facilities, and local appeals are in motion nationwide.

The Birmingham appeal is for seven new specialist Macmillan posts added to the existing services, based in local hospitals. £550,000 is needed to fund these posts. This amount funds the salary, training and travel costs of seven Macmillan nurse specialists, including one for head and neck cancer to be based at Queen Elizabeth Hospital, and another for bone tumours at the Royal Orthopaedic Hospital in Northfield. A Macmillan paediatric nurse to support children with brain and spinal cancer will be based at the Birmingham Children's Hospital. Any funds in excess of the target will be used for Macmillan services in the region. As with all Macmillan nurses, after the initial funding of these posts by Macmillan, the appropriate NHS trust will take on the long-term funding.

Prices: Unspecified

John Rayner, Birmingham Appeals Director, Suite 3, Arena Studios, 126 Morville Street, Birmingham B16 8DG. Tel.: 0121 454 5499

British Heart Foundation

The British Heart Foundation finances much of the research carried out into all aspects of heart and circulatory disease, which is the biggest killer in Britain. In this area of work, eighty per cent of which is research, the foundation is able to name, for example, fellowships after a deceased person. This would involve very significant sums of money, as research projects typically run from five to twenty-five years. Therefore, if a person is considering a bequest of, at 1995 value, £200,000 or above, he or she is invited to enter into discussion with the director-general about suitable areas of work.

At a lower level of finance, the foundation may also fund items of equipment, such as defibrillators. However, the foundation needs the utmost flexibility where it applies funds and, in general terms, welcomes the same flexibility to decide how a legacy should be spent at the time it comes into effect so that it can be directed to the most urgent need. In the past, unnecessary restrictions have meant that the foundation was unable to satisfy the conditions in the will and so lost the legacy. Contact C.J. Ellison to discuss possible bequests and the best way to match a benefactor's requirements with the society's needs.

Prices: Up to £500,000, up to £1 million and beyond

C.J. Ellison, Legacy Manager, 14 Fitzhardinge Street, London W1H 4DH. Tel.: 0171 9350185

British Lung Foundation

Lung diseases – bronchitis, pneumonia, emphysema, asthma and cancer – form the most common group of diseases in Britain. Research into these disorders would lead to earlier diagnosis and more effective treatment. The foundation does receive legacies and in memoriam donations and these form a vital form of funding. As yet, it does not have a book of remembrance for small donations.

All donations and bequests, however small, are nevertheless welcomed and can be put towards a research project. For larger donations, the project could be carried out in someone's name. The cost of a research project does depend on the amount of activity, but £50,000 would be the minimum sum to cover a project for two to three years. A large donation would be recorded in the newsletter and the foundation is happy to negotiate commemorating a name in a project, if that is desired. The society would like to emphasize that it is not looking solely for legacies over £50,000 as that would exclude ninety-nine per cent of its bequests. The reason for not having formal memorials is to divert as much money as possible towards research. Should a donor want a specific project that was not planned as part of ongoing research, for example research into lung cancer, the foundation would need more money and would have to advertise for funds to aid running costs, unless perhaps £80,000 or more were bequeathed. More general donations can be added to an existing area of research. The foundation emphasizes that it is always pleased to talk and advise potential benefactors.

Prices: Up to £50,000, up to £100,000

Susan Kaye, Appeals Manager, 78 Patten Gardens, London EC1N 8JR. Tel.: 0171 831 5831

Cancer Relief Macmillan Fund \

Douglas Macmillan founded the Cancer Relief Macmillan Fund in 1911 after the death of his father. Its role is to help improve the lives of people with cancer, at any stage in their illness and in any setting – their own home, the hospital or a specialized cancer unit. Its services reach more than 20,000 people each year. Macmillan nurses are at the centre of this care.

There are four kinds of Macmillan nurse; currently most are based in the community, caring for patients at home, although a growing number are working in hospitals. Some support women with breast cancer while paediatric nurses care for children with cancer and their families. Funding for Macmillan nurses is provided by the Cancer Relief Fund usually for the first three years and includes the cost of specialist training. After that time, financial responsibility is taken over by the health authority. Although more than 1,000 Macmillan nurses now work in the UK, many patients still do not have access to their specialist care. The plan is to have a complete countrywide network of home-care nurses. The fund also wants to have Macmillan hospital nurses and breast-care nurses in each health district and Macmillan paediatric nurses in each health region. Macmillan doctors use their skills to diagnose, advise on pain and symptom control and manage the day-to-day care and support of their patients and families. Some are also involved in teaching and research. Macmillan buildings are specially designed to meet the needs of people with cancer. The fund's role is usually to build and equip specialist cancer centres, including day-care units, while the NHS takes on the running costs. In addition, the charity undertakes major refurbishment projects, improving cancer wards and treatment areas in NHS hospitals. It also awards one-off patient grants to help with such items as extra fuel bills, clothing and convalescent holidays. The charity believes that all health care professionals should have a better understanding of the needs of cancer patients. To this end, it funds a medical and educational programme which includes an educational unit at the University of Dundee.

The Macmillan fund does not have strict guidelines on named memorials, which are only given if relations or the terms of a will request it and then only for a substantial legacy. For example, when a legacy of £273,000 helped to build a £1 million day-care centre for cancer patients and an education centre for Macmillan nurses, a room was named after the benefactress. As £48,000 of the legacy was used to finance a nurse tutor post for three years, the nurse used the name of the legator for the three year period, beginning in 1987. The current cost of a Macmillan nurse for three years is £81,000. The Macmillan fund needs permission from the NHS to name anything after legators as they work so closely together. Although the fund has few requests for anything to be named after a person, it would be willing to discuss this if the question arose.

Prices: Up to £100,000, up to £1 million
Janet Livermore, Legacy Development Manager, Anchor House, 15–19 Britten Street, London SW3 3TZ. Tel.: 0171 351 7811

Colon Cancer Concern

Colon Cancer Concern, founded in 1987, is a unique specialist charity dedicated to caring for people with advanced colorectal cancer, particularly patients with resulting secondary liver cancer. It is itself a memorial charity, originally called the Britta Dolan Cancer Fund, started by her husband Pattrick and a surgeon, Tim Allen-Marsh, to introduce American secondary liver cancer treatment into the UK. The charity supports pioneering research and provides treatment for suffers. Colorectal cancer is the second most common cause of cancer death in the UK and it affects more than 30,000 people every year. Early detection of its spread to the liver is the key to successful treatment. It is also a subject that generally is found to be embarrassing and therefore is not often publicly discussed.

The charity has been treating patients with colorectal secondary liver cancer for seven years. The first trials reported in *The Lancet* showed that survival and quality of life of patients with advanced colorectal cancer were considerably prolonged and improved by the implant of a small pump to deliver chemotherapy. All treatments are given at home with the help of three chemotherapy nurses who travel throughout the British Isles to visit patients. The society welcomes all legacies, donations and in memoriam gifts and is happy to discuss commemoration with potential benefactors or their families. Several ongoing needs would lend themselves to commemoration, whether sponsoring a nurse, a scientist, a research project or purchasing equipment. The society is aiming to raise £2 million by the turn of the century to continue its work. At the moment, although it has the technology to help sufferers it has the resources to help only a small percentage of them. Its ultimate aim is to help everyone who develops colon cancer and secondary liver disease live longer and have a better quality of life. Support for a nurse for 'quality of life' studies would cost £30,000; a cryoprobe freezing machine for treating secondary liver tumours, £25,000; hepatic artery pumps for patients, £4,000 each; liver scans for patients, £450 each; a double viewer microscope, £2,000. There is a variety of items for patients' use ranging in price from £500 up to £8,000. A day's research by a scientist costs £60. A day on the road for a nurse visiting and treating patients costs £35. The charity's ultimate goal is the endowment of an academic chair.

Prices: Up to £10,000, (also per annum), up to £50,000 (also per annum)

Caroline Grantham, Fund-raising Manager, Department of Surgery, 3rd Floor, Chelsea and Westminster Hospital, 369 Fulham Road, London SW10 9NH. Tel.: 0181 746 8809/8468/8469

CORDA

CORDA, the Coronary Artery Disease Research Association, is a specialist charity dedicated to the prevention of cardiovascular disease. This disease of the heart and arteries is a major killer in people of pre-retirement age as well as older people. But it is believed to be largely preventable, and research centres on ways of discovering who is most at risk and of developing safe, effective, painless screening so that early preventive action can be taken.

The executive director is very willing to discuss individual bequests and in memoriam donations individually to see how the wish for appropriate commemoration can coincide with the needs of the charity. He wishes to stress that a donation is welcomed and valued, however small, and that it could contribute to necessary research. On a larger scale, £5,000 would contribute towards a research project; £10,000–£25,000 would buy a piece of high-technology equipment of the kind that would aid research; £10,000+ would also contribute to the costs of projects on the early diagnosis and prevention of cardiovascular disease at the Royal Brompton Hospital in London and on the causes of heart disease in children at Great Ormond Street Hospital, also in London; a research fellowship costs £50,000 a year to fund, for salary and associated costs in consumable materials; £500,000 would provide a complete mobile magnetic resonance scanner to help diagnose heart disease in people in the early stages before it can do harm; £1 million would guarantee the future of an entire project for four to five years. An endowment of £5 million would provide sufficient funds to create an entirely new Chair of Preventive Medicine in the field of cardiovascular disease and open up research in exciting new ways.

Prices: Up to £5,000, up to £10,000, up to £50,000 (also per annum), up to £100,000, up to £500,000, up to £1 million and beyond

Anthony Burns, Executive Director, Tavistock House North, Tavistock Square, London WC1H 9TH. Tel.: 0171 387 9779

Cystic Fibrosis Trust

The society offers support for sufferers of cystic fibrosis and research into the disease. Donations in memory of loved ones are allocated to the projects researching cystic fibrosis that are funded by the society on an ongoing basis.

When a cystic fibrosis sufferer dies, parents or spouse are given the opportunity to have his or her name entered in the book of remembrance, now in its second volume. There is no charge for this. The book was created in the society's Silver Jubilee (1989). The first volume opens with the words: 'This Book of Remembrance records, with respect and affection, the names of those who lost their lives because of Cystic Fibrosis.' The frontispiece and binding are decorated in gold-leaf. The first book is bound in white and the second in dark blue leather. The first volume was blessed at the Silver Jubilee service in Westminster Abbey by the Archbishop of Canterbury and throughout the year it was an integral part of services held in Belfast Cathedral; St Giles's Cathedral, Edinburgh; Durham Cathedral; St Margaret's Church, King's Lynn; and Llandaff Cathedral in Cardiff. When the society has collected approximately twelve names, they are sent to the society's calligrapher who travels to the Resurrection Chapel at Holy Trinity Church, Brompton Road, London, to make the additions. Glenda Waddell, assistant to the Revd J.A.K. Millar, is the contact at Holy Trinity Church and if telephoned (0171 581 8255) will arrange viewing appointments for a family or confirm the entry has been made. The books are kept in a glass cabinet.

Prices: Memorial Book, Unspecified
Deirdre Ashenden, Alexandra House, 5 Blyth Road, Bromley, Kent BR1 3RS. Tel.: 0181 464 7211

Fight for Sight

Fight for Sight was established in 1965 to raise funds for research into the prevention, treatment and cure of eye disease and blindness. Its main beneficiary is the Institute of Ophthalmology, research partner to Moorfields Eye Hospital, which has received more than £7 million for its research. In 1992, the institute moved into a new building on the same site as Moorfields. Many internationally respected scientists have been attracted to work at the site which, with more than 170 researchers, is by far the biggest eye research centre in the UK. Moorfields has the biggest ophthalmic population of any hospital in the Western world and this, together with the institute's research expertise, makes the site unique. A recent success has been the development of a new, simple, computer-based test by Fight for Sight supported scientist, Dr Fred Fitzke, for the early detection of glaucoma, two to three years earlier than ordinary methods. The charity is committed to providing long-term funding for research scientists at the centre and the total future commitment to the institute for research salaries is now approximately £3.5 million. In 1996, the charity needed to raise £400,000–£750,000 for research salaries and £350,000 for specialized equipment.

There are several ways of commemorating legacies. A name can be placed on the plaque located at the entrance to the Institute of Ophthalmology for legacies, in memoriam gifts and major donors, such as companies, who give £50,000 and more. Items of equipment needed range from £2,000 to £50,000 and can have an individual commemorative plaque attached. Research salaries can be named in memory of the legator. For example, a research student can be funded at a cost of £15,000 per year for three years, including the student's stipend, university fees and consumables needed in the laboratory. Research salaries are Fight for Sight's major expenditure and posts can be named, for example, the Rothes Chair was named in honour of Lord Rothes, the founder chairman. After his death, his family and friends gave donations and the charity held an appeal to raise funds for the chair in his honour. Similar donations can be made in the form of an endowment which produces enough interest to fund the post indefinitely. Quite a large donation is required for this, especially for the high-level posts of professor or senior lecturer.

Alternatively, it is possible to fund the post for the duration of the donation. As Ph.D. studentships last for three years, it is possible to have one or more of them named after the legator until the donation is used up. Laboratories can be named for legacies, also major donors, for £200,000 or more. These are needed when a new building is being built or there is a major refurbishment of existing space. The Francis and Renee Hock Laboratory in the most recent building development was named in honour of a legacy of £500,000. If the legator lets the society know in his or her will or a covering letter that he or she wishes the legacy to be commemorated in an appropriate way with his or her name or that of a loved one, the society would be delighted to oblige. A bequest of any size can be directed towards a chosen research area. If the legator or a loved one suffered from a particular eye disorder, it is natural that he or she would wish a bequest to be channelled towards research into that condition. This can best be done using a form of words (which Fight for Sight or the solicitor can advise on) that leaves the charity with some latitude in the event of there being no research into the particular condition when the legacy comes into effect.

Prices: Up to £5,000, up to £50,000, up to £100,000, up to £500,000, up to £1 million

Dr Claire Walker, Secretary, Institute of Ophthalmology, Bath Street, London EC1V 9EL. Tel.: 0171 490 8644

Hearing Research Trust

The trust funds research into hearing difficulties and is convinced that if sufficient quality research is funded, most if not all forms of deafness can eventually be abolished. Current concerns include improving established treatments, developing more effective hearing-aids, attacking the problems of tinnitus and glue ear, and improving procedures for recognizing and improving deafness in babies. However, the chief hope for many of Britain's eight million deaf and hard-of-hearing people lies in research into the intricate nerves and cells of the inner ear, an investigation which may eventually lead to stimulating the natural repair and regeneration of the inner ear's vital cells.

Because the Hearing Research Trust is a small charity, its officers can be very flexible about specific memorials. A plaque at a research centre could be provided for donations of about £500. Those contributing £1,000 would have their names listed in the trust's accounts and annual report in addition to a plaque. For £5,000, a room or laboratory would be possible. Larger sums could be directed to particular projects or centres, or pieces of equipment. The appropriate naming of a research studentship would cost around £30,000 while full project funding costs £40,000 and over. For example, £6,000 would support a key project into tinnitus for three months and £500 would pay the researchers' travelling expenses for a year. The Deafness in Babies Project costs £1,500 a month or £18,000 a year to run. £55,000 would establish studentship for investigation of the inner ear. In research into more effective hearing-aids, £5,000 will buy essential testing equipment and £35,000 support a research fellow for one year. The trust is continually seeking support for a whole range of hearing research work, which provides the opportunity for gifts of all sizes to be accommodated.

Prices: Up to £500, up to £1,000, up to £5,000, up to £10,000, up to £50,000 (also per annum), up to £100,000

David Godfrey, Appeals Executive, 330–332 Gray's Inn Road, London WC1X 8EE. Tel.: 0171 833 1733

Imperial Cancer Research Fund

This is the largest independent cancer research institute in Europe, employing about 1,000 scientists, doctors and technicians in its own laboratories or hospital units. It studies the causes, cure and prevention of cancer of all kinds – there are more than 200 different types. Imperial Cancer carries out more than a third of all UK cancer research as well as helping hundreds of patients every year in its hospital research units.

Everyone who leaves a legacy, irrespective of amount, is entered in the book of remembrance, kept in the foyer of the central laboratories. The person's name, place of residence and age at death are recorded. However, the amount bequeathed is not mentioned and for this reason the society is unwilling to put forward any price ranges for memorials, emphasizing that all bequests and donations are precious. In the case of a bequest or memorial gift, the society would do its best to arrange a suitable memorial, whether for a piece of equipment or naming a laboratory. A donation of £1,000 or more leads to the offer of a life governorship of the fund. The fund's scientists are at the forefront of international efforts to develop gene therapy for cancer patients. It is hoped to begin initial clinical work with those with malignant melanoma and breast cancer, part of the annual £5 million breast cancer programme. There is room for named funds inside the Imperial Cancer Fund. The Bobby Moore Fund for Imperial Cancer was set up after the death of the former World Cup footballer in 1993. Football fans in the UK and around the world raised £225,000, which has been used to set up a new bowel cancer research programme at the Imperial Cancer Oncology Unit at Edinburgh's Western General Hospital, whose director, Professor John Smyth, treated Bobby Moore. Stephanie Moore, Bobby's widow, launched the new venture, which includes the Bobby Moore Research Fellowship, supporting the work of a clinical researcher into ways of improving the treatment of bowel cancer. Donations large and small are welcome. For example, £5 buys a box of twenty disposable scalpels, £10 buys an electronic timer or box of one hundred disposable gloves, £16.48 funds a scientist's salary for sixty minutes and £50 buys fifty tissue culture dishes. £200 buys a magnetic stirrer for the laboratory, £2,000 buys a laboratory incubator, £3,500 a cabinet for sterile tissue work, £5,000 buys a research microscope or a −70°C laboratory freezer. In the higher price range, £10,000 buys a scintillation counter for counting radioactivity, £26,000 would buy a special computer system which, fitted to a microscope, enables the image being viewed to be captured and stored for more detailed analysis by scientists, and £35,000 a year meets the basic salary for a clinical fellow, with a further £30,000 needed to support this work fully. A fellow is contracted for a particular research project usually for three years. There is a need for more scientific staff to expand the laboratory programme. £40,000 would buy a DNA synthesizer for synthesizing fragments of DNA, £100,000 would fund the cost of a bowel screening pilot study for a year, saving perhaps 3,500 lives a year. £100,000 would also buy a laboratory robot to help with DNA analysis. Objects of value are also welcome bequests.

Prices: Memorial Book, up to £1,000, up to £5,000, up to £100,000, up to £500,000

Josie Golden, Senior Information Officer, PO Box 123, Lincoln's Inn Fields, London WC2A 3PX. Tel.: 0171 242 0200

Marie Curie Cancer Care

Marie Curie Cancer Care provides more than 6,000 Marie Curie Cancer Nurses across the UK each year, giving practical care at home to about 20,000 people with cancer, without charge. It also provides specialized medical and nursing care at eleven Marie Curie Hospice Centres which care for more than 4,000 patients a year. The Marie Curie Research Institute investigates the causes, prevention and detection of cancer.

Marie Curie Care currently receives more than £13 million a year from legacies and £1 million from 'In Memory' donations. The vast majority of these donations go into the general fund but sometimes there is a request for the money to be used for specific purposes, usually one of the Marie Curie Hospice Centres, the Marie Curie home nursing services or the Marie Curie Research Institute. The society is happy to allocate any donation towards a specific project if requested and it has used substantial donations to buy specific items that were urgently needed. Some of the rooms, wards and laboratories were provided by individuals. It is common for the society to name larger gifts, for example a room or piece of scientific equipment, if requested. However, donors must be sensitive to the hospice environment and the wishes of a donor must be balanced with the needs of the seriously ill patients, who may find it difficult to be in an environment where large quantities of the equipment and furniture have memorial plaques. The most useful gift is that which enables the society to provide more nurses or scientists; this is the major area of cost and one that directly benefits future patients. A donation of £60 would provide one night's nursing at home for a seriously ill patient. The Sponsor-a-Nurse Scheme has been very successful, with people making a monthly donation of between £2 and £7 towards the cost. The only regular memorial that the society maintains is a book at head office listing all individuals who have left the society at least £1,000. The Field of Hope Scheme has also been a great success. This involves buying four daffodil bulbs from the society for £1. These are then planted in every conceivable place, from motorway embankments, parks, schools, and even at Stansted Airport. The size of each Field of Hope can vary from a window-box to a million bulbs. The daffodils coming up each spring offer a continuing living memorial and reflect hope. Half a million bulbs line one and a quarter miles of the Melrose bypass in the Scottish Borders. The Marie Curie Cancer Care Society recently rebuilt the Liverpool and Newcastle Marie Curie Hospice Centres at a cost of £5 million and £4 million respectively. In both centres there are areas funded by individuals whose names they now carry. Marie Curie Cancer Care is happy to receive all legacies and to consider any special requests for memorial items. The organization is always very willing to discuss the wishes of potential legators and could accommodate most requests.

Prices: Memorial Book, up to £100, up to £1,000, up to £5,000
Helen Smith, Support Services Manager, 28 Belgrave Square, London SW1X 8QG. Tel.: 0171 235 3325

National Kidney Research Fund and Kidney Foundation

The foundation aims to finance and promote research into the causes, diagnosis and treatment of kidney disease and kidney-related illnesses, such as high blood pressure, diabetes and cystitis, as well as into improvements in kidney machines and transplants.

Although it has not yet been asked to commemorate a person's name, it would be possible for a memorial book or a plaque to be established depending on the size of the donation; a building could be named for a very substantial amount. It would also be possible to endow annual prizes; for example, there is a sponsored walk every May across the London bridges from Battersea to the Tower of London and back. There is also an opportunity for a donor's name to be linked to a research project or fellowship grant. Endowing a research project into kidney disease and related problems would cost a maximum of £65,000. Special research projects would be £150,000. A senior fellowship for three to five years would cost £200,000. Training fellowships for three years would be £170,000 and studentships £50,000. Funds are urgently needed for dialysis machines in all the major hospitals throughout the country.

Prices: Up to £50,000, up to £100,000, up to £500,000
Leslie Rout, Director-General, 3 Archers Court, Stukeley Road, Huntingdon, Cambs. PE18 6XG. Tel.: 01480 454828

National Library for the Blind

The library has more than 5,000 readers and sends out 1,000 volumes free every day. The material in its catalogue ranges through bestsellers, Booker Prize winners, biographies, reference books, gardening guides, knitting patterns and children's books.

Eighty-five volunteers transcribe books into Braille and the Royal Mail covers postage costs for the society to send books around the world. A gift of £20,000 from an anonymous donor enabled it to buy a new Braille embosser to increase production. Two-way books combine Braille text with pictures and printed words so that, for example, a visually impaired person can read a book to sighted children while they look at the pictures. Books can also be produced in large print or Moon, an alternative to Braille for less sensitive fingertips. The highlight of 1993–94 was the publication and launch of the Oxford Children's Encyclopaedia in Braille. £5 pays for a new strong postal bag or £100 for twenty; £11 pays for the sturdy binding of one hardback volume; £20 will provide a transcriber with a year's supply of computer discs; £60 pays for the transcription of three chapters into Braille or for a novel to be copied so that more than one reader can enjoy it at the same time; £100 purchases a specially designed Braille keyboard for a transcriber to use. For £250 a name can be inscribed in the front of a Braille or two-way book. This is the amount needed to produce it. £1,000 will produce a new four-volume novel for the library (Braille takes more space than conventional writing), while £5,000 will cover the cost of a year's supply of print books required for transcription. The NLB publishes an annual list thanking its legators and those who give donations, including those who give in memoriam donations for family members. The society's leaflet on making and changing a will, called *Spelling out your Wishes*, is available in Braille as well as print. The society is exploring new ways of including dedications in Braille book production.

Prices: Up to £500, up to £1,000

Pat Lynn, Chief Executive, Cromwell Road, Bredbury, Stockport SK6 2SG. Tel.: 0161 494 0217

Royal College of Physicians

This independent professional association of doctors was founded in 1518 by Royal Charter. In the modern world it ensures, through continual research, training and education, that specialists and hospital doctors are up to date with the latest medical developments. Its research reports have influenced modern health care and ideas on such varied topics as the dangers of smoking, the needs of the young disabled, alcohol abuse and the importance of dietary fibre in the prevention of disease. The college research unit undertakes collaborative research into the causes and cures of diseases of all kinds and problems such as diabetic renal failure and mental impairment in the elderly. As a registered charity, the college depends for a proportion of its income on donations and bequests. Sometimes these are given to endow named memorials in the form of prizes and medals, lectures and orations, fellowships and scholarships. Many of them are given in commemorative terms and for diverse purposes.

Additionally, there are occasions when fund-raising activities may contribute significantly towards part of a building or refurbishment appeal in memory of an individual, and these will be acknowledged by naming a room or mounting a wall plaque. In 1995, the college mounted an appeal for £1.9 million to build an extension. One major grant has been received from a charitable foundation to name a new meeting room after a late benefactor and friend. More recent examples of college trusts and special funds include the Graham Bull Prize, founded in 1988 by a gift from the Clinical Research Centre, Northwick Park, in honour of Sir Graham MacGregor Bull. It endowed an annual prize of £1,000 for an individual under the age of forty-five who has made a major contribution to clinical science. The Sir Michael Perrin Lecture was established in 1988 by deed of covenant in memory of Sir Michael Perrin who died in 1988. The money, £3,000 annually over a period of four years, endowed a lecture to be given by a medical scientist based in Europe. The Dr J.D. Ramsay Scholarship was founded by a bequest received in November 1993 from the estate of Dr James Duff Ramsay, leaving funds to be invested. The income is to be used to support a lecture or symposium relating to cardiology and organized by the college in Dr Ramsay's name. Part of the income is also to be used towards travel grants to enable junior doctors to attend lectures and meetings held by the college.

Prices: Unspecified

Patrick Jackson-Feilden, Appeal Director, 11 St Andrew's Place, Regent's Park, London NW1 4LE. Tel.: 0171 935 1174

Royal National Institute for the Blind

The institute, the largest organization of its kind in the world, was founded in 1868 by a surgeon who was forced to give up work when he lost his sight. It provides many services for the visually impaired, including the Sunshine House School for blind, partially sighted and often severely disabled children. It also funds holiday homes, an employment service and retraining facilities for newly blind adults, specially adapted equipment, materials on tape and in Braille and the talking books service, offering over 9,000 books. Two thousand staff are employed, from teachers to Braillists, from sound engineers to car staff, and there are over 10,000 volunteers who read books on to tape, help in the RNIB homes and schools, service talking book machines and raise funds.

Each legator who informs the society of his or her intention to leave money, an item of value or property to the RNIB receives – as well as formal thanks – a cassette featuring songs and music by blind and partially sighted children. Every person who leaves a legacy to visually impaired people through the RNIB is commemorated in the institute's book of remembrance. This beautiful leather-bound book is given pride of place in the main reception area at the RNIB's headquarters in London and can be viewed there. Each page in the book is dated and the name of the donor is recorded on the day he or she dies. An experienced calligrapher updates the entries regularly. There is no charge for entering the name of the donor in the book and all donors' names are recorded, no matter how small or large their gift. Will booklets are available in large print as well as in standard size print, in Braille and on tape for visually impaired legators, and parallel information exists for donors living in Scotland. There is a special service for blind and partially sighted legators, and home visits are available on request. Specific wishes can be discussed. For example, one gentleman left a legacy of £83,000 to help children at the Sunshine House School in Southport. It costs £5 to provide a white cane, £15 to print one copy of a Braille magazine for young children, £69 to give a blind person a week's holiday in an RNIB hotel and £500 to record one talking book. To keep services running for a day, the cost is £175,000.

Prices: Memorial Book, Unspecified

Heidi Nash, Wills and Legacies Advisory Service, 224 Great Portland Street, London W1N 6AA. Tel.: 0171 388 1266

Royal National Institute for Deaf People

This is Britain's only charity that works for people with all degrees of hearing loss and for deaf–blind people. Almost one in six people in the UK has some degree of hearing loss.

The institute provides many services, including Typetalk, the National Telephone Relay Service, funded by BT, that enables deaf people to communicate with hearing people on the telephone. Its community support units provide interpreting links for deaf people at job interviews or hospital visits. In addition, the RNID provides residential care, both long and short term, and rehabilitation and training for deaf people with special needs. In Northern Ireland, the RNID is working with Habinteg Housing Association to provide the first residential centre for deaf people with special needs in the province. The RNID also undertakes medical research with particular emphasis on people with tinnitus, as well as specialist research into products and applications of new technology. The RNID remembers supporters who have left a gift to the charity in their will. If an individual wishes, his or her name, town and county is included in the Book of Friends, which is updated every six months by a calligrapher. No charge is made for this. The book is displayed in the reception area at headquarters. In some circumstances a plaque will be erected for a donation or legacy which has contributed to a particular project, for example the opening of an occupational development unit. However, this would be done only when it has been specifically requested or as a condition of the gift.

Each year the RNID has different projects for which funds must be raised, and part of a legacy could be used to contribute to a project. £200 could help to buy four special telephones to enable residents in the institute's residential centres to call their families and friends. £250 could help to purchase lifting equipment for physically disabled residents, to buy a textphone in a communication support unit or to pay for a two-day specialist interpreter course. £300 could sponsor twenty hours of research into a new type of hearing-aid which blocks out background noise – £56,000 would fund the full cost of the development of its prototype. This new hearing aid could change the lives of four million hard-of-hearing people. £15,800 (at 1995 prices) could be used to buy a minibus for one of the residential centres to provide safe transport for residents with other disabilities. £60,000 could be used (at 1995 prices) to pay for calls to the free advice line, RNID Tinnitus Helpline. Two million people suffered from tinnitus (intrusion of unwanted noise) during 1995. £65,000 was the approximate cost of opening a communication support unit in 1995, which provides sign language interpreters, notetakers, deaf-blind interpreters and speech-to-text reporters for deaf people in all walks of life and any situation where communication support is required. Legacies between £1,000 and £15,000 could be used to contribute to any of the more costly projects.

Prices: Memorial Book, up to £500, up to £50,000, up to £100,000
Vickie Kemp, Appeals Executive, 105 Gower Street, London WC1E 6AH. Tel.: 0171 387 8033

15 Museums

Commemoration in this field comes most usually through donated artefacts and requires individual discussion with curators as to their suitability. This is not usually because the museum is being obstructive, but because it is undertaking to care for the artefact in perpetuity. The most imaginative scheme in the higher price range is probably the National Tramway Museum, where you can endow a restored Victorian Street.

American Air Museum in Britain

More than half a million US airmen were based in the UK in the Second World War, many in East Anglia. The American Air Museum in Britain, scheduled to open in mid-1997, will be based at Duxford, part of the Imperial War Museum and home of one of the finest collections of historic aircraft in the world (see entry on Duxford below). During the Second World War it was a USAF fighter base.

The museum will be a memorial to the 30,000 US airmen who lost their lives while flying from British bases. Designed by Sir Norman Foster, it will be set in the existing museum complex, alongside the preserved First World War hangars. Duxford is already the home of the finest collection of historic American combat aircraft outside the US. The museum will use the aircraft and supporting exhibits to explain the significance of American air power and its part in twentieth-century history. Fund-raising under the joint chairmanship of Charlton Heston and Field-Marshal Lord Bramall in the US and Britain aims to find £7.2 million for design, building, exhibit research and installation. There is a scheme whereby US donors, paying a minimum of $25, are known as Founding Members of the American Air Museum in Britain Campaign (there are now more than 50,000). Their names and the name of one other person in whose honour they may have made the contribution are entered in the Founders' Register of Honor, which will be on permanent display in the new museum. All donations from the UK and abroad are recorded in the roll of donors. Those who make more substantial donations, in memoriam gifts or bequests will be given prominent recognition. A suggested figure for such commemoration is over £10,000, whether corporate or individual. One suggestion is that names might be commemorated on a board or plaque on commemorative walls, and there will probably be opportunities for plaques for those who give substantial amounts. UK legacies and donations follow the standard charities tax exemption rules and come under the Imperial War Museum Trust. However, US contributions should be made payable to the American Air Museum and are tax deductible under Section 501(c)(3) of the US Internal Revenue Code. The Federal Tax Exemption Number is 52-1326048.

Prices: Memorial Book, up to £100, up to £50,000

The Director, The American Air Museum in Britain, Duxford Airfield, Duxford, Cambridge CB2 4QR. Tel.: 01223 835000; or The American Air Museum in Britain, Kessler and Associates, 510 11th St, SE Washington DC 20003, USA. Tel.: 202 543 4226

Birmingham Museum of Science and Industry

Items given as an in memoriam gift or in a bequest will be marked with an appropriate label commemorating the owner and will be cared for in perpetuity by the museum. Some items cannot be accepted, but the principal curator is pleased to advise at the time of the gift.

If money is given as an in memoriam gift for a chosen area, then what is bought will again be marked appropriately with a plaque or label. For example, a widow gave a donation in memory of her husband who loved trams. After discussion with the widow, a good-quality video machine and monitor were purchased, on which a video about old trams is constantly on show to visitors. The machine is labelled to commemorate the name of the man. Government grants can be used to double the value of a bequest or in memoriam gift, so a vehicle or similar that is restored from the money from a legacy or in memoriam gift will have two plaques, one commemorating the testator or person to be remembered, the other the body that donated the extra money. At 1995 prices, a £5,000 bequest could be used, together with an extra grant, for a restoration job of repainting and re-upholstering a vehicle in need. In this case the name of the benefactor or the person commemorated by the in memoriam gift would be on one of the plaques, while the others would be to the original donor of the vehicle and to the grant-aid body that had assisted with additional grants. £25,000 would replace a fire box on a steam-roller. £100,000 would pay for the complete redecoration of a gallery or the installation of facilities, for example a children's picnic area with plumbed-in washing facilities. £250,000–£1 million would pay for the refurbishment of galleries which could, subject to discussion, be named after the donor.

Prices: up to £5,000, up to £50,000, up to £100,000, up to £250,000, up to £500,000, up to £1 million

The Principal Curator, Newhall Street, Birmingham B3 1RZ. Tel.: 0121 235 1661

Chatham Historic Dockyard Trust

The historic dockyard comprises more than a hundred buildings and structures, many scheduled as ancient monuments, on an eighty-acre site. The trust has resisted the temptation to soften the industrial atmosphere and, wherever possible, working craftsmen are keeping alive traditional maritime skills.

For example, the Ropery at Chatham is now the last working naval ropeyard of its kind in Europe. Rope is made in a building dating from the eighteenth-century, using nineteenth-century machinery. Sailmaking and flagmaking are similarly encouraged and on display for the visitor, thanks to tenants who are keen to be part of the regeneration of the site. A number of people have made donations for memorials such as benches or garden areas, and there remains great scope for individual donations to assist the work of the trust and to develop facilities. As a museum development, the site is young and there is much to be done in terms of preserving the past for the future. Two major galleries telling the story of iron warship construction and submarine construction have been planned. They await funding and could provide lasting and unusual memorials, as a donor could be remembered in the name of a gallery. The trust is looking for ways of funding research and development of the collections. Donations could help preserve key artefacts in the collection, enable much-needed cataloguing, restore smaller boats possibly to working condition and assist in the preservation of maritime skills within the North Kent area.

Opportunities exist to restore the dockyard steam railway to working condition, providing transport for visitors. The church is badly in need of redecoration and enhancement. An endowment could enable active musical, artistic or lecture programmes to be organized. The trust would also like to commission appropriate sculpture and artwork inspired by the site, for the public spaces. The site has a full-time education officer who could use endowments from bequests to enhance visits for schoolchildren, students or adult learners. This could be done in traditional ways through the provision of additional activities or resources, publications or even play facilities. More innovative educational work could be considered if substantial funds were available – including publications for schools and colleges in traditional format or on CD ROM. Another project awaiting sponsorship is a huge interactive technology area where the exhibits reflect some of the large artefacts around the site, such as cranes, winches, capstans, pulleys, dry docks and caissons. Alternatively, a donor could fund and name university-based scholarships at the University of Greenwich, recently established in the former naval barracks at Pembroke, or the University of Kent, which also has a college in the historic dockyard.

The Administrator, Chatham Historic Dockyard Trust, Chatham, Kent ME4 4TE. Tel.: 01634 812551

Duxford Aviation Museum

Duxford is a preserved Battle of Britain fighter station, originally opened in 1917, and a former USAAF fighter base. Today, as an outpost of the Imperial War Museum, Duxford has become a leading aviation museum, housing one of the best collections of historic aircraft in the world. More than 140 historic aircraft are on show, from First World War biplanes to Gulf War jets. The museum undertakes a huge programme of aircraft restoration and conservation and is world-renowned as a centre for the flying of historic aircraft. More than thirty of the aircraft, mainly Second World War models, are kept in flying condition. Much of the airfield is preserved as it was in the early 1940s.

One of the major exhibits is itself a memorial. The Jesse Lumb Lifeboat was built in 1939 with a legacy of £9,000 by Miss A. Lumb, whose family owned a high-quality textile works in Huddersfield, West Yorkshire. A condition of the legacy was that the boat should be named after her brother Jesse. This was the last wartime lifeboat of this type in service with the Royal National Lifeboat Institution; it was moved to Duxford for display in 1980. The restoration and conservation programme at Duxford not only of aircraft but also of vehicles, artillery, missiles and equipment is one of the largest operations of its kind in the world. Any individual or organization that is able to help by giving money, materials or time is invited to contact the conservation manager on

01223 835000. This is a potentially fruitful area for commemoration of bequests and in memoriam gifts. Donations are also
recorded in the book of donors. The museum has an active
collecting policy and items on its acquisitions list can turn up from
many sources. In memoriam gifts and bequests of any possible
suitable items should be discussed with the curator.

Prices: Memorial Book, Unspecified
*The Curator, Duxford Airfield, Duxford, Cambridge CB2 4QR.
Tel.: 01223 835000*

Imperial War Museum

This museum illustrates and records all aspects of the military
operations involving Britain and the Commonwealth since 1914.
Founded in 1917, it also manages HMS *Belfast*, the Air Museum at
Duxford and the Cabinet War Rooms. The museum itself is
divided into a number of different departments, each with its own
speciality.

The Department of Film: the department is eager to add to the
collection of amateur (home movie) film, which can offer a
different viewpoint or extra coverage to balance official or
professional material. Private owners of this and other film footage
or posters, press cuttings, stills and similar material and those with
written or oral testimony of the making of such films, are asked to
contact the acquisitions officer.

The Department of Documents: this department houses a vast
collection of records of all types relating to warfare in the
twentieth century. The collections fall into two main groups, one
consisting of British private papers and the other largely of
captured German material. A principal aim is to preserve the
personal diaries and letters of servicemen and civilians who did not
rise to high positions but whose recorded experiences reflect the
activities and thoughts of ordinary people in wartime. Again this
might be a repository for a tangible bequest of any personal or
military wartime records of the twentieth century. Potential
donors should contact the acquisitions officer.

The Department of Printed Books: this is a national reference
library holding more than 100,000 books and 25,000 pamphlets,
15,000 volumes of periodicals and 15,000 maps and technical
drawings. The collection includes detailed coverage of the two
World Wars, more limited inter-war conflicts such as those in
Abyssinia and Spain, the Falklands War and other post-1945
conflicts, including Korea, the Middle East and Vietnam. Contact
the acquisitions officer to ascertain whether privately owned books

and printed material concerning war would be suitable as a memorial gift to this department.

The Department of Exhibits and Firearms: this department is responsible for the acquisition, cataloguing, conservation and storage of all three-dimensional material held by the museum. It operates two loan services, one for other museums and another more limited one for schools. The department is very pleased to acquire those items that it needs to complete its collection, but the cost of storage, record keeping and conservation necessitates a careful selection policy. Anyone considering offering an object to the department should telephone or write beforehand to establish whether the museum can accept it.

In many ways the Imperial War Museum is itself a national memorial to those who have been killed or have served in twentieth-century conflicts. A large amount of material in a range of departments originated as gifts from individuals. Anyone who gives money, whether as a bequest, in memoriam gift or donation, has their name inscribed on the Roll of Benefactors, a book specially kept for this purpose. The museum is delighted to receive legacies towards its work or in memoriam contributions for particular projects and exhibitions. An example would be the building of the American Air Museum at Duxford (see above).

Prices: Unspecified

Robert Crawford, Director-General, or Angela Godwin, Museum Sponsorship Co-ordinator, Lambeth Road, London SE1 6HZ. Tel.: 0171 416 5000

National Army Museum

The museum is delighted to accept both objects and money in memory of members of the Army both at home and abroad. Under the terms of its Royal Charter, it covers not only the British Army, both volunteer, regular and territorial, but also the forces of the Dominion and Colonies and the former British Indian Army.

Because the museum was founded in 1996, it is too young to have had new wings or extensions built by bequests, but there is certainly the possibility of galleries being refurbished by future legacies. The majority of bequests fall into the category of objects for the collections; all items are acknowledged by letter. Where requested, the director is happy to acknowledge the gift or bequest with a caption that accompanies the object. Every object on display at the museum has a short sentence indicating who provided the object concerned. War medals, memorabilia, archives and any other relevant objects will be gratefully received as well as money. Outside the museum, next to the flagstaff is the Tyndareus Stone, shipped back from Hong Kong where it commemorated a First World War tragedy. The men of the Plant Section, 70 Support Squadron, Queen's Gurkha Engineers, recovered the three-foot-high stone from its position high on the Peak on Hong Kong Island. It had been there for 70 years, erected by the commanding officer of the 25th Battalion of the Middlesex Regiment, Lieutenant-Colonel John Ward, in memory of the men of his battalion who died when their troopship *Tyndarios* struck a German mine off South Africa in 1917 while taking the men to the Hong Kong garrison. Also outside the museum is a modern memorial tablet erected by the Royal Corps of Transport upon its absorption into the Royal Logistic Corps in 1993. It traces the history of the RCT from its origins in the Royal Waggon Train. In the collections are a number of memorials, including a stained-glass window in memory of Lieutenant-General Sprot's service to the 83rd County of Dublin Regiment. There are also many pieces of mess silver which were once presented to messes now closed, disbanded or amalgamated by particular officers in memory either of their service or the service of their colleagues. The museum holds the original full-sized plaster maquette for Adrian Jones's bronze of a light horseman in the Australian Contingent of 1899–1902, the South Australian Volunteers Memorial which stands in North Terrace in Adelaide.

Prices: Unspecified
Ian G. Robertson, Director, Royal Hospital Road, Chelsea, London SW3 4HT. Tel.: 0171 730 0717

National Maritime Museum

The museum preserves superb collections relating to Britain's sea heritage, especially the history of the Navy and of shipping. It is also responsible for the landscaping and the upkeep of the buildings in Greenwich Park and former palace including the seventeenth-century Queen's House and the Royal Observatory, home of Longitude 0 degrees and Greenwich Mean Time.

Shipbuilding, sea battles, sea trade and great seafarers such as Drake, Anson, Cook and Nelson are represented among the museum's paintings, models, boats, charts, silver, weapons, uniforms and vast library of documents. The museum was founded from an endowment and the collection of Sir James Caird, the main hall and library being named after him. The endowment has since supported research work through grants, fellowships and awards. The main building in the east wing is named after the founding director, Sir Geoffrey Callender. The new education wing and lecture theatre were built from funds from the Leopold Muller Trust, who left £1.5 million to the museum; both new structures are named after him.

The museum welcomes bequests, which can be spent in a specified area or according to current need. These will be commemorated suitably. All legacies will be recorded in a book of remembrance. Some legacies will also be recorded on plaques elsewhere in the museum if appropriate. Although neither the museum nor the Friends has a formal memorial scheme, there are many opportunities for commemoration even for modest amounts. For example, from £100 upwards, a book could be bought and dedicated with a chosen name. The friends have a scheme whereby an artefact's restoration can be sponsored and this could be done in memoriam. In the case of a book, for example, this would cost from about £100. Recently, a company gave a lifetime gift of £25,000 to repair the roof of the observatory where the telescope is housed. For £50,000 part of the museum could be renovated and this would be commemorated with a plaque. For £100,000 upwards, a picture that the museum especially wanted could be purchased and acknowledged with a plaque.

At present, the museum is trying to raise £4 million for major restoration and extension of large areas of the museum, galleries and displays, because only twenty per cent of the collections can be displayed at any one time. The museum appeal is naming bricks for a minimum of £1,000 each, again a possible in memoriam dedication. Each brick entitles the donor to leave five lines in the archive records that can be used to commemorate a person, an animal, people at sea or for more general dedications. For a significant sum, £500,000 or more, it would be possible to name part of a building or a specific area, while for £1 million a whole gallery could be named. Artefacts are more difficult as a bequest since the museum has limited space. Such gifts should be discussed in advance, whether as part of a legacy or an in memoriam gift to see whether the museum could care for them. Contact the development director or initially the Friends' Office at the museum to discuss bequests and suitable commemoration.

Prices: Up to £100, up to £500, up to £1,000, up to £5,000, up to £50,000, up to £100,000, up to £500,000, up to £1 million and beyond

The Development Director, Greenwich, London SE10 9NF. Tel.: 0181 858 4422

National Tramway Museum

The National Tramway Museum depends upon the support of the members of the Tramway Museum Society, the charitable company that has built the museum and now owns and operates it. The museum shows trams in the surroundings in which they once operated and many of the buildings are transferred from their original settings. Trams run each day, manned by volunteers in traditional dress.

The board of management is made up entirely of volunteers, most of whom are also involved in other aspects of running the museum. Scores of volunteer workers have over the years formed a huge extended family and come from all over the country to spend weekends and holidays working in the museum. Many people, upon retirement, have moved house to be near the museum. In such circumstances, it is natural that people should wish to be associated with the museum after their death. At the request of the family, the museum's board usually agrees to commemorate the lives of active volunteer members in several ways. Dedication of a tree or bench may be sponsored by the family of the deceased. The ashes of the deceased may be scattered at the museum, a ceremony overseen by the museum chaplain. The most notable example took place in 1985, when the museum's board made arrangements for the coffin of Richard Fairbairn, a member who had made an outstanding contribution to the museum, to be carried by electric tram-car on the way to his funeral and his ashes to be scattered among the trees planted to commemorate his ninetieth birthday.

As a charity, the museum also welcomes gifts and bequests from members of the public, and any projected gifts, bequests and in memoriam donations together with suggested suitable memorials, should be discussed in advance with the museum board. Bequests that support the general work of the museum are particularly welcomed, since running the museum is very complex and regular work cannot be put aside to respond to specific wishes expressed in a bequest – even a generous one. It is important to talk over timescales and possible areas where the needs of the museum coincide with the wishes of the testator. The museum has a strict restoration policy governing the choice of tram-car to be restored. Donations must comply with this. A tram partially restored through the bequest of a member had a very discreet plate underneath in order not to interfere with the authenticity of the vehicle. A discreet plaque, perhaps not on the artefact itself, could be found, to commemorate the benefactor. To sponsor total tram-car restoration costs £180,000–£240,000. The restoration materials would cost from £60,000 to £80,000. Repainting a tram-car would cost £5,000–£10,000. To re-upholster the seating would be £8,000–£12,000. A tram-car motor rewind would be between £5,000 and £10,000. Workshop equipment is in constant demand and items would cost anything from £250 to £30,000. An extension to the workshop building would cost £250,000.

The Tramway Museum is also aiming to recreate a Victorian street. The cost of building terrace housing would be from £180,000–£500,000. A feature building, such as a school, fire station, garage, Co-operative shop or a chapel would cost from £100,000 to £300,000. A fountain or statue in the bandstand/park area would be from £2,000 to £10,000. To create a Victorian rose garden near the bandstand would be from £1,000 to £3,000. The annual maintenance cost of the park and rose garden would be from £250 to £500. Street furniture, such as lamps, railings, gates and fittings, signs and seats would cost from £1,000 to £20,000. There would obviously be opportunities for commemoration.

There is also a sponsored scheme for rebinding library books. The museum has one of the leading libraries on urban transport and many volumes in the collection are very old and falling apart. Members sometimes choose to pay for a book to be rebound and this could be marked with a commemorative bookplate. The library is therefore another suitable area for bequests from the general public. Bookbinding varies between £250 and £2,500. Shelving and fittings would be £250–£5,000. Acquisitions funding ranges from £250 to £5,000. The salary of a research/conservation assistant would be £15,000 a year. Site development and facilities are another area that would benefit from bequests and donations. A building to house a major exhibit would cost about £300,000. Planting trees and flower-beds, cutting grass and relandscaping the entrance and carpark could involve sums of £250–£50,000. Creating a children's play area is another project for possible funding, including rubber matting, play equipment and baby changing facilities, which would begin at £500 and go up to £20,000. Facilities for the disabled and visually impaired such as improved access, an induction loop, Braille guides, wheelchairs, etc., from £1,000 to £50,000. Provision of free entry for disabled visitors and those with special needs would involve funding from £2,000 to £60,000. New terminus visitor facilities would cost from £500,000 to £1 million. Land/property purchase to extend the area of the museum would be from £200,000 to £2 million. As for running costs, housing one tram on site involves a sum of £2,500. The traction supply to run trams is £4,500 for a year.

Prices: Up to £500, up to £1,000, up to £5,000, up to £10,000, up to £50,000, up to £100,000, up to £250,000, up to £500,000, up to £1 million and beyond

R.J. Clarke, Honorary Secretary, Crich, Matlock, Derby. DE4 5DP. Tel.: 01773 852565

National Waterways Museum at Gloucester

At the National Waterways Museum, display labels on exhibits are used to carry memorials. Currently none of these are dedicated to individuals but are for groups who have collected money to put some item on display or who have presented an item for display. However, labels could equally commemorate an individual bequest or in memoriam gift.

The museum makes memorial benches which are used on site for picnics or resting in the outside area of the museum. Currently, two such projects are being carried out in conjunction with the work schedule of the museum. One bench is being created to commemorate a man who used to visit the docks in his lunch-hour as a retreat from work. The second memorial bench will commemorate the *Maria Assumpta* which sank on the Devon coast with the loss of three crew after sailing from Gloucester in 1995. Outdoor benches cost about £150 and provide work for the museum's blacksmith and for volunteers who fit the woodwork. A plaque commemorating a person or event can be fitted to the bench or perhaps located elsewhere in the museum. The museum is also remembered in people's wills and this is one way of ensuring that a piece of heritage does not disappear when its owner dies. Although suitable artefacts are obviously welcome, it is much preferred if potential donors contact the museum in advance to discuss the bequest, since items bequeathed vary from collections of archives to a tug. These rarely come with a financial bequest, although of course this would help with future maintenance. Any bequests of an object will carry the donor's name and some detail. Bequests – whether to buy a new building or a piece of furniture for the museum – would be very welcome and appropriately commemorated. The National Waterways Museum is interested in any items connected with canals, canal people, river nagivation and the like, and would welcome discussion of any bequests or donations so that requests for memorials can be established.

Prices: Up to £500

A.J. Conder, Curator, Llanthony Warehouse, Gloucester Docks, Gloucester GL1 2EH. Tel.: 01452 318054

In Loving Memory
Victoria and Albert Museum

The V&A has a long history involving bequests of all sizes. The support of the public in this manner is very much appreciated, especially in these financially difficult times. Unlike some of the other national galleries and museums, the V&A does not have any sizeable endowment funds. This means that the cost of basic building maintenance, together with conserving objects in its care, absorbs more than the government funding it receives. Many people are not aware that the museum is a charity, and that by leaving a legacy to the V&A they can reduce the tax burden of their estate. The V&A recognizes that commemorating a loved one is important and is pleased to discuss various options, depending on the donor's particular interest. It is difficult to give a price element because of the variety of options available. The museum stresses that it is essential that the wording of the terms of a gift is suitable – it could not accept a gift if the terms were too restrictive. The trustees of the V&A also have an obligation under the National Heritage Act to ensure that the objects received are appropriate to the collection before accepting a bequest.
Prices: Unspecified
Lipi Khan, Legacies Officer, V&A Museum, South Kensington, London SW7 2RL. Tel.: 0171 938 8500

16 National and Regional Arts Boards

This is the area where for even a reasonable sum of money you can endow a prize or one-off grant. However, although there is plenty of information on past projects, prospective endowments do need to be tailored to available funds and areas of interest. For a substantial sum, there would be many opportunities for a notable and exciting contribution, especially in a local arts region. The regional centres may also offer access to those elusive local craftspersons who can create individualized memorials.

Arts Council of England

The Arts Council of England was set up to develop and improve the understanding of the arts and encourage their practice and accessibility throughout England. It helps to fund the English Regional Arts Board and encourages dance, drama, mime, literature, music, opera and the visual arts – including photography and documentary films and videos on the arts nationally.

There is a variety of bursaries, awards and funds, including fifteen annual bursaries valued at £7,000 each for writers, and a fund using about £100,000 per annum for translating published works. Its support includes schemes to establish writers' residencies in prisons and to promote literature in libraries and education. The Arts Council of England has been the recipient of bequests and donations in the past, with which it has set up awards, for example the Chrissi Bailey award for photography.

Prices: Unspecified
Mary Allen, Secretary, 14 Great Peter Street, London SW1P 3NQ. Tel,: 0171 333 0100

Arts Council, Ireland

The Irish Arts Council has a strong commitment to creative artists in Irish society and offers awards to individuals in recognition of their achievements and to assist them in the pursuit of their art. It funds bursaries, awards, travel and training awards, apprenticeships and scholarships in many fields, including the visual arts, music, opera, dance, literature, community arts, education, drama, and film and video.

Within the literature department of the Irish Arts Department there is a memorial prize, the Denis Devlin Memorial Prize for Poetry. This is given to the best book of poetry to be published by an Irish citizen every three years. It commemorates the distinguished Irish poet and diplomat, Denis Devlin, who was one of the Modernist Irish group of writers who started their work in the 1930s and included Samuel Beckett, Brian Coffey and Flann O'Brien. There is a trust fund which generates the £1,500 allocated every three years. The Tyrone Guthrie Centre is a workplace for artists in the late Tyrone Guthrie's home in Annaghmakerrig, Co. Monaghan; it is supported by the two arts councils in Ireland. There are a variety of painting and sculpture studios, a large music room and rehearsal space, and artists contribute what they can afford towards the cost of their stay.

A new scheme involves bursaries (at present two) of up to £5,000 for established artists and younger artists who wish to gain practical work experience. Artists can be working in any media, on a specific project or continuing with regular studio practice. This might be a suitable area for endowment. The Alice Berger Hammerschlag Trust Award was set up to continue her work assisting young and unappreciated artists. The award is made to an artist, normally resident in Northern Ireland or the Republic of Ireland and practising one of the visual or plastic arts, to enable him or her to travel abroad. Contact the council to discuss possible bequests and in memoriam gifts and appropriate commemoration.
Prices: Unspecified
Laurence Cassidy, Literature Officer, 70 Merrion Square, Dublin 2, Ireland. Tel.: 00 353 16611840

Arts Council of Northern Ireland

The council encourages the arts throughout Northern Ireland. There are several memorial trusts offering awards. For example, the Alan Astin Memorial Fund was established by friends of the late Professor Alan Astin, who died in June 1991 after a career in education, scholarship and the arts. He was Chairman of the Arts Council of Northern Ireland, was Professor of Ancient History at Queen's University and was at various times a pro-Vice Chancellor, Dean of the Faculty of Arts and Dean of the Faculty of Theology. The fund's purpose is to help young people to travel in the Mediterranean world for reasons connected with ancient historical or architectural scholarship. One bursary is available annually for first and second year students at Queen's University, available in alternate years to students of ancient history and architecture. The Thomas Dammann Junior Memorial Trust Awards were set up to honour the late Thomas Dammann Junior. They are given to Irish students resident in Ireland, North or South, and registered for a postgraduate or undergraduate award at a third level institution in Ireland. Travel awards up to £2,000 annually are available to individuals and groups for the purpose of travelling abroad to visit exhibitions, museums, galleries and buildings of architectural importance. The Stewart Parker Trust is to encourage playwrights in Ireland. Stewart Parker came to be recognized as one of the leading theatrical stylists of his generation, but for many years after he gave up his academic job he was struggling to have his work read and considered for production. The trust therefore concentrates its resources on helping playwrights working in Ireland for two years after the first professional production of one of their plays. The primary objective is to support them through to a second production, whether this is another production of premier work or a second play. Contact the Arts Council to discuss ideas for named bursaries and awards and other forms of possible commemoration for gifts and bequests.

Prices: Unspecified
Noirin McKinney, Director of Creative Arts, Stranmillis Road, Belfast BT9 5DU. Tel.: 01232 381591

East Midlands Arts

This covers Derbyshire, except for the Peak District, Leicestershire, Northamptonshire and Nottinghamshire. See the entry for the English Regional Arts Board for more details.

Prices: Unspecified
John Buston, Chief Executive, Mountfields House, Epinal Way, Loughborough, Leics. LE11 OQE. Tel.: 01509 218292

Eastern Arts

This arts board covers Bedfordshire, Cambridgeshire, Essex, Hertfordshire, Lincolnshire, Norfolk and Suffolk. See the entry for the English Regional Arts Board for more details.
Prices: Unspecified
The Director, Cherry Hinton Hall, Cherry Hinton Road, Cambridge CB1 4DW. Tel.: 01223 215355

English Regional Arts Board

The board acts as a co-ordinating secretariat and representing body for the ten Regional Arts Boards that now cover England. The secretariat provides project management, services and information for members. The ten regional boards are autonomous and work in partnership with local authorities and many other local organizations.

Each region has separate charitable status and is concerned with all forms of arts and crafts, performing arts, visual arts, media and published and works in close conjunction with the Arts Council of England, the British Film Institute and the Crafts Council, who between them provide most of the funds. The English Regional Arts Board assists new initiatives in areas of perceived need in the different regions. A regional board may fund an award in memory of a person who had a close connection with the arts in the region, for example the David Althuai Film Award, which is awarded annually by Southern Arts. However, a member of the public could discuss with the local regional board the naming of an award or prize in an area of interest or the funding of a local performance or project. In addition, local craftspersons or artists may be commissioned to create memorials of many different kinds, whether a painting, a piece of sculpture or a memorial bench, and the Regional Arts Board is a good source of locating such expertise. An example of this is the Hampshire Sculpture Trust (Southern Arts Board), which can commission craftspersons/ sculptors to make memorial seats and other artefacts to be put in local beauty spots (see entry below). Contact either the English Regional Arts Board at Winchester or the executive director at one of the regional boards to discuss any of the issues above.
Prices: Unspecified
Carolyn Nixson, 5 City Road, Winchester, Hants SO23 8SD. Tel.: 01962 851063

Hampshire Sculpture Trust

Although not primarily an organization for memorials, the Hampshire Sculpture Trust does offer a core of craftspersons who can offer creative memorials in the environment, not just in Winchester but around the south-east of England and even beyond.

Recently, the Hampshire Sculpture Trust erected a commemorative seat on St Giles's Hill on the outskirts of Winchester to a young woman who had died two years earlier. This prompted the renovation of the whole hillside. The seat cost £2,300; half was raised by family and friends and the trust contributed the rest. The trust was approached by colleagues of the girl and this venture proved a catalyst for an interest in seating, as well as the hill. The seat was made by an artist/blacksmith of forged metal. Its back represents a fox running through trees – the girl had red hair and was known as Foxy.

Another memorial was erected in 1994 to celebrate D-day at Netley on Southampton Water, the spot from which D-Day invasion forces left. Alex Peever, a local stone-carver, erected the piece. The trust is happy to produce effigies but also advises potential donors to consider the vast array of useful wayside memorial artefacts in Victorian times that added to the local environment as well as serving a commemorative function. For example, there is a drinking fountain on St Giles's Hill, Winchester, that has gone into disuse and that could be restored as a lasting and useful memorial. This is also true of church memorials, such as stained-glass windows. Instead of purchasing existing works of art for cathedrals and churches that may not be appropriate, the trust suggests commissioning some appropriate piece from a local artist, sculptor or craftsperson.

Prices: Up to £5,000
Contact the trust through the English Regional Arts Board, 5 City Road, Winchester, Hants SO23 8SD. Tel.: 01962 851063

London Arts Board

This covers the area of the thirty-two London boroughs and the City of London. See the entry for the English Regional Arts Board for more details.

Prices: Unspecified
The Chief Executive, Elme House, 133 Long Acre, Covent Garden, London WC2E 9AF. Tel.: 0171 240 1313

North West Arts Board

This covers Lancashire, Cheshire, the Peak District, Greater Manchester and Merseyside. See the entry for the English Regional Arts Board for more details.
Prices: Unspecified
Sue Harrison, Chief Executive, 12 Harter Street, Manchester M1 6HY. Tel.: 0161 228 3062

Northern Arts

This covers Cleveland, Cumbria, Durham and Northumberland, and the Metropolitan Districts of Newcastle, Gateshead, North Tyneside, Sunderland and South Tyneside. See the entry for the English Regional Arts Board for more details.
Prices: Unspecified
Peter Hewitt, Chief Executive, 9–10 Osborne Terrace, Jesmond, Newcastle upon Tyne NE2 1NZ. Tel.: 0191 281 6334

Scottish Arts Council

The Scottish Arts Council is the principal channel for government funding of arts in Scotland and is funded by the Scottish Office. It aims to develop and improve the knowledge, understanding and practice of the arts and to increase their accessibility throughout Scotland. It offers about 1,300 grants annually to arts and arts organizations concerned with the visual arts, drama, dance and mime, literature, music, festivals and traditional, ethnic and community arts.

Most people living in Scotland who make a bequest want it to benefit Scotland and this follows the principle of government funding. All funds go to the arts and the council does not, for example, set up plaques outside writers' homes. On the whole, the council prefers bequests to go to living art. Some years ago, the council was left about £300,000 to be directed towards the arts in a way it thought appropriate. The income from this donation enabled a new scheme of support to be drawn up whereby young people between the ages of sixteen and twenty-five would apply for grants towards activities that might otherwise have been ignored. The SAC also funds an important biennial lecture, called the Neil Gunn Lecture, which forms the climax to the visit of an internationally acclaimed novelist. The Scottish Arts Council has set up a trust to advise and suggest ways in which people might leave funds for use by artists and organizations in Scotland. Contact the trust to discuss bequests and in memoriam gifts and possible commemoration through naming prizes, awards, lectures, etc.

Prices: Unspecified
Walter Cairns, Director of Literature, 12 Manor Place, Edinburgh EH3 7DD. Tel.: 0131 226 6051

South East Arts

This covers Kent, Surrey, West Sussex and East Sussex. See the entry for the English Regional Arts Board for more details.

Prices: Unspecified
Christopher Cooper, Chief Executive, 10 Mount Ephraim, Tunbridge Wells, Kent TN4 8AS. Tel.: 01892 515210

South West Arts

This covers Avon, Cornwall, Devon, Dorset (except for the districts of Bournemouth, Christchurch and Poole), Gloucestershire and Somerset. See the entry for the English Regional Arts Board for more details.

Prices: Unspecified
Graham Long, Chief Executive, Bradnich Place, Gandy Street, Exeter EX4 3LS. Tel.: 01392 218188

Southern Arts

This covers Berkshire, Buckinghamshire, Hampshire, Isle of Wight, Oxfordshire, Wiltshire and the districts of Bournemouth, Christchurch and Poole. See the entry for the English Regional Arts Board for more details.

Prices: Unspecified
Sue Robertson, Executive Director, 13 St Clement Street, Winchester SO23 9DQ. Tel.: 01962 855099

Welsh Academy

The Welsh Academy is the English arm of Yr Academi Grymreig, the national society of Welsh writers. It exists to promote literature in Wales, in Welsh or English. Currently, it administers the John Tripp Literary Award, paid for by the interest from a bequest of £5,000. Another memorial award is the Rhys Davies Trust, set up by the author's brother. The academy welcomes any suggestions for bequests, in memoriam awards or bursaries and potential donors should contact the director.

Prices: Unspecified
Kevin Thomas, Director, 3rd Floor, Mount Stuart House, Mount Stuart Square, Cardiff CF1 6DQ. Tel.: 01222 492026

Welsh Arts Council

The Welsh Arts Council has departments for music, art, literature, drama, crafts and dance and runs the Oriel Gallery in Cardiff. It uses both the English and Welsh languages in its work. Contact the executive director to discuss bequests, in memoriam gifts and possible suitable commemoration through named awards, prizes, bursaries etc.

Prices: Unspecified
Emryr Jenkins, Executive, Holst House, 9 Museum Place, Cardiff CF1 3NX. Tel.: 01222 394711

West Midlands Arts

This covers the counties of Hereford and Worcester, Shropshire, Staffordshire, Warwickshire and the districts of Birmingham, Coventry, Dudley, Sandwell, Solihull, Walsall and Wolverhampton. See the entry for the English Regional Arts Board for more details.

Prices: Unspecified
Michael Elliot, Chief Executive, 82 Granville Street, Birmingham B1 2LH. Tel.: 0121 631 3121

Yorkshire and Humberside Arts

This covers the districts of Barnsley, Bradford, Calderdale, Doncaster, Kirklees, Leeds, Rotherham, Sheffield, Wakefield and North Yorkshire and Humberside. See the entry for the English Regional Arts Board for more details.

Prices: Unspecified
Roger Lancaster, Executive Director, 21 Bond Street, Dewsbury, W. Yorks. WF13 1AX. Tel.: 01924 455555

17   Nature

This was one of the most fruitful areas of exploration with an almost one hundred per cent response to my initial enquiries and a noteworthy set of enthusiastic contacts who seem to love their work. Trees are obviously the most common and a very reasonable form of commemoration. Careful forms of identification ensure that memorial trees will always be found.

AB Wildlife Trust Fund

The trust has a philosophy, rooted in its work with dying and bereaved people and with wildlife conservation. It is an entirely new type of charity, bringing together the concepts of a natural setting where people may die in peace with a natural bereavement period and burial with the creation of nature reserves for the living to enjoy. It would welcome donations, in memoriam gifts and legacies.

An ideal project would create a large nature reserve with woods, glades, pastures and ponds, and a homely cottage for dying and bereaved people to stay. They could live in the holiday cottage setting with 24-hour help near at hand if required. If the death was not imminent, the trust would hope to provide care of the same quality at home. Those who are dying could enjoy the setting and wildlife before merging with it at the time of burial, returning to a very old idea of going to a chosen place of beauty to die. Friends and relatives could work together after the death as part of a natural mourning period, digging the grave at their own pace and sharing memories while cooking meals or resting. The aim of the trust is to increase the amount of land available for nature reserves, giving them permanent protection, along with protection of graves in perpetuity. In cemeteries graves are only leased for a set number of years and in 1995 the trust took up in court the case of a cemetery being turned into a carpark and the graves dug up. Nature reserves of all shapes and sizes will eventually be provided, radiating from the Harrogate area outwards. At present the trust can arrange a small number of burials on nature reserves near Harrogate. However, when funds exist to create and own new nature reserves, beautiful settings will be created for wildlife and animals. The combination of graves with a wildlife habitat is both practical and easy. Graves can be mounded for flowers, such as bee orchids and wild thyme or left with hiding places for frogs, toads, newts and lizards. The number of graves on these reserves would vary from one grave per acre to 450 graves per acre, depending on existing wildlife and ground condition. There will be no rows of headstones, and graves will quickly merge into the surroundings, particularly when permanent broad-leaved woodland is developed. The site would be accessible to frail or disabled visitors. The trust therefore needs to buy its own land for burials and nature reserves. It also needs to buy a homely cottage or cottages on the reserves and employ staff to be available twenty-four hours a day to cater for every physical, mental and spiritual need of the dying and afterwards the bereaved. A cottage on such land might cost £100,000 to be restored and specially adapted. Land suitable for a nature reserve might cost £30,000+. Those making large donations may be able to have areas named after them. Others could have features created in their memory, such as wild-flower areas, ponds, bat caves and artificial badger setts. The trust is happy to discuss such possibilities at any time for bequests and in memoriam donations, large and small. Gifts of land anywhere in Britain are very welcome. An ideal requirement would be in an area of natural wildlife, perhaps a large ploughed field, that could be converted to a burial ground/woodland next to a natural habitat such as a wildlife pond or an area conducive to wildlife conservation. The idea is that the area should have natural amenities for walking so that, as well as visiting the grave, visitors can wander along footpaths and by hedgerows or among wildlife breeding areas. The trust publishes *Green Burial – The DIY Guide to Law and Practice* at £9.85. It can also offer advice on all aspects of dying, bereavement and burial.

Prices: **Up to £50,000, up to £100,000**

John Bradfield, Honorary Adviser, 7 Knox Road, Harrogate, N. Yorks. HG1 3EF. Tel.: 01423 530900

Aberfoyle Forest District

In the depths of Loch Ard forest within the Aberfoyle Forest District, a memorial to women and children lost at sea due to U-boat action during the First World War has been carved by a

stonemason on the water board aqueduct. See also the entry for
the Forestry Commission below.
Prices: Unspecified
*N.H. Clayden, Forest District Manager, Aberfoyle, Stirling FK8
3UX. Tel.: 01877 382383*

The Book of Oaks

The Book of Oaks, dedicated on 14 May 1993, was established by
Peter Webb, East Midlands Conservator for the Forestry
Authority, the Forestry Commission's grants and licensing arm.
The heavy, leather-bound volume rests in a place of honour in
Lincoln Cathedral. In it are listed the names of people who have
dedicated single oak trees or plantations to the future restoration
of Lincoln Cathedral's roofs. The Book of Oaks, which is inscribed
with each name by a calligrapher, will be on permanent display in
the cathedral. In eighty to one hundred years' time, each tree will
be transferred to the cathedral roof where it will lie for ten years
until it is seasoned. If wood for such purposes is not seasoned then
it may crack. The idea of the Book of Oaks arose because
cathedral craftsmen were faced with rapidly dwindling supplies of
English oak. Each year alone, seven tons of top-quality timber are
needed to maintain the rafters, some of which date back to the
thirteenth century. Securing a new source of raw materials was
vital if Britain's finest run of medieval oak roofs were to survive
into the future. A certificate of dedication is issued for each tree
planted. Farmers and landowners in the region have begun
establishing new woodlands containing native tree species. Among
them are the oaks which will one day go to the cathedral. As a
further memorial, the woods will create new habitats for wildlife
and recreation facilities for future generations. Anyone can
dedicate an oak-tree to Lincoln cathedral through the Book of
Oaks. People with trees on their land can specify one which is
already growing, enabling the pledge to be realized earlier, during
their own lifetime or by their children, or they can plant new ones.
Those without land can have a tree in Lincoln's new cathedral
wood, dedicated to their name or in memory of a loved one. The
wood is being established in partnership by the Forestry
Authority, Lincoln Cathedral and Lincoln City Council. There is
no charge for such a dedication. The Forestry Commission has
given a designated oak-tree to be planted in the cathedral grounds
at Lincoln and it is the intention to encourage young people in
Lincoln to plant such trees. It is hoped the scheme will eventually
be widened to include other cathedrals. The East Midlands

Forestry Area covers Lincolnshire, Nottinghamshire, Derbyshire and Leicestershire but in theory people from other areas can participate.

Prices: Memorial Book, Unspecified

Peter Webb, Conservator, East Midlands Forestry Conservancy, Willingham Road, Market Rasen, Lincs. LN8 3RQ. Tel.: 01673 843461

The British Trust for Conservation Volunteers

There are more than 85,000 conservation volunteers from all walks of life, who work on more than 15,000 sites in England, Wales and Northern Ireland, in urban as well as country settings. One of the aims of the trust is to recreate the former great native woods.

Since the Second World War, more than half the broad-leafed trees of Britain have been lost and – along with the destruction of the woodlands – the habitat of many wild animals, including the red squirrel. For example, during its lifetime an oak tree can act as host to over 32 species of mammal, including badgers, fieldmice, deer and hedgehogs, 68 species of bird, 34 species of butterfly, 271 species of insect, 168 species of fern and 31 species of lichen. A tree can be planted in the name of a donor, friend or relative and will be nurtured for the early part of its life for five years. The planting season starts on 1 November each year and ends with Woodland Action Week at the end of March. Illustrated material is sent with the application. There is also an opportunity to plant a memorial to someone who was not a close friend or family, without offending the immediate family. For example, one donor dedicated a tree in memory of a former war hero. For £17, BTCV will plant a tree and for each additional £17 donated an extra tree will be planted. There are eight species from which to choose: beech, oak, ash, hazel, wild cherry, field maple, guelder-rose and willow. For £135, BTCV will create a copse of traditional trees. An invitation will be issued to the family of a deceased relative or to a living donor to see the trees planted by skilled volunteers or learn how to plant them. For £250, BTCV will plant and care for an individual site of fifteen trees, created in the donor's name or that of a loved one. Donors can select the site of their choice. During the years the chosen sites may change and donors are given a wide selection. The following sites were available from 1995 onwards for tree planting: In Charter Wood, Norwich, an eleven-acre wood is being planted in the Yare Valley to celebrate the 800th anniversary of Norwich City's Royal Charter, designed to symbolize past, present and future. In Appleton Park,

Leicestershire, an informal parkland has been developed on more than three acres of derelict land. It consists of a children's play area, woodland and meadow. In Northfleet Country Park, Kent, 500 trees will be planted and community copses developed at this recreational area near Dartford. At Ham Green Wood, Forest of Dean, Bristol, pupils from St Katherine's Secondary School, Forest of Dean, will augment their curriculum studies by finding ways to develop the wood. Upper Westland Wood is a special feature of the Clandeboys Estate. Thousands of young people visit it every year as they walk along the Ulster Way footpath. Volunteers will help to maintain this popular woodland by replanting many of the trees which have been lost in the past. Moore Nature Reserve, Warrington, Cheshire, was once a sand quarry situated between the Manchester Ship Canal and the River Mersey. It is a popular destination for people from Warrington and further afield. Thousands of trees will be planted here to develop the reserve and encourage a similar transformation of the adjacent landfill sites. Hammond Farm, Burgess Hill, West Sussex, is a twenty-acre site recently acquired by Mid-Sussex District Council. BTCV helped to plant 1,000 trees there in 1995 to develop it as a new community area. A former site was Two Storm Wood in Richmond Park in Surrey, planted to replace some of the trees lost in the hurricane of 1987. A scheme also exists to dedicate trees for birthdays and anniversaries, and special dedication cards will be sent for the occasion.

Prices: Up to £100, up to £500

Andrea Mannings, Public Relations Officer, 26 St Mary's Street, Wallingford, Oxon. OX10 OEU. Tel.: 01491 839766

Chilterns Forest District

At Cowleaze Wood, near Stokenchurch in Buckinghamshire, in the Chilterns Forest District, a memorial was unveiled to the crew of a Halifax bomber on the fiftieth anniversary of its crash while returning from a mission over Germany in the early hours of the morning of 31 March 1944. Representatives of the families of crew members, members of the squadron, a member of the salvage team and of the Forest Enterprise were present at the unveiling.

Some eighteen months earlier, after finding a poppy attached to a tree in Cowleaze Wood, the forestry district manager was approached by the nephew of the crew members regarding placing a memorial on the site of the crash. A stone was donated by the Trustees of Lincoln Cathedral and inscribed with the names of the crew. See also the entry for the Forestry Commission below.

A.J. Dauncey, Forest Manager, Upper Icknield Way, Aston Clinton, Aylesbury, Bucks. HP22 5NF. Tel.: 01296 625825

Forestry Commission

Within the woodlands of the Forestry Commission are many memorials. Each forest manager will consider all requests for memorials if appropriate and in keeping with the woodland surroundings. One advantage is that the memorial is on land that will be protected in perpetuity; it is also less likely to suffer vandalism than a memorial in a park or urban open space, since the rangers are vigilant and visitors tend to have travelled to enjoy the quietness.

Although many of the memorials are collective ones, it is possible to erect a modest personal tribute. For more information on the types of memorial available see the entries for the Aberfoyle, Chilterns, Moray and Wester Ross Forest districts, the Book of Oaks and the Sherwood Forest Initiative.

Prices: Unspecified
Dawn McNiven, Press Officer, Department of Forestry, Corstorphine Road, Edinburgh EH12 7AT. Tel.: 0131 334 0303

Moray Forest District

In the Moray Forest District, Speymouth Sign Workshops have created a large number of commemorative memorials in the form of seats. These cost from £200 plus VAT and delivery.

Also in Moray, staff of BP donated and erected three barbecues for one of the recreation sites, each with a small plaque in memory of one of their colleagues. See also the entry for the Forestry Commission above.

Prices: Up to £500
R.L.A. Bryson, Forestry Manager, Balnacoul, Fochabers, Grampian IV32 7LL. Tel.: 01343 820223

National Memorial Arboretum Appeal

The appeal was launched by John Major to create a living tribute to the wartime generations of this century and to be a gift, in their memory, for future generations to reflect upon and enjoy.

It is being established on 150 acres of land provided by Redland PLC on the banks of the River Tame in Alrewas in Staffordshire.

Living memorials can take several forms. A commemorative tree can be planted and the name of the donor entered in a book of remembrance at the site's visitor centre. For an individual, a tree would cost on average £30. Arrangements for plantings can be made by writing to the National Memorial Arboretum. Each tree will be planted and dedicated individually and its exact location recorded at the visitor centre. The director says that the arboretum will be delighted to dedicate groves of trees on a pro rata basis, i.e. ten trees for £300. The arboretum is intended to commemorate all the wartime generations of this century, not only those who lost their lives. In the long term it will become a central place, where the great and the good and the ordinary men and women of the nation can be remembered in a positive way. Groups or associations are welcome to have trees or groves planted and can have a dedicatory plaque placed at the spot. Groups making use of this facility include ships, regiments and squadrons of the Services, the Royal British Legion and other veterans' associations. The Merchant Navy is having a wood planted in which each tree will represent a ship lost to enemy action, while the site will also feature a rose garden dedicated to the war widows of Britain. A Garden of Innocence will be planted in memory of all children killed in wars. Capital projects include the chapel, which will need £250,000, the visitor centre for £750,000 and a parking area for £90,000. Landscaping will cost £80,000 in total and the rose garden £50,000. The arboretum is pleased to have memorial benches donated and dedicated. This cause offers a living memorial and the emphasis is on trees rather than cost. Says David Childs, the director: 'We would rather plant commemorative trees than have people who wish to do so be put off by cost.'

Prices: Up to £50, up to £50,000, up to £100,000, up to £250,000, up to £1 million

David Childs, Europa House, 13–17 Ironmonger Lane, London EC1V 3QN. Tel.: 0171 250 1700

Sherwood Forest Initiative

The Sherwood Forest Initiative, a partnership between the Forestry Commission, local authorities, conservation interests, landowners and country organizations, aims to restore vast parts of the forest that have disappeared, using new areas of oak-trees and heathland to join the forest together so that it will be as it was originally.

Once Sherwood Forest stretched from Nottingham Castle to Worksop, twenty miles long and up to eight miles wide. Now covering an area of less than 500 acres, scattered with gnarled and decaying oaks, the Shire Wood is often regarded as the only remaining part of the forest, although in fact there are scattered fragments across its former expanse. It is a forest with worldwide significance, as focus for the Robin Hood legends. Visitors are disappointed when they visit Nottingham and cannot find the forest. The project is described in the official pamphlet as 'Putting back Britain's Heart of Oak'. Austin Brady, the project's director, says that the scheme offers scope for imaginative and enduring memorials. A new wood created from an open field can be named after a relation or oneself and once it has been recorded on Forestry Commission documentation, over time the name becomes enshrined and appears on Ordnance Survey Maps.

Memorials in all price ranges are possible. Fifty acres of new oak forest, to be set up and maintained, would cost £500,000. In all such projects there is the initial cost for capital outlay and the need for money to be invested to pay for future management. Much smaller areas of woodland can also be purchased. An acre of woodland would range from around £10,000 upwards. The trust will aim to buy land and plant it with oak-trees in memory of a loved one or a living donor. A tree can be planted for £10. The trust expects to plant groups of 1,000 trees, of which 200–300 would be endowed. Rather than endowing a specific tree which could be destroyed by deer, die or need to be cut down, the trust will keep the same number of trees as memorials, replacing any that die, with a plaque in that area commemorating people who have bought a tree. One plan is to have a little picnic area by the memorial plaque so that relatives of those commemorated by the trees could wander in the appropriate area of woodland. Picnic sites are another suggested tangible memorial. A picnic site in the forest would cost initially around £2,000 to set up with heavy picnic tables and all the other paraphernalia, with the total cost being £5,000–£10,000 to allow for maintenance. A visitors' centre would cost upwards of £500,000 to allow money for it to be publicized as well as maintained, in order to bring people back into the forest.

Prices: Up to £100, up to £5,000, up to £10,000, up to £50,000, up to £500,000, up to £1 million

Austin Brady, Project Director, Cuckney Road, Carburton, Worksop, Notts. S80 3BP. Tel.: 01909 472965

Wester Ross Forest District

The Wester Ross Forest District receives a regular donation of £100 towards work at the Kylerhea Otter Haven. In memoriam donations have also been used to have trees planted and dedicated to family members. The forest ranger is especially interested in donations for creating artificial otter holts and wetland restoration. See also the entry for the Forestry Commission above.

Prices: Unspecified

R.C.B. Johnstone, Forest District Manager, Balmacara, Kyle of Lochalsh, Ross and Cromarty IV40 8DN. Tel.: 01599 566321

Woodland Creations

Woodland Creations is a non-profit-making organization, although not a registered charity, dedicated to restoring broad-leafed native woodland in Cornwall, using native trees such as oak, ash, beech, wild cherry and sweet chestnut.

Britain has lost forty-five per cent of its semi-natural woodland during the last fifty years and in one of the least wooded countries in Europe. Much of what remains is, according to Tim Reed of Woodland Creations, under threat from development and lack of management. Although the Forestry Commission has managed to increase Britain's woodland to ten per cent from an all-time low of five per cent when it was set up in the early 1920s, Tim says that this tends to be in the upland regions of Britain and involves planting of non-native trees as well as native ones. Only three per cent of woodland in Britain is native broad-leafed cover. Woodland Creations is planting native woodlands on existing farmland to create a woodland habitat, and trees can be dedicated in memory (or for other reasons) for £15 per tree. For this amount, Woodland Creations will nurture the tree to maturity. If the tree dies the organization will replace it. The trees are tagged on site with a requested dedication and recorded in a dedication book, with a mapped reference number. Sponsors receive a dedication card with this reference number. Only every other tree is dedicated, so that in ten–fifteen years time, when the woodland matures, the undedicated trees can be cut back to allow the commemorative trees to grow to full maturity. A sponsor can choose the type of broad-leafed tree required and is welcome to visit the site to see the dedicated tree. It is possible to sponsor several trees to form a small copse or even a whole larger copse which can be named in memory of the chosen person. Copses would cost between £1,000 and £5,000, according to size and situation. Woodland Creations would keep the name of the original field, which may be centuries old, but the new copse would be named after the chosen person.

Prices: Memorial Book, up to £100, up to £1,000, up to £5,000

Tim and Nicky Reed, The Guildhouse, Tredethick, Lostwithiel, Cornwall PL22 OLE. Tel.: 01208 873618

18   Overseas

This proved a difficult category for tangible memorials, since overseas work tends to be carried out by local organizations who are less conducive to naming projects or buildings after an unknown benefactor. Aid too may be in the form of seeds and tools rather than permanent structures. Jewish World Relief can offer tangible commemoration in many forms and prices, as can the Commonwealth Society for the Deaf. Oxfam has a memorial book and Christian Aid is considering memorial photographs. It may be that with the competition for resources, this is one area where rapid improvements in commemorative projects will take place, perhaps through memorial books at organizations' headquarters.

ActionAid

ActionAid is the fourth largest overseas charity, working to improve the quality of life in some of the poorest parts of the world by helping some two million people to find a future through long-term projects which benefit the whole community. A legacy gift is seen by ActionAid as an enduring memorial that could affect many generations to come.

It might be used to help provide safe water, equip schools, train teachers or enable a community to develop a more secure financial base from which to tackle farming, health care and vital income-generating trade in Asia, Africa and Latin America. The costs of such projects are very substantial and it is unlikely that any one legacy could fund them in their entirety. However, the combined income from legacies, however small, is vital to the work of ActionAid and makes a substantial contribution to funding these projects. The society will always give feedback on projects if requested and will do its utmost to direct money to the area specified. For example, ActionAid's biggest legacy to date, £189,000 from a supporter in Norfolk who did not wish to be named, carried the request that it was used towards a project in the Far East. It was directed towards the Son La project in Vietnam and is being used to fund work in health care, credit and savings schemes, water and agriculture. The Vietnam project began in 1991 and targets over 19,000 people. The legacy has not only ensured that planned activities will be carried out but has also helped to create a more secure funding base. The legacy gift and project were reported in *The Common Cause*, ActionAid's supporters' magazine. In ActionAid's Cordillera Negra programme in Peru, it costs £1,833 to provide teaching materials to eight education centres, benefiting 650 children at a cost of £2.82 per child.

Prices: Unspecified

Chrissie McCall, Marketing Manager, Hamlyn House, Macdonald Road, Archway, London N19 5PG. Tel.: 0171 281 4101

ActionAid, Sponsor a Child

Sponsoring a child in memory of a loved one or even as a lifetime gift is another possibility. Regular reports from fieldworkers are sent on the sponsored child plus a photograph and messages from the child. Every three years a new photograph is sent.

The cost of sponsoring a child is £15 a month and can be paid either directly, by direct debit or deed of covenant by taxpayers (see chapter 2 for details of covenanting), which enables ActionAid to claim back tax at the basic rate in addition to the £15. A typical child might be a six-year-old girl in Bangladesh, where ActionAid works in partnership with local organizations to provide health care and basic education for children like the sponsored child and also general help with small business and agricultural projects to help to raise the level of family income. Children can be sponsored throughout Africa, Asia and Latin America. Communities and specific projects can also be sponsored.

Prices: Up to £500 per annum

Janice Ball, UK Supporter Development Department, Chataway House, Leach Road, Chard, Som. TA20 1FA. Tel.: 01460 62972

Baptist Missionary Society

The Baptist Missionary Society works with Christians in more than thirty countries in Africa, Latin America, Asia and Europe and also helps them to come to Britain to study.

More than half the BMS workers are involved with Evangelism, while others engage in teaching, discipling new Christians, health work, agriculture and development, social projects and administration. In Latin America, for example, Baptist missionaries work in the city slums as well as carrying out development and agricultural work in remote communities. In the slums of Brazil, pre-schools are set up to prepare disadvantaged children – potential street children – for the state education system. The schools are held in a bus, and in every place that a school is started, a Christian church is also being established. The society receives a number of legacies each year, principally from members of Baptist churches. Although the society does not have any formal schemes for remembering legators, it would consider some form of memorial for an individual who has been deeply involved in the work of the organization over a number of years. Details of legacies and their givers are also published in the *Missionary Herald*. Over the years a number of properties have been left to the society for specific purposes, such as missionary home assignment accommodation. It is always useful if those considering leaving a legacy to the society are not too specific on how the money or property is to be used. The society can then be free to use it in connection with its ongoing work and the particular needs at the time the legacy becomes available.

Prices: Unspecified
Michael J. Quantick, Administration Manager, PO Box 49, Baptist House, 129 Broadway. Didcot, Oxon. OX11 8XA. Tel.: 01235 512077

British Red Cross

The organization spent more than £30 million in 1994 on international relief and development aid. An example of its work abroad includes its Aid to Rwanda programme. By the end of 1994, the British Red Cross had supplied fifty-five skilled delegates including a sixteen-strong medical team, medical equipment, vehicles, blankets and tarpaulins for shelters. Over a million people were slaughtered, including Red Cross workers, and two million refugees fled the country. In all, there were twenty-three relief flights and a total cost of over £8 million. Zaire, which borders Rwanda, took in more than a million refugees, and the British Red Cross assists in supporting camps to provide shelter and aid. From 1992 to 1995, in the former Yugoslavia, £22 million was spent by the British Red Cross on aid and personnel and on such projects as major water and sanitation programmes in

Mostar, Pale and Sarajevo, providing essential medical supplies and assisting in more than fifty hospitals and medical centres in the UN Protected Areas and the Banja Luka areas. The British Red Cross provided hot meals in community kitchens to many thousands in need and delivered essential food parcels and wheat flour to people who had been months without supplies.

In Britain in 1994, the British Red Cross trained more than 175,000 people in First Aid. In 1994, Fire Victim Support Schemes were set up in Berkshire, County Durham, Humberside and Merseyside and the service continues to expand. It offers specially adapted mobile units equipped with basic essentials such as baby food, clothes, money, a mobile phone, toilet and shower facilities, children's toys and refreshments. Trained volunteers give practical and emotional support to those whose homes have been partially or completely destroyed by fire. The British Red Cross also provides transport for the elderly and infirm, and is creating new medical loan centres to provide vital home nursing aids, and additional home care teams to help the disabled and those returning from hospital. Much of the work of the Red Cross is paid for by money received in the general fund. Calls for help can come from one-off disasters such as the Herald of Free Enterprise tragedy or emergency appeals throughout the world and in Britain.

For this reason, a general donation is the most helpful form of bequest in a fast-changing world, where a sudden need may demand instant response by the Red Cross. Even small amounts of money are helpful. For example, £15.30 buys five blood bags to treat people injured in crossfire; £30 provides blankets to keep families in war-ravaged areas warm and dry; £47 keeps a First Aid Team on twenty-four hour alert over one weekend; £75 keeps one emergency vehicle dedicated to the new Fire Victim Support Scheme on the road for a day. The Book of Gratitude kept at national headquarters contains the names of people who have died and made a bequest to the Red Cross. The book is printed in copperplate type by computer, and relatives may come and see the entry. One possible memorial to a loved family member, friend or colleague would be to purchase a Humanity red rose, grown specially to coincide with the 125th anniversary of the Red Cross in 1995. For each rose bush sold, the British Red Cross receives a donation of £1.67 and a local branch can be nominated. One rose bush – the roses bloom from early summer until early autumn – costs £8.45, two cost £14.40, three, £20.35, with additional rose bushes at £5.75, including postage and packaging. Details and orders from Humanity Rose Offer, Harkness New Roses Ltd., The Rose Gardens, Cambridge Road, Hitchin, Herts., SG4 0JT. Tel.: 01462 420402
Prices: Memorial Book, up to £100

David M. Noble, National Headquarters, 9 Grosvenor Crescent, London SW1X 7EJ. Tel.: 0171 235 5454

CAFOD

CAFOD (Catholic Fund for Overseas Development) is the official overseas aid agency of the Catholic Church in England and Wales, and helps people in need regardless of their race or religion. It has made possible more than 1,000 projects in seventy-five countries in Africa, Asia, the Pacific, Latin America, the Caribbean and Eastern Europe. It funds development projects inspired and managed by local people and responds to emergencies worldwide, often through its membership of the church's network of relief agencies, Caritas International.

Development projects supported by CAFOD include food production and agriculture, water development and irrigation, preventive health care, leadership and skills training, especially among refugees, and adult education and literacy programmes. CAFOD does not keep an in memoriam book or name rooms after legators. However, in its magazine, published three times a year, it does publish a list of names of those supporters who have died. If a person specifies an area of the world in which he or she would like a legacy to be spent or a family who give money in memoriam specify an area of concern to the person being remembered, CAFOD will do its utmost to direct money as requested. If a legacy specifies that the family would like feedback on a project to which the legacy has made a substantial donation or if the family request such knowledge, again this will be provided. On occasions CAFOD has been asked if, for example, it would be possible for a well to be dug in memory of someone who has died. Such requests are extraordinarily difficult to fulfil, especially if photographs are wanted. The society is anxious not to create extra burdens on its partner organizations, such as the Catholic Church networks in the Third World. However, if, for example, it was requested that money given was spent in the Sudan, the society would, on request, provide examples of similar projects in the chosen area. The society tries to dissuade legators from making too specific their directions towards a particular project, as the legacy may not be realized for many years, by which time that project may no longer be a current area of work. Sometimes families ask friends to send donations in lieu of flowers as a memorial to a loved one and this is greatly welcomed. Even relatively modest amounts can have great effect. In Kenya in 1994, a grant of £6,000 enabled the House of Peace, a centre for street children in Kwetu, to buy a grinding mill.

This will provide a service to the people of the surrounding slum area and at the same time help the centre to become self-sufficient. In Burma, CAFOD made a grant of £33,548 for a rehabilitation programme for Karenni people who had been forcibly displaced by the military from their villages in 1993. On a larger scale, CAFOD made a grant of more than £200,000 from its own funds for the purchase of seeds, agricultural tools and fishing equipment in Southern Sudan, to help people regain their self-sufficiency.

Prices: Unspecified

Judith Rees, Head of Support Services, Romero Close, Stockwell Road, London SW9 9TY. Tel.: 0171 733 7900

Christian Aid

Christian Aid is funded by the general public as well as churches in Britain and Ireland to whom it is responsible. It works in more than sixty countries where the need is greatest, regardless of race or religious belief. It does not run its own programmes overseas but works through local churches in areas of need and through other organizations which alleviate poverty and help poor people to find their own solutions. The society is committed to alleviating the root causes of poverty anywhere in the world and spends up to ten per cent of its income on education and campaigning in the UK and Ireland.

In the Third World, grants are made towards development to enable workers to buy and farm land as community endeavours, to irrigate land and to provide training in crafts and local industries. For example, in Southern India, workers from Seelanthanalar Village were helped to buy their own plots of land to grow rice after their landlord, who had paid them very low wages, ploughed flat the rice fields because the workers were seeking fair pay. They were assisted by Krishnammal Jagannathan, who runs a project called Lafti, a scheme that earned her the Gandhi Peace Prize. She began Lafti with a grant from Christian Aid of £14,000 and has helped hundreds of people to buy their own plots of land. Lafti helped to secure the land at a fair price and to find low interest loans, which enabled the workers to buy a plot each. The Sangham (village committee) has started a community hire service that enables villagers to rent ploughs and tractors. A shop has also been set up, selling seeds and fertilizers at favourable prices. The villagers have set up committees to see that loans are repaid and to discuss how they can begin dairy farming, brickmaking and house building. In India, £2,400 will pay for four bore wells to be sunk; £5,000 will pay for sufficient seedlings to plant one hundred acres; £10,000 will pay for thirty-five cyclone-resistant houses.

224

In Loving Memory

In Ethiopia, Christian Aid supported groups such as the SOS Sahel Project, where women spin cotton for blankets which they then sell, providing much-needed income for their families. Grants totalling £900,000 supported Christian Aid's partners' work in Brazil in access to land and rural credit, black communities and street children. Christian Aid is considering a scheme of memorial photographs for people who have made generous bequests. The photographs would be of some of Christian Aid's projects in the Third World with a suitable in memoriam message.

Prices: Memorial Photographs, Unspecified
John Ranford, PO Box 100, London SE1 7RT. Tel.: 0171 620 4444

Commonwealth Society for the Deaf

The society aims to work in partnership with developing countries in the commonwealth to increase awareness of and assist in the prevention and treatment of deafness in children. This is achieved by working parties of specialists answering calls for help from commonwealth governments and their national associations and institutes which care for deaf people, and training individual teachers of deaf people, audiologists and audiology maintenance technicians. The society provides hearing-aids, audiological and educational equipment, and works towards preventing deafness by research projects into the prevalence and causes of infective ear disease and the development of simple, cost-effective treatment of it.

The society does not have any established programme for remembrance of legators but will try to meet the wishes of donors on an individual basis. Contributions are acknowledged with memorials and plaques, if appropriate. The annual report lists legacies and other donations. There is plenty of scope for donations, as children in many commonwealth countries still have no access to hearing assessment, hearing-aids, schools for deaf people or an ear specialist. For example: £15 will buy a diagnostic chart to identify ear disease; £25 will buy high-frequency rattles to identify ear disease; £40 will buy professional journals for a group of teachers of the deaf for one year; £45 will buy an otoscope to identify ear disease; £50 will buy a battery charger/rechargeable batteries for hearing-aids; £80 will buy a medical kit to treat infected ears and prevent deafness in sixty children under seven; £120 will buy books and equipment for a classroom of deaf children; £200 will buy a sound-level meter to determine noise levels; £325 will buy a paediatric audiometer to screen babies and children from three months onwards; £650 will buy a speech trainer to encourage children's speech development; £1,500 will buy a diagnostic audiometer to measure hearing loss; £2,500 will buy an equipment calibration system; £4,000 will train one student in audiology maintenance technology; £5,000 will keep a hearing assessment unit running for one year in Africa. The Commonwealth Society for the Deaf has carried out a range of more expensive projects, such as the establishment of an ear-mould laboratory for £12,000 and the building of an assessment centre for £220,000.

Prices: Unspecified

Elizabeth Lubienska, Project Administrator, Dilke House, Malet Street, London WC1E 7JA. Tel.: 0171 631 5311

Karuna Trust

The Karuna Trust is a Western Buddhist charity, set up in 1980 to support the work of its sister charity in India, which is supplementing projects among former untouchable communities. These projects include nineteen hostels for school-children from very poor rural families, medical and informal literacy work in slum localities and cultural projects. Karuna supports work in five Indian states, encouraging Indian authorities and individuals to support the projects. All the work is carried out with local involvement and run by Indians from the sister charity, Bahujan Hitay, which means 'for the welfare of many'. There are just two Western liaison officers in the field.

The projects are open to all who are in need. The Karuna Trust supports primary health care in five states and funds a clinic in the Dapodi district of Pune, treating thirty patients a day. In 1995, Karuna was also supporting nine sewing classes for 145 women, three shops, a handicraft project, two horticultural/agricultural projects and social work training schemes for up to forty men and women each year. These measures are aimed at promoting self-sufficiency. A project current in late 1995 was the building of hostels for children affected by earthquakes in Maharashtra. The trust also supports specific Buddhist work, such as retreat centres and Buddhist classes; Karuna is a Sanskrit word meaning 'compassionate action based on wisdom'. The Karuna Trust does not have a specific programme for instigating memorials. However, one regular supporter who died in 1993 left a large bequest for the Tibetan refugee school in North India. Some of the money was used to make a publicity video about the school and the film was specifically dedicated to the memory of the lady who left the legacy. The direct cost of supporting a child at a hostel is £8 per month. The direct cost of supporting a kindergarten for thirty-nine children is £20 a month. Prospective donors and benefactors should contact Darryl Cowley to discuss the bequest and any possible memorial, which would need to be negotiated through him with the charity operating in India.

Prices: Unspecified
Darryl Cowley, Administrator, St Mark's Studio, Chillingworth Road, London N7 8QJ. Tel.: 0171 700 3434

Oxfam, United Kingdom and Ireland

The aim of Oxfam is to be a partner to ordinary men, women and children in alleviating the crushing burden of starvation and poverty, disease and exploitation in Africa, Asia, Latin America and the Middle East through relief, development, research and public education. Oxfam works with the people under crisis, not to give them charity but to help them overcome the crisis and to find practical ways of alleviating their suffering.

An in memoriam book is kept in the reception area of Oxfam's headquarters in Oxford. When a donation is sent in memory of loved ones or supporters of Oxfam who have died, it is put into the general funds unless otherwise stated. Gifts in kind can be bequeathed to Oxfam. Such artefacts, whether golf clubs, stamp collections, musical instruments, books, clocks and so on, can be converted into cash, whether for digging wells or planting trees. The difference between an in memoriam donation and an ordinary donation is that the names of the deceased and those who donated are put into the memorial book. An in memoriam card of thanks is sent off with the receipt. If it is specified that a memorial donation should go to a particular project, this can sometimes be arranged. However, because of the complexity of allocating gifts to a particular project, the amount has to be of a size that warrants the extra work involved.

A little money can go a long way: £11 would provide a year's schooling for a girl in Bangladesh; £20.36 would provide emergency IV kits for an emergency team in Zaire; £50 would provide thirty hoes for farmers in Mozambique; £106 would provide tools and equipment to build latrines for 200 people. These prices are subject to change.

Prices: Memorial Book, Unspecified
Andrew Macdonald, Operations Centre, 274 Banbury Road, Oxford OX2 7DZ. Tel.: 01865 313131

World Jewish Relief

World Jewish Relief exists to advise and assist Jewish refugees in the UK who have escaped from racial and religious persecution anywhere in the world. It offers aid to Jews in need who live outside the UK and helps Jewish communities abroad in their social, educational and religious work.

Jewish World Relief offers several forms of memorial. The simplest form is a certificate. This is used in several ways: on the occasion of a celebration, hosts will invite their guests to make a donation to the charity in lieu of gifts. A certificate is issued to acknowledge the donations. Donors may mark special occasions, birthdays, anniversaries, the birth of a child or grandchild, with a donation to the charity, for which a certificate would be issued. Sometimes a legacy comes with special requirements and the society is always happy to honour these. The sums involved vary considerably from a few hundreds to many thousands. At the request of an executor, the society has erected a building and named it after the deceased. More often this type of bequest is used to establish educational or scholarship funds, which bear the name of the deceased. On occasion, the society is approached by a donor to discuss the contents of a will so that the society is very clear about his or her wishes. The society currently administers two educational funds, which will benefit when their benefactors are deceased. Programmes of assistance to emergent Jewish communities in the former Soviet Union and Eastern Europe lend themselves to memorial projects. Buildings can bear the name of a donor who provides funds for renovations; rooms can bear the name of a donor who provides equipment, for example a library or computer laboratory. Capital funds used for provision of social services can bear the name of the donor, as can training programmes and youth camps and facilities.

The majority of memorial requests come from people with whom the society has no relationship but who know of its humanitarian work, trust its discretion and integrity and know that their wishes will be carried out. Programmes change constantly in response to current humanitarian situations. Therefore, people wishing to contribute to projects should contact Cheryl Mariner for more details as costs are only given as a rough guide: £50 will provide a food parcel or provide books or educational material; £100 will provide food parcels or medication; £1,500 will provide a pension supplement, enable a child to attend a summer camp for a week, provide educational materials or provide one work station for a computer laboratory; £10,000 will provide a dedicated room within a community centre redevelopment; £300,000 would provide a physiotherapy wing in a haemophilia centre in Israel (such a project could be dedicated as the donor desired).

Prices: Up to £10,000, up to £50,000, up to £500,000

Cheryl R. Mariner, Drayton House, 30 Gordon Street, London WC1H 0AN. Tel.: 0171 387 3925

19   Religious

The days of placing plaques or memorials in churches are generally past, unless you have a strong local connection with a church. However, certainly in the higher price ranges and sometimes for more modest cost, cathedrals offer more scope. The most modest permanent religious commemoration is probably the Eternal Kalendar of Remembrance at Prinknash Abbey and some of the most imaginative projects centre around Lincoln Cathedral and include being named on a bell, on a beam in the roof or through the Book of Oaks (listed in chapter 17), a scheme for endowing trees for the roof beams one hundred years hence.

The Abbey, Caldey \

The Isle of Caldey has been the site of monastic traditions for many centuries. In 1928, the present order of Cistercian monks took over the abbey from the Benedictine community, who moved to Prinknash in Gloucestershire.

The most recent in memoriam gift received by the abbey was for a young boy who died in September 1995, after suffering for many years from muscular dystrophy. He visited the island each year with his family and found great solace and peace on Caldey. His family donated the sum of £1,000 in memory of their son to pay for a new organ for the abbey church. The abbey buildings are in a fine Italianate style but are in need of much repair, in particular the roofs. There is also a medieval priory and church, St Illtyd's, that requires substantial renovation. Contact the Father Abbot to discuss legacies, in memoriam gifts and donations and appropriate commemoration.

Prices: Unspecified

The Father Abbot, Caldey Island, Tenby, Dyfed SA70 7UH. Tel.: 01834 842632

Apostleship of the Sea

The Apostleship of the Sea was founded in the 1920s by a group of dedicated laypeople in Glasgow. Its aim from the outset has been to care for the spiritual needs of the seafarer, who spends much of his life far away from any parish.

The network of chaplains throughout the world endeavours to offer the seafarer a parish where he can find support and encouragement. It offers hospitality to any stranger visiting the UK and supports the seafarer in his struggle for justice and human rights where these are being violated. Traditionally the Apostleship of the Sea has focused on the needs of the crew of the merchant ships but in recent years the commitment has widened to all who depend upon the sea for their livelihood, irrespective of nationality, creed and colour. For merchant seamen, the AOS provides chaplains for the SS *Canberra* and the *Sea Princess*. The Apostleship of the Sea has a home for retired seafarers at Gateacre Grange, Liverpool. It also cares for seafarers who are sick or injured and extends hospitality to the seafarer in port through centres that provide recreational facilities. Seafarers are welcomed by a chaplain and laypersons, who visit the ships as they arrive at port. The Apostleship of the Sea (England and Wales) has a memorial book which lists the names of seafarers who have died at sea and on land as well as deceased workers and helpers of the AOS. If a seafaring member of your family has died or if you know of a seafarer who has died, send the name, date of birth, date of death and the circumstances of death. The names will then be entered into the memorial book, ensuring that they are never forgotten and are prayed for daily by the members of the organization. As such, there is no fee for entering a name. However, people do generally give a donation, the size of which varies. The money is then used to support the ministry among seafarers visiting the many ports along the coastline.

Prices: Memorial Book, Unspecified

Fr. John Maguire, National Director, Episcopal Agency for England and Wales, Stella Maris, 66 Dock Road, Tilbury, Essex RM18 7BX. Tel.: 01375 845641

Cathedral Church of Canterbury

Canterbury Cathedral is the Mother Church not only of England, but of eighty million Anglicans throughout the world. The cathedral was founded in AD 602, when St Augustine arrived in Kent, and rebuilt in the eleventh century by Archbishop Lanfranc.

St Thomas à Becket was murdered in the cathedral in 1170 and there is a shrine to him as well as a chapel for twentieth-century martyrs. The tomb of the Black Prince is there and the cathedral is famous for its Norman crypt and beautiful stained glass as well as the unusual way the choir is raised above the nave and the altar above the choir. The Dean and Chapter do not have a standard policy on memorials, but there are frequent opportunities for people who wish to commemorate loved ones. Some who do not wish to spend very much can make a donation to the cathedral's flower fund. The names of those so commemorated are kept in a book in the treasury which is always available for inspection. Any donation to the flower fund, no matter how large or small, is entered in the book. People sometimes leave money for a particular project or object which is needed and many people's families arrange after their deaths to donate objects to the cathedral in memory of their relatives. For example, a gift of new missals cost less than £100, a new chalice and paten for everyday use cost about £1,500 and a lectern for the cathedral archives was made by the cathedral carpenter as an in memoriam gift. The decision on the nature of the gift should be discussed through the Dean and Chapter. From time to time, the cathedral does carry out private fund-raising for major projects and there are often opportunities for naming. For instance, £4 million is needed for a new education centre and there are many opportunities to contribute for those who wish the names of their family to be recorded. Sums ranging between £50,000 and £1 million would ensure a particular space in the education centre having the appropriate name attached.

Prices: Memorial Book, up to £100,000, up to £250,000, up to £500,000, up to £1 million

Rear-Admiral David Macey, Cathedral House, The Precincts, Canterbury CT1 2EH. Tel.: 01227 762862

Cathedral Church of St Peter in Exeter

The original church, founded by Athelstan about AD 932, was superseded by a Norman building in 1120–1206. The transformation of the Norman church began about 1270. The western façade is decorated with sculptured figures, the central theme being the Enthronement, flanked in the upper tier by Apostles, Evangelists, Patriarchs and Prophets. In the lower tier are the chief persons of the Royal line of Judah.

Exeter Cathedral contains many fine tombs and memorials and a large number of memorial ledger stones. At the time of writing, it is not the policy of the Dean and Chapter or of the Fabric Advisory Committee to add to the number of memorials within the building. There are, however, four existing cathedral charities which are open to donations, devises or bequests. These are the Dean and Chapter of Exeter Account, the Friends of Exeter Cathedral, the Exeter Cathedral Preservation Trust and the Exeter Cathedral Music Foundation Trust. The friends provide help with the fabric, music and library of the cathedral and contain within their capital fund one bequest for the restoration of the cloister. The Preservation Trust provides funds for the restoration and maintenance of the fabric of the cathedral and properties and could accept bequests for special purposes, such as the restoration of the cloister. The Music Foundation Trust provides funds for the support of cathedral music and includes an appeal for choristerships. The trust seeks twenty-four choristerships but has so far achieved only fifteen. Each costs £25,000. The donor is named on a board kept in Oldham's Passage beside the South Quire Aisle. The Dean and Chapter have commissioned a concept for the restoration of the cloister and have a first estimate that the whole project, which would include reordering inside the cathedral and the stoneyard, would amount to £3 million. It would be possible to include in the renewed cloister a stone with names of donors inscribed. The Dean and Chapter have already much improved the situation by many working economies and by the trading activities of the shop and refectory. These are limited, however, by size and location. Relocating the shop to a site in the cloister would greatly extend the hours it could open, its accessibility and size, and an extension of the space available to the refectory in the cloister would not only improve its profitability but also give better service to the visiting public. Another major project would be the development of an education and interpretation centre with displays, models and space for large visiting groups.

Prices: Up to £50,000

Michael Woodcock, Chapter Clerk, Cathedral Office, 1 The Cloisters, Exeter EX1 1HS. Tel.: 01392 55573

Church of Scotland

The Committee on Artistic Matters advises and approves alterations of any kind to interiors and exteriors of Church of Scotland buildings. Churches are very often seen as appropriate places for memorials. Prices will vary according to the size, quality and nature of the item offered.

In addition to wall plaques, the gift of a suitable item is now often accompanied by a small plaque, commemorating the donor. Items may be stained-glass windows, pieces of furniture, such as a lectern, a set of new hymn-books for the congregation, pew bibles or anthem books for the choir. Memorial trees may be planted in the churchyard. Examples of a different kind of memorial are prizes for the Sunday School or a prize given to the local school for pupils or teams who research into the history of the local community and its churches. Contact individual churches or Douglas Galbraith to discuss in memoriam gifts, bequests and memorials.

Prices: Unspecified

Revd Douglas Galbraith, Administrative Secretary, Advisory Committee on Artistic Matters, 121 George Street, Edinburgh EH2 4YN. Tel.: 0131 225 5722

Grail Centre

The Grail Centre is the home of a group of Christian women who have made a long-term commitment to a simple lifestyle, to help individuals grow spiritually and to care for the earth on a small scale. Other men and women sharing this ethos and the work that comes from it become part of the Grail community for longer or shorter periods of time. Some community members run the centre. 'Poustinias', small hermitages, are available throughout the year for those seeking solitude.

Each summer the Grail Centre runs family weeks which combine holiday with spiritual input and exchange. The centre always needs to subsidize some families, and donations and in memoriam gifts as bursaries towards this would be very helpful. Family weeks, held at Pinner and other venues throughout the country, cost £110 for an adult and £54 for children between four and eleven. Young People's weeks for those aged between sixteen and twenty cost £95 per person. Possible methods of commemoration could be through the Family Network Newsletter, the Grail Bulletin or a memorial book kept at the Grail headquarters at Pinner. Another area where the Grail Centre could use help would be in providing bursaries for the workshops held by the centre. These focus on belief, education, healing and social responsibility. Commemoration again could be through the bulletin and memorial book. A third area where financial help would be greatly valued would be to increase the centre's ability to have 'poustiniks' all the year round. This would mean putting up at least one new chalet, a very expensive operation because the land is clay and therefore foundations have to be dug deep. This would cost £60,000 at current prices. Commemoration could be a plaque on the new poustinia. The most general need is for money to enable people who are seeking for meaning in life to get together to share their experiences, to support one another and to feel valued. Modest donations to establish group gatherings are appreciated as much as more substantial financial gifts and would again be commemorated in the memorial book and bulletin.

Prices: Memorial Book, up to £100,000

Jackie Rolo, 125 Waxwell Lane, Pinner, Middx. HA5 3ER. Tel.: 0181 866 2195/0505

Handicapped Children's Pilgrimage Trust and Hosanna House Trust

The Handicapped Children's Pilgrimage Trust was formed in 1956 after a young doctor, Michael Strode, took four disabled children to Lourdes. This revolutionized the way that disabled children could enjoy the experience – not, as previously, staying in hospitals and hospices but in proper hotels and enjoying treats such as trips to cafés and a donkey ride in the mountains. Nearly forty years later the HCPT takes almost 2,000 children annually from England, Scotland, Wales and Ireland, as well as children from Slovakia and their helpers who are being sponsored by the British and Irish trusts. The children, aged seven–eighteen, have a wide range of physical and mental disabilities or are physically and emotionally deprived or neglected. Together with helpers, the total size of the Easter Pilgrimage is about 5,000 and there is a smaller one at Whitsun.

From the HCPT grew the Hosanna House Trust. Hosanna House, the trust's residential centre for adults, just outside Lourdes, provides accommodation for nearly 2,000 pilgrims in groups of forty or fifty, many of whom are disabled or have special needs. The older part of Hosanna House, Notre Dame, is being refurbished and access is being improved. A lift was installed in 1993 and there are plans to widen doorways to make it easier to get into bedrooms and bathrooms; this will entail major civil engineering works and is an area where donations are welcomed. A wheelchair is the trust's only official memorial as such and supporters are invited to purchase one of these for £285 for the use of children at Lourdes. The cost of sending a child to Lourdes is £419 and it is possible to sponsor a child for a week, so this could be done in memory of a loved one. An adult can be sponsored for a week at Hosanna House at a cost of £310 and this might again be an appropriate in memoriam gift. A donation can be made towards a Parker bath with hydraulic seat for the disabled at Hosanna House and the total cost is £4,000 for similar aids. Deceased supporters and members are remembered in the newsletter. Bequests for general use are especially welcome; these are placed in a reserve fund, which is invested to produce a good income and appreciation of capital, and this underpins much of the trust's work.

Prices: Up to £500

Michael Orbell, Communications Manager, 100A High Street, Banstead, Surrey SM7 2RB. Tel.: 01737 353311

Lincoln Cathedral

Remigus, the Norman bishop, built a church on rising ground that became the triple-towered cathedral of today. Bishop Hugh of Avalon, who died in 1200, was responsible for the Early English work in the aisled choir, apse and transept. Lincoln's copy of the Magna Carta is kept in the chancel of Bishop Longland.

The Lincoln Cathedral Fabric Fund is an arm of the Preservation Council, which is concerned with the conservation and preservation of the cathedral. This is very different from the idea of restoration, as conservation repairs what is existing so that people can see the original beauty. For Lincoln, as for other cathedrals, however, there is a dearth of skilled craftsmen. Lincoln Cathedral puts money bequeathed for general purposes into an investment fund to train apprentices to use old crafts on the cathedral. Funding an apprenticeship would cost about £18,000 a year. Glass conservation is the rarest skill of all. There are only three craftsmen in the country, one of whom is at Lincoln Cathedral, and this is an area of expertise where the cathedral is especially dedicated to providing training to carry on the work. There are a variety of ways in which a legacy or gift in memory can be recorded. A benefactions book, in which gifts over £500 are recorded, is displayed within the cathedral. Some years ago, a stained-glass window was conserved with a donation of £35,000 and the donation was acknowledged on the window. The cathedral is beginning work on one of the oldest and largest bells in the country, Great Tom of Lincoln. Refurbishing Great Tom will cost £20,000 in total; significant benefactors, who give £5,000 or more, will be recognized by having their names inscribed on the headstock. A length of oak for the roof could cost anything from £150 to £1,500 and donors could have their initials and the date of donation or of the death of a loved one carved in it (see also chapter 17 entry on the Book of Oaks). The cathedral has a prioritized and costed programme of work over the next fifteen to twenty years and, with consultation beforehand, gifts towards specific projects could be recognized.

Prices: Up to £500, up to £1,000, up to £5,000, up to £10,000, up to £50,000

Bob Snookes, Executive Director, Lincoln Cathedral Fabric Fund, 4 Priorygate, Lincoln LN2 1PL. Tel.: 01522 548125

Prinknash Abbey

The monks at Prinknash Abbey are members of the Subiaco Congregation of the Order of St Benedict, a contemplative order. They originally lived on the Isle of Caldey in South Wales, where they attempted to establish the Benedictine life in the Church of England.

However, in 1913 the Order made its corporate submission to the Holy See. In 1928, financial difficulties compelled the Order to move from Caldey to its present home in the Cotswold Hills. The Prinknash Kalendar of Eternal Remembrance is the only commemorative memorial maintained at the abbey and has proved to be of great comfort to many people. When asked, the monks celebrate masses for the repose of the souls of the dead. In the days of primitive Christianity, the names of the dead were written on tablets laid upon the altar for the priest to commemorate at mass. The Order now has the Kalendar, a large book kept in the church near the high altar of the monks' Chapel until the crypt of the new monastery church is built. This will be set aside for the everlasting remembrance of the dead. In the Kalendar of Eternal Remembrance are inscribed the names of the living and the dead, Catholic and non-Catholic alike, who will be remembered by intention at every mass said by the priests of the community so long as Prinknash stands. In addition, a requiem mass is said each month for the souls of those enrolled in the Kalendar whose death occurs during that month. To enrol names in the Kalendar, the full name should be given and in the case of the deceased, the date of death should be added, if known. For their records, the monks would appreciate being told of the relationship of those involved and the occasion that has prompted the enrolment. Certificates of enrolment are normally sent to the donor but can be addressed elsewhere if requested. An offering of £10 for each name enrolled is asked, £5 per name in the case of multiple enrolment, to cover administrative costs and contribute to the maintenance of the monastery. The donors themselves are remembered in the prayers of the community, the conventual mass on Sundays being offered to all benefactors and friends. For this purpose the donors themselves are entered upon the Roll of Friends. Write to the Secretary to the Abbot for an enrolment card.

Prices: Memorial Book, up to £100

The Secretary to the Abbot, Cranham, Gloucester GL4 8EX. Tel.: 01452 812455

Salisbury Cathedral

Nearly all of the cathedral was built between 1220 and 1280 and in the next decade was added the great spire, which can be seen from many points of Salisbury Plain. The cathedral still stands by itself in the middle of its own river-meadow close, where the foundation stone was laid in April 1220. The cathedral trust's objective is to ensure its long-term survival as a building, as a priceless part of our heritage and as a centre for Christian worship. In the 1990s, the trustees' prime concern was for the fabric of the building.

The trust is considering ways of commemorating donors, including the idea of recording names and addresses in a specially made book that can join the other fascinating records of cathedral history in the Dean and Chapter vault. This contains records running back century upon century and there can be few places where such records have been kept so well and for so long. By the year 2008, the trust hopes to fully restore the cathedral. It has sufficient money to complete the spire, tower and west front by the year 2000 (at a cost of £6.5 million) and is now trying to raise funds for the next century's work. 1999 will be a special landmark for the cathedral as the west front is expected to emerge from scaffolding, fully refurbished. The stonework of the great elevation will reappear, identical to that of 1315, the year in which it was completed. Before the end of the first decade of the new millennium, at least a further £4 million will be needed. Many of the forty-five craftsmen employed by the cathedral works department are apprentices in the maintenance of the cathedral. The Radcliffe Trust provides a sponsorship for apprenticeship in cathedral building skills valued at £750 per annum. It would be helpful to have a second sponsorship valued at £1,000 per annum. For further details of sponsorship needs, contact Andrew Robertson, Head of Building Works, The Close, Salisbury, Wilts.

Prices: Up to £1,000 (per annum)

Robin Gamble, Trust Director, Salisbury Cathedral Trust, The

King's House, 65 The Close, Salisbury, Wilts. SP1 2EN. Tel.:01722 332004

Winchester Cathedral Trust

In the mid-seventh century, the West Saxon leader Cenwalh built the church known as the Old Minster on the south side of the old Roman forum. Within a quarter of a century, the West Saxon bishopric was transferred from Dorchester upon Thames to Winchester and so the minster achieved cathedral status.

Cenwalh's modest minster church was greatly enlarged towards the end of the tenth century under Bishop Ethelwold and later by his successor Alphege. In 1070, Bishop Walkelin began the new huge Romanesque cathedral and in 1070 William the Conqueror wore his crown at Winchester for the first time, an important symbolic gesture that confirmed Winchester as his administrative centre as well as marking the cathedral as his principal royal church. Winchester Cathedral Trust exists primarily to raise funds to assist the Dean and Chapter in repairing and conserving the fabric of the cathedral. Gifts exceeding £250 are recognized by an entry in the register of donors, which is maintained by the cathedral curator and can be inspected on request. Entries are handwritten by the cathedral calligrapher. In the case of memorial plaques, each request would be treated on its merits. In a recent successful fund-raising campaign, donors contributing £50,000 or more have been commemorated on a stone tablet positioned on the wall of the north nave aisle. In 1990–92 there was a successful campaign to raise £7 million. The restoration of the tower was completed at a cost of £1,106,000. New workshops for stone-masons, joiners and other trades were built for £349,000. A north aisle window, combining medieval and modern glass cost £26,000 and was a personal memorial gift. The 1995 restoration of the cathedral's west front cost £600,000 as opposed to the envisaged £200,000 because the glass and stone were in such poor condition. Other work in hand includes the conservation of the medieval tiles in the Retroquire and the medieval decoration of the Lady Chapel. The campaign also provided a substantial endowment for the choir. Major work on the south transept roof started at the end of 1995 and will be followed by the restoration of the south nave clerestory and the nave high vaults. The programme is due to be completed by the year 2010. The cathedral still needs financial support to maintain the fabric of the building and to offset the substantial day-to-day running costs.

Prices: Memorial Book, up to £500, up to £100,000

Keith Bamber, Secretary to the Trustees, 5 The Close, Winchester, Hants SO23 9LS. Tel.: 01962 868647

Worcester Cathedral Appeal Trust

Worcester Cathedral, which stands on the banks of the River Severn, dates back to AD 680. Its greatest architectural treasures include Wulstan's crypt and King John's tomb.

As a result of a thorough survey in 1986, it became apparent that extensive repairs were needed to the cathedral fabric, including the 4,100-ton central tower, which was in danger of collapsing. £10 million is needed to cover the total cost of restoration. By the beginning of 1996, half the work was completed, including stabilizing the central tower. However, considerable work remains and it is becoming increasingly important to complete restoration as soon as possible, as the fabric is deteriorating at an alarming pace. An ongoing fund-raising programme is essential. If preferred, bequests and significant gifts can be dedicated on request. At a more modest level, the cathedral has several specific themes for dedication. Benefactors can pay £250 to link their names to gargoyles, which will replace eroded figureheads on the south side of the nave. The new stone gargoyles are based on wood-carvings on the medieval choir-stalls. If successful, the sponsorship of gargoyles may be repeated on the nave's north face. A previous offer involved etching names in restored clerestory stained glass for £10. New schemes may be introduced throughout the restoration programme.

Prices: Up to £500

Jean Armstrong, Appeal Co-ordinator, Chapter Office, 10A College Green, Worcester WR1 2LH. Tel.: 01905 611002

20 Social Welfare and Housing

This category offers good commemorative opportunities, including an engraved brass tally on a naval rum tub from the Royal Naval Benevolent Trust for £500. The Anchor Housing Trust and the YWCA offer a list of commemorative opportunities, beginning with quite modest sums. Jewish Care has a wonderful Book of Life as well as several other options. The Royal Star and Garter Home too has an incredibly detailed and well thought-out memorials scheme. The concern that residential homes for the elderly should not be filled with plaques commemorating those who have died is understandable and leads the way for more imaginative remembering.

Age Concern

Age Concern exists to promote the well-being, quality of life and happiness of older people. It was founded in 1940, prompted by the hardships endured by thousands of elderly people during the Second World War.

Today, Age Concern is the largest organization providing direct services for elderly people in Britain, with more than 1,400 independent groups, staffed by 250,000 volunteers. Its services include day centres, lunch clubs, transport and help with everyday problems such as heating, gardening and household repairs. Age Concern tries to meet the needs of older people – from shopping trips for housebound pensioners and cookery lessons for older men who have lost their wives to information on how to keep warm in winter and mobile day centres for those living in remote areas. There are many potential opportunities for memorial gifts. For instance, £15 can help run a Good Neighbour scheme to give older people a regular visitor; £25 can help to buy a new heater for an elderly person; £50 would help an Age Concern group draughtproof a pensioner's house to make it more energy efficient; £50 can also provide new equipment for an Age Concern day centre; £10,000 would help partially fund an information officer to provide advice at an Age Concern group; £20,000–£30,000 would pay for a minibus to transport otherwise housebound older people to a day centre or on trips. £1 million would help considerably to either refurbish or build a day centre which could be named after the donor.

Prices: Up to £1 million
The Director, Astral House, 1268 London Road, London SW16 4ER. Tel.: 0181 679 8000

Anchor Housing Trust

Anchor Housing Trust has built more than 21,000 sheltered flats all over Britain to rent to older people who need support and security. It also runs a Staying Put scheme to help older home owners and provides special flats for very frail people who need care but do not wish to live in a residential home.

Since 1968, it has run a scheme for naming flats in memory of a special friend or loved one, in return for a donation to help the trust continue its work. Common rooms or even whole buildings have also been named, usually for a company or charitable organization. For £300, the trust will mount a plaque above the door of a chosen flat. The plaque is finished in gold with black lettering and will be maintained in place for at least ten years. Should it need to be moved for any reason, such as a major refurbishment of the building, the family would be informed at once. Any of the 21,000 flats can be chosen, providing they do not already bear a plaque. Many thousands already carry the names of those who have been remembered. Up to fifty letters can be used on the plaque for the chosen wording. The trust will send a full list of housing schemes, giving exact locations, and the administration staff will be pleased to accompany lifetime donors or family members to see the plaque once it is in place. A quiet room can be named for £600 and a common room for £2,000. Some buildings can also be named (contact Christopher White, the fund-raising manager, for further details). Buildings have been named for as little as £10,000 and as much as £1 million. In this case consideration is given to the other benefits that might accrue from association with a particular name, for example someone who is well known in the locality. Another consideration would be the effect such a gift would have on completing the project ahead of schedule. Anchor has an ongoing building programme which means that up to a dozen buildings will be completed or refurbished over a year, most of them eligible for specific namings. Gifts are also used to add value to the environment of the buildings, for example to enhance landscaping, to provide garden features or to improve interior decor. Some donations are used to upgrade kitchens or to add communal amenities that can be used by others not resident within the scheme. Any donation will be spent in expanding the work of the trust through the Sheltered Housing and Housing with Care programmes as well as the Staying Put programme.

Prices: Up to £500, up to £1,000, up to £5,000, up to £50,000, up to £100,000, up to £250,000, up to £500,000, up to £1 million

Chrissy Durnell, Fund-raising Administrator, Fountain Court, Oxford Spires Business Park, Kidlington, Oxon. OX5 1NZ. Tel.: 01865 854000

British Limbless Ex-Servicemen's Association

BLESMA caters specifically for limbless serving and ex-service men and women. It also accepts responsibility for the dependants of its members, in particular their widows, who number some four thousand. Six thousand surviving ex-servicemen have lost one or more limbs as a result of their war service, including the Falklands, the Gulf, Northern Ireland and in support of the United Nations. During 1994, two servicemen lost limbs serving in Bosnia and one in Rwanda, so the work of the society is ongoing. It provides permanent residential and respite accommodation through its two nursing and residential care homes at Blackpool and Crieff in Perthshire. Among its many functions, the association offers financial assistance to members and widows in the form of grants or by the provision of equipment and aids. It also plans and organizes rehabilitation programmes for amputees and, with an influx of young amputees from service, includes sporting activities such as ski-bobbing, golf and sailing. BLESMA is also involved in research and development of artificial limbs and the training of prosthetists and orthotists. The BLESMA Pain Clinic was established at Guy's Hospital as part of a two-year project to research stump and phantom limb pain and advise on treatment for BLESMA patients.

Over many years the association has adopted various forms of commemoration. A few examples are given but the association is happy to talk to any potential testator or giver of an in memoriam donation about suitable commemoration and projects that might welcome support. Each piece of equipment is usually tailor-made but approximate costs for disabled transport are: a fifteen-seater minibus, £25,000, a basic twenty eight-seater coach, £58,000. On occasions BLESMA has inserted a named plaque within a coach or minibus. Parts of the two residential homes are named after individuals who made a substantial contribution to the building work. Rooms within buildings have been furnished from legacies and therefore dedicated to a named individual, as have specific items of equipment. Building projects in recent years have included one wing, tacked on to the residential home, which was a two-storey building with twelve single rooms with *en suite* facilities on each floor. The cost was about £350,000 plus an additional £2,500 per room for furnishing. Many elderly amputee members have difficulty in getting up and down from chairs and BLESMA has invested in a number of motorized units for use by permanent residents and others. These vary in cost from £1,500 to £2,500.

Prices: Up to £5,000, up to £50,000, up to £100,000, up to £500,000
R.R. Holland, General Secretary, 185–187 High Road, Chadwell Heath, Romford, Essex RM6 6NA. Tel.: 0181 590 1124

Church Army

The Church Army was founded in 1882 by Prebendary Wilson Carlile, an Anglican clergyman. Today, officers work in the dioceses and parishes of the Anglican Church in the UK and Eire and in many other ecumenical settings, such as the Forces and prisons.

The social evangelism of the Church Army is co-ordinated with local authorities and other voluntary organizations, providing residential establishments for unemployed young people, single homeless people and the elderly. The society is also concerned with the rehabilitation of addicts of whatever form of abuse. Although the Church Army does not have a specific way of commemorating a loved one, it does have an in memoriam fund, whereby a donation is made in lieu of flowers at a funeral. The Church Army sends an acknowledgement to the donor and tells the next of kin of the gift and the total amount of donations sent in a loved one's name. Very occasionally it is left a bequest where the family of the deceased ask if the money received can be used as a specific memorial to their relative, and the management committee will consider such options. Quite often specific bequests to a particular project or a particular area of work are made and usually this is not a problem. However, there are instances where a bequest cannot be paid by the executors because the project for which it was left no longer exists. For this reason the Church Army asks people to state a preference without making a binding clause, thereby allowing a more personal tribute while leaving control with the trustees. During 1994, work began on renovating and improving Marylebone House, a hostel for homeless women. Plans include a day centre, the first in London exclusively for women. The development aims to change the institutionalized atmosphere and to cater imaginatively for both long- and short-stay residents and those with psychiatric needs, aiming to provide care and training so that residents can eventually move on to individual accommodation. A total of £2.2 million would be required, of which £890,000 is being funded by the Portman Housing Trust, a housing association of which the Church Army is sole trustee. The residential homes for the elderly run at a deficit, so are another cause for funding.

Prices: Memorial Fund, Unspecified
Kevin Hawkes, Legacy Officer, Independents Road, Blackheath, London SE3 9LG. Tel.: 0181 318 1226

Corrymeela Community

The Corrymeela Community, founded in 1965, is a dispersed community of Christians from all the main denominations in Ireland who have bound themselves together as instruments of peace in church and society, through prayer, mutual support and commitment. They come from a wide spectrum of political and cultural backgrounds. There are approximately 170 members and 2,200 friends, living throughout Northern Ireland and further afield, committed to promoting peace and reconciliation and the healing of social, religious and political divisions that still exist in Northern Ireland and throughout the world. Members renew their commitment to the community every year. The focus of the community has been the development of a residential centre/open village on the north-east coast of Northern Ireland near the town of Ballycastle. In the early years only one or two people were resident full-time at the centre but gradually the community has established a small residential core of ten annual volunteers and five or six permanent staff, in addition to day staff. There is room for up to 120 people. The Corrymeela Community has also established a non-residential resource centre in the city of Belfast as a base for preparation and follow-up of programmes and as a communication centre for members, friends and sympathetic organizations or groups. The two centres act as a resource to the dispersed community, to friends and to the community at large. The members of the community are largely laypeople with a few clergy.

The community works with schools, youth groups and offers holidays, respite care and a wide range of activities for families in difficulty, whether through family breakdown, troubles with children, single-parenthood pressures, domestic violence or a partner in prison. The community interweaves different groups informally at the centre. Work with schools has developed with support of the Department of Education and the centre has become a resource for a wide variety of inter- and intra-school encounter programmes, often followed up by ongoing community relations projects. Young adults in urban areas of social disadvantage, who may be influenced by paramilitary organizations, are especially helped and encouraged to mix with people of other traditions and the wider world and even on international exchanges. Members of the community are encouraged to keep their links with their local churches and neighbourhood and to live out their commitment in the family, at work and in local social and political situations.

The Corrymeela Community receives many donations every year, some as in memoriam gifts. The community does not generally set up plaques or ask for certain items to become memorials unless someone who has been very close to the membership of the community is involved. However, the community is considering a memorials donation book where loved ones' names could be inscribed in remembrance. Daily expenses for the community are quite high; it costs £1,000 a day to run the centre at Ballycastle, £110 per week to pay the expenses of the year-long volunteers and £50 to provide a weekend of respite care, as part of Corrymeela's cross-community work in Northern Ireland. The community is also undertaking a major building campaign in 1996 and will need to raise £1.3 million in order to redevelop the main residential house. Half the amount has already been secured.

Prices: Unspecified
Heather McMaster, Appeals Director, 8 Upper Crescent, Belfast BT1 7NT. Tel.: 01232 325008

Distressed Gentlefolk's Aid Association (Homelife)

The Distressed Gentlefolk's Aid Association has eleven homes and one sheltered housing unit, offering a range of facilities including nursing care and residential care.

The DGAA Homelife does not as a rule commemorate donors. Where there is a specific request for a tangible memorial, the association will comply, usually with a discreet plaque or a room name in one of the residential and nursing homes. Where a substantial bequest has been made, the DGAA would name the building or part of a building after the donor; an example is the Florence Balls House in Tunbridge Wells in Kent, home to twenty-four residents. It can be quite depressing for a nursing home patient to see lots of memorial plaques and plates around what is his or her home. The association has to bear this in mind when refurbishing the homes and is thus considering setting up a memorial book.

Prices: Unspecified
Hilary Watt, Director of Appeals and Publicity, 1 Derry Street, London W8 5HY. Tel.: 0171 396 6700

Ex-Service Fellowship Centres

The centres aim to help ex-service personnel, including ex-merchant service men, women and their dependants in immediate need. At its London relief centre, the fellowship provides immediate relief in the form of advice, money, travel warrants, food vouchers, clothing and accommodation. Between 1,000 and 1,600 applicants are seen every year.

The society also runs a hostel for homeless ex-service personnel in Stepney in London and two residential care homes, one in London and another in Bexhill on Sea, for aged and infirm ex-service persons and their widows and widowers. There are facilities for the disabled at the home in Bexhill. There is also a block of eighteen retirement flats at Bexhill, for those who can still look after themselves, which are let at fair rents. Any gift is always acknowledged, both privately to the donor and his or her family or executors and publicly through the annual report. In addition, the fellowship would be very happy to accept any plaque or memorial that a donor or legator would wish. Colonel O'Dea can be approached to discuss any bequests and appropriate memorials. Some of the projects undertaken in 1994/5 are as follows: at New Belvedere House in Stepney, London, refurbishment of hostel rooms at a cost of £10,000, reroofing at £18,000, improvements to rooms and installation of additional showers at £9,000 and purchase of new dishwasher, freezer and fridge at £2,800; at Hollenden House, Bexhill on Sea, internal work to create three additional single rooms at a cost of £16,500 and external maintenance at £20,400; at Whitworth House, at Bexhill on Sea, installation of fire alarm system at £12,000 and external maintenance at £11,200. During the year 1 October 1994 to 30

September 1995 the fellowship received 983 requests for assistance at the London relief centre and gave financial grants of £7,290, issued seventy-five travel warrants at a cost of £1,500, placed forty-six homeless ex-servicemen in DSS hostels and twenty-nine in the fellowship's own hostel and made 221 issues of clothing, thus indicating the need for further donations to this worthwhile cause.
Prices: Unspecified
Colonel M.J.M. O'Dea, 8 Lower Grosvenor Place, London SW1W 0EP. Tel.: 0171 828 2468

Jewish Care

Jewish Care is Anglo-Jewry's largest domestic charity, caring for more than 5,000 people every day of the year. The charity has sixteen residential care homes and five day centres. Its services take care of increasingly frail people and those with special needs, including people with visual impairment, physical disability and Alzheimer's disease.

The society also provides domiciliary care. Three of the day care centres are for Alzheimer's sufferers, one is a resource centre for younger physically disabled people and there is a centre for survivors of the holocaust. There are no set criteria for naming rooms, areas or buildings. The society will discuss projects with a potential donor and always try to accommodate a donor's wishes. Wherever possible, the society tries not to place names on individual bedrooms but to acknowledge donations and bequests in one central area, as this is seen as most appropriate with regard to residents' dignity and independence. Jewish Care does have a Book of Life to formally commemorate memorial gifts. This is a beautiful volume on permanent protected display in Stuart Young House, the headquarters. On receipt of one or more donations, whether from immediate family, relations or friends, the name of the person so commemorated is entered for all time in the Book of Life and the bereaved family receive an inscribed scroll, honouring the loved one. At a later date, a list of contributors' names will be sent to the bereaved family with an accompanying letter, and the money will be used for giving a better life to those the charity helps. The bereavement need not have been recent and the entry can commemorate a loved one who died many years before. Donations may be made by individuals, families or organizations in memory of colleagues. There is no upper or lower limit on the size of gift to Jewish Care and all are treated equally, with just one donation ensuring entry. All donors are thanked by letter and are welcome to inspect the Book of Life.
Prices: Memorial Book, Unspecified

Jeff Shear, Campaign Director, Stuart Young House, 221 Golders Green Road, London NW11 9DQ. Tel.: 0181 458 3282; ext. for Book of Life: 346

Royal Naval Benevolent Trust

The Royal Naval Benevolent Trust exists to help serving and ex-service ratings in the Royal Navy, their Royal Marine equivalents and all dependants. The trust was established by Royal Charter in 1922 and much of the work is carried out by men of the Royal Navy and Royal Marines, supported by the trust's governors and staff.

It carries out its work in four main ways: cash grants to those in need – about £1.5 million yearly; regular annuities of some £400,000 a year; financial support to other organizations that provide assistance to those eligible to assistance from the trust; and the running of Pembroke House, its own residential home for elderly ex-naval men, in Gillingham, Kent. The grants committee meets twice weekly and gives swift assistance to 100–150 people a week. Grants are made for accommodation, food, clothes and heating bills, medical treatment and disability aids, respite and recuperative holidays, child care, house repairs and training courses for second careers. The annuities scheme offers a modest regular supplement to income for elderly people and widowed mothers. The number of annuities is limited to just over a thousand but there are always new needs. The RNBT also offers financial support to children's homes, training colleges for the disabled, hospices and residential and nursing homes. Pembroke House has a nautical atmosphere and maintains some of the Royal Navy traditions including, on special occasions, 'Splicing the Mainbrace', the issue of an extra tot of spirits. In addition to long-term residents, Pembroke House offers temporary care. There are several ways in which in memoriam gifts and bequests as well as donations can be commemorated in a tangible way. A gift of £500 will be remembered by an engraved brass tally screwed to the original Royal naval rum tub at Pembroke House. The rooms at Pembroke House are being refurbished and a room will be named after a donor for £5,000. A sum of £50,000 could, at the donor's wish, be used to fund a scheme, named after the donor in perpetuity, to provide eight to ten annuities to very needy people at the trust's current rate.

Prices: Up to £500, up to £5,000, up to £50,000
The Chief Executive, Castaway House, 311 Twyford Avenue, Portsmouth PO2 8PE. Tel.: 01705 690112

Royal Star and Garter Home for Disabled Sailors, Soldiers and Airmen

The home, established in 1916 mainly for young men under thirty who had been seriously injured in the Great War, has had an established memorial scheme for some years.

The whole building was dedicated by the Women of the British Empire through the British Women's Hospital Committee, as the Women's Memorial of the Great War, 1914–1918. It offers nursing and rehabilitation for anyone physically disabled or incapacitated who has served in the regular or reserved forces, irrespective of rank, length of service or whether the disability was caused on active service or through accident or illness in civilian life. It can cater for up to 185 residents for permanent rehabilitation or respite care and has a staff of over 300 in total. The commemoration of loved ones is particularly important to the home as well as to their families. The memorial scheme covers three main areas: donations to the home in lieu of flowers at a funeral, legacies and endowments. Donations in lieu of flowers can lead to quite large memorial funds. If donors wish to buy specific items, the home has a shopping list ranging from physiotherapy or occupational therapy aids to furniture, pictures, garden benches and flower troughs. Once an item has been purchased, the home can arrange for a plaque bearing an inscription to be placed on or near the item. Home residents today tend to be older and more infirm than in earlier times; a number therefore tend to require systems that utilize pressurized air to relieve pressure points on a recumbent patient. These systems can cost from £817 to £3,260. Beds with electrically operated tilts to assist in lifting patients can cost £2,000 each.

Legacies form an extremely important part of the home's income and are entered on the roll of honour. The Royal Star and Garter Home is also arranging for a sundial to be erected in the garden so that names can be inscribed on a plaque of honour. In 1993, the home began an extensive refurbishment programme for which endowments, donations and grants are sought. The project included the renovation of eight wards to provide a stock of single and double rooms and bathrooms as well as converted bay areas which allow nursing staff to monitor frailer patients who are dependent on 24-hour nursing care. The total cost of the project has been estimated at £3.2 million over three years. Two wards have already been completed and work has commenced on a third. Any assistance with this project, however small, is welcome. For example, a donation of £15 would enable the home to purchase a vase or other soft furnishings to brighten up a resident's room. The

home is pleased to receive memorial tributes specifically for this
project. Endowments will be noted with an entry on a roll of
honour located in one of the refurbished areas and, if appropriate,
the naming of a wing or room on one of the wards. Some examples
of costs for the refurbishment of a ward include: structural work
£250,000; bedrooms £80,000; bathrooms £25,000; non-slip flooring
£15,000; beds £12,000; nurse call system £25,000; nursing and
catering equipment £15,000; lighting £3,000; furnishing £15,000.

A list of permanent and special memorials is inscribed on
plaques on each side of a recess in the front hall. These record the
many gifts and endowments received from all over the world. The
home's Chapel of St Mary was the gift of the first Viscountess
Cowdray, a member of the Women's Hospital Building Fund, who
donated it as a memorial to her son, Captain Francis Pearson, who
died of wounds in France on 6th September 1914. The Jack
Cornwall VC Memorial commemorates the young sailor mortally
wounded at the Battle of Jutland who was posthumously awarded
the Victoria Cross. Five rooms in one of the wards at the home
were endowed in his name by the Navy League. Among
endowments received from all over the world was one for £180,000
from Mrs H. Douglas Ives, of New York City, USA, in memory of
her husband, Captain H. Douglas Ives of the Royal Highlanders of
Canada. One of the small ambulances is nearing the end of its
working life and must be replaced, at a cost of £20,000, as it is
critical to the home's transport needs. It is used daily to take
residents for hospital check-ups and eye examinations as well as on
shopping and leisure trips. The vehicles are also used for
emergencies. Lifts (at a cost of £50,000) are the vital means of
access to the home, transporting residents from ward to
dining-room, physio-, hydro-, speech and occupational therapy,
the library, bar and garden. The E Lift is in urgent need of
refurbishment. There are many practical ways of commemorating
a loved one and a visit to the home would allow potential donors to
gain even more ideas.

**Prices: Memorial Roll and Sundial, up to £100, up to £5,000, up to
£50,000, up to £100,000, up to £250,000**
*Flora E. Rogers, The Royal Star and Garter Home, Richmond,
Surrey TW10 6RR. Tel.: 0181 940 3314*

Woking Homes

Woking Homes provide residential care for those retired
employees and their spouses from British Rail and associated
companies who find it increasingly difficult to take care of

themselves. Until 1988, Woking Homes also provided residential care for children of employees from British Rail and associated transport industries, to assist families in overcoming their problems.

Over the years the organization has received many legacies and large donations and has had garden seats purchased in memory of people. The society does not encourage plaques on rooms or walls, because it makes the place look like an institution rather than a residential home for the elderly. When the children's home existed, there were plaques above all the beds.

At present Woking Homes are in the process of making all the residents' rooms *en suite* and this is being financed from the development fund. The cost per room is approximately £5,000. One project that Woking Homes are keen to progress with is the building of a swimming pool on site for the use of residents and short-stay guests. The cost for a totally built-in swimming pool of the kind to be erected in an outbuilding was estimated in the early 1990s at about £25,000, but the problem of ongoing maintenance would be a major expenditure. At one time there was the Evergreen Book, in which the names of people who contributed to the homes for a very long time were entered. However, since the demise of the children's home, it has not held the same importance. Woking Homes tend to recognize the good work people do in the minutes, by letter and through presentations.

Prices: Unspecified

Mrs M.E. Taylor, Director, Oriental Road, Woking, Surrey GU22 7BE. Tel.: 01483 763558

Young Women's Christian Association of Great Britain

The YWCA aims to identify and respond to the needs of all women regardless of race or religion. It is part of the largest and oldest women's ecumenical organization in the world.

Every year, 100,000 young women come to the YWCA for practical and emotional support. By offering secure affordable housing and addressing issues as wide-ranging as homelessness, unemployment, single parenthood, domestic violence, sexual abuse and drug addiction, the YWCA provides a life-line to help young women learn to help themselves. The YWCA offers the following suggestions for memorials: for £100, the loved one's name could be included on a permanently displayed list of supporters in a hostel which offers safe, affordable accommodation to young people; for £250, an area of a hostel garden offering a relaxing refuge could be named after a relative or friend; for £1,000, a room in a women-only hostel offering a secure home to a young survivor of abuse or violence could be named after a loved one; for £2,500, a central meeting place in a hostel or project, where young women have the opportunity to exchange ideas and discuss problems, could be given a loved one's name, ensuring that he or she is permanently remembered within a women's centre; for £10,000, a named annual bursary could be set up offering financial support to one young woman each year who plans to return to training or education; for £50,000, a family workshop offering young families the chance to work, play and learn together could be named after a mother, family or friends.

Prices: Up to £100, up to £500, up to £1,000, up to £5,000, up to £10,000, up to £50,000

Dawn John, Clarendon House, 52 Cornmarket Street, Oxford OX1 3EJ. Tel.: 01865 726110

21 Sporting, Seagoing and Adventure

In this category, the Royal National Lifeboat Institution provided one of the most helpful and detailed entries in the book. It may be no coincidence that they rank very high in the most popular charities. The adventure organizations the Jubilee Sailing Trust and the National Playing Fields Associations offer detailed imaginative projects involving commemoration in all price ranges and show the scope for clear and creative thinking in this field. There can be variations even in similarly orientated organizations. For example, the Scouts had a very detailed system for memorials while the Guides favoured individual negotiations.

Chelsea Football Club

The club offers various opportunities for memorials. One of the restaurants in the East Stand, Bentleys, is named after Roy Bentley who played for Chelsea in the 1950s. Drakes in the North Stand, a huge bar and restaurant, is named after another old Chelsea player Ted Drake. Dixons is named after Kerry Dixon and Tamblings after the 1960s captain Bobby Tambling.

The club should be contacted to discuss any bequests or in memoriam gifts and suitable memorials. It is possible to sponsor many things connected with the club, including a memorial match. A Premier League match costs somewhere in the region of £8,500 plus VAT to sponsor. Chelsea Youth Team are seeking shirt sponsorship which would cost around £10,000 plus VAT per season. Sponsorship of the schoolboys would cost from £2,500 plus VAT per season. A five-year season ticket is available and this might be a good in memoriam gift, perhaps to a child or grandchild in memory of a parent or grandparent who was a football fan. For £1,995, the CFC premium five-year season ticket guarantees a chosen seat in the upper tier of the new £9-million stand, plus

membership of Chelsea Football Club for the period and the guaranteed right to buy Cup Final and European match tickets in which Chelsea is involved. The club does not have charitable status.
Prices: Up to £5,000, up to £10,000
Carole Phair, Commercial Manager, Stamford Bridge, London SW6 1HS. Tel.: 0171 385 5545

Guide Association

The Guide Association is Britain's largest voluntary organization for girls and young women, with more than 750,000 members. It also has nine branch associations within the Commonwealth as well as numerous independent Commonwealth associations. Ages for the Guiding Movement range from four years old to twenty plus.

The Lone Guiding Scheme opens up Guiding to girls and women between the ages of ten and sixty-five who cannot attend a local unit if, for example, the nearest unit is too far away or work, training schedules, long-term illness or disability prevent regular attendance at unit meetings. In October 1994, the President, HRH Princess Margaret, visited the Commonwealth Headquarters for the official launch of the Look Wider programme for the 14–26-year range of Guiding's Senior Section. It aims to appeal not only to association members but also to young women who are not involved in Guiding, to reach young mothers, young women living away from home in hostels or bedsits, those who have come through the care system, those of ethnic origin who may find it difficult to become involved with the wider community, and those who have been in trouble with the law. Names have been associated with a particular bequest or memorial but this is not the norm.

Examples of memorial gifts include the furbishment of the council chamber at Commonwealth Headquarters in 1930 by Sir James Cargill in memory of his wife. In 1941, Restrop Hostel, situated at Blackland Farm, was given and equipped in memory of Sylvia Kemm, camp adviser for Berkshire. In 1972, two permanent shelters at Blackland Farm were given in memory of Violet Synge, Girl Guider of 1st Buckingham Palace Company. However, even substantial bequests have been used for the benefit of the association and its members without attribution. All donations and legacies are recorded in the annual report.

The association does have substantial assets which were gifted to it. Some of these are lifetime gifts. For example, the association has a large country property, Foxlease Training Centre, Lyndhurst, Hampshire, given to the Guide Association by Mrs Archibald Saunderson in 1922, on the occasion of the marriage of HRH Princess Mary, the former Princess Royal who was president of the association at the time. Projects can be stipulated and the Guide Association will try to comply. In 1980, the Edwards' Legacy of £5,000 was received with the stipulation that it should be used for Guides or young Guiders from high-rise flats to go to the association centre at the Guide Chalet at Adelboden in Switzerland. The executors agreed that only the interest should be spent and that opportunities would be offered on a regular basis but that the executive committee would have the power to change this. The grant would cover the full cost of the accommodation at the chalet and all travel expenses. The main concern was to send Guides/Rangers/Guiders who would not otherwise be able to afford a visit of this kind. Because it was difficult to find Guides from high-rise flats, the legacy was used by others, with preference given to those from high-rise accommodation. With the exception of 1991, when no applicants were forthcoming, the interest on the legacy has been used in this way ever since. Hilary Williams would be very happy to receive any suggestions for attributed bequests or planned memorials for individual consideration within the association's management structure. Potential donors can also contact their local Guide Association about legacies, in memoriam gifts, suitable projects and needs and possible memorials.

Prices: Unspecified

Hilary Williams, Chief Executive, 17–19 Buckingham Palace Road, London SW1W 0PT. Tel.: 0171 834 6242

Jubilee Sailing Trust

The Jubilee Sailing Trust was founded in 1978, based on the vision of teacher Christopher Rudd that physically disabled and able-bodied people should be able to sail together at sea. The STS *Lord Nelson*, a tall, square-rigged, purpose-built sailing ship, named after Britain's most famous sailor, undertook its maiden voyage in October 1986.

This venture was very successful with great demand for berths to locations including the Canary Islands, the Scottish Western Isles, Brittany, the Channel Islands, Belgium, Holland, Ireland and the Isles of Scilly. The *Lord Nelson* has ten full-time crew and an additional forty voyage crew, half of whom will be physically handicapped. A second ship, made of wood, is being built at a total projected cost of £6.8 million. A grant of just over £4 million

from the Sports Lottery Fund will meet sixty-five per cent of
the cost, but the Jubilee Sailing Trust has to come up with the rest.
The ship will take three years to complete and will need funding
after that for maintenance and to provide berth fees for those in
need. In addition to the extra £2.8 million, the trust has to raise
money for increased running costs of the *Lord Nelson*, including
essential refits, maintenance and a fund to assist those who find it
impossible to raise the full berth fees. The *Lord Nelson II* Project
will create a living, working shipyard involving mixed teams of
physically disabled and able-bodied volunteers, who will help to
build the ship under the guidance of professional shipbuilders. The
names of those who leave legacies or money in memoriam are
inscribed in the memorial log, a hand-bound leather book kept on
board the *Lord Nelson* at all times. When the ship is in port, it is put
on display in a specially made display case. The amount of money
given is not put in the book, only the name of the deceased person
and whether the money has been given as a legacy or in memoriam.
Occasionally, a berth fund has been set up in the name of a deceased
person. This can enable other people to sail who would otherwise
not be able to afford it. Future fund-raising will centre around the
new ship and, for a legacy or donation of a seven-figure sum, the
ship could be named after the testator; £20,000 would name a cabin
and the first 200 people to buy a plank for £400 for the new ship will
have their names placed on a plaque. Plank prices start at £5 and go
up to £400 for a yard of planking with the name of the donor or a
chosen name on it. The location of the plank will be given and
families or living donors can visit the site and see their piece of plank
going into place. Cover for the dock is £150,000 while special tools
to enable disabled students to be involved cost £10,000. Designers'
fees are £450,000. Wind-tunnel and tank testing of ships' models
would be £50,000. The hull, deck and superstructure amount to £1.9
million, spars and rigging, £590,000 and navigational equipment,
£125,000. Sponsorship of the sick bay would be £26,000, five
chairlifts, £20,000. Fitting out the laundry would be £2,000 and two
main engines, £60,000. Sails (donation received from the Clothwor-
kers' Foundation) will cost £40,000. Smaller amounts are needed to
buy necessary equipment such as basins, taps and wet-weather gear.
All donors will receive a parchment certificate denoting their gift.
£5,000 would pay for one berth per year for five years. Larger
amounts could pay for more than one berth or for a longer period of
time. The *Lord Nelson* runs company voyages and sponsorship
schemes, whereby commercial organizations can sponsor voyages
and send employees. One or two schemes might adapt well to an in
memoriam gift, sponsoring a voyage which would cost £5,000–
£15,000 or sponsoring a professional crew member, costing

£15,000–£20,000 per year. Such ideas would have to be discussed with the trust but might be an unusual way of remembering a sailor relative.

Prices: Memorial Log, up to £100, up to £500, up to £5,000 (per annum), up to £50,000, up to £100,000, up to £1 million and beyond *Elizabeth Wakeman, Fund-raising Manager, Test Road, Eastern Docks, Southampton SO14 3GG. Tel.: 01703 631388*

National Playing Fields Association

The association acquires, protects and develops play, sport and recreation space for local communities throughout the UK, protecting around 2,000 playing fields.

The most notable of these are the King George V Memorial Playing Fields. In addition, there are a number of playing fields which have been given to the NPFA in memory of a local person, for example the Robert Ann Memorial Field in Burghwallis, South Yorkshire, the Harry Hewlett Memorial Field in a high-density housing area in Manchester and Michael's Field in Hannington, Hampshire. In the London area there is the Eleanor Shorter Playing Field in Croydon and a field at Crockham Hill which was given by the Crockham Hill War Memorial Committee. Memorials that lend themselves to naming or dedicating might include: a gift of land for sport and recreation in a local community; a pavilion or pitch in memory of a legator; seating, trees, roses or park gates on NPFA fields. The NPFA has its own rose, called Playtime, a *Rosa rugosa* with a rich mid-green foliage and cyclamen-pink single blooms, which flower repeatedly in clusters throughout the season. It was conceived to enhance entrances, boundaries and other areas on playgrounds and sports fields. Details are available from the NPFA.

There are many opportunities for making commemorative gifts. For example, you could provide an NPFA Multigames Wall to be located in an area of discerned need with a plaque to commemorate the benefactor. Costing £24,863, the wall is designed to provide the opportunity for ball games for individuals and groups of children, for practice or organized team games, such as tennis, basketball, netball, football and cricket. It takes the space of half a football pitch and can be installed in corner areas of parks and sportsgrounds. The first Multigames Wall was built at Tidworth in Wiltshire, a town with a high proportion of young families. The wall was opened by the Queen in June 1993. During 1994, a further thirteen walls were installed in different locations including Lambeth, which was opened by Mike Gatting.

Endowing the NPFA's Playground of the Year competition, a national event, would cost around £5,000 per annum to organize. Funding a Schools' Sports Award competition on a regional basis would cost around £7,000. There is also the chance of endowing a fellowship in the benefactor's name in sports-field management, children's play safety or playing-fields development. This would cost around £20,000.

Prices: Up to £5,000, up to £10,000, up to £50,000
Elsa Davies, Director, 25 Ovington Square, London SW3 1LQ. Tel.:0171 584 6445

Royal National Lifeboat Institution

'It is better to have one's name on a boat than on a gravestone', said a legator to the RNLI. The RNLI has provided the lifeboat service for the UK and the Republic of Ireland since 1824, and its boats can reach any point up to fifty miles off the coast. There are 214 lifeboat stations and their lifeboats were launched 6,092 times in 1994, saving 1,621 lives. More than fifty-four per cent of all services were to pleasure-craft. The cost of running the RNLI in 1994 was £56 million.

The lifeboat stations are manned by highly trained volunteer crews and all the money needed to maintain the lifeboat service is raised by voluntary contributions. Although the institution is proud of its independent status as a registered charity, it works closely with HM Coastguard and other organizations to provide a co-ordinated rescue service. Modern lifeboats are sophisticated vessels and range from high-speed inflatable inshore lifeboats to all-weather boats almost fifty-six feet in length. The larger all-weather boats are capable of high speed in atrocious weather, are self-righting after a capsize and are fully fitted with modern navigation, location and communication equipment. Donations to the RNLI, however small, will be used at the donor's chosen location and in the manner requested. Thanks will be in the form of a letter with a plaque, if appropriate. The RNLI aims to please donors. Recently, money in lieu of flowers at a funeral was used for a specific requested project at Appledore Lifeboat Station. A D-class inflatable lifeboat can be purchased for about £11,000 (1995 prices). It seats two to three crew and is suitable for moderate seas and daylight rescues, or exceptional conditions, such as bright moonlight or operations with an all-weather boat. If that amount is donated, the boat can be named as requested after a person. For £61,250, a new-style Atlantic 75-class lifeboat can be purchased and named. This lifeboat responds to the increasing problems associated with leisure sailing as it can operate in inshore waters at high speed with room for a three-man crew plus survivors. It is the fastest lifeboat in the RNLI fleet and it is hoped by the year 2000 that half of the existing Atlantic stations will have the new Atlantic 75 to replace the Atlantic 21. The current large boats being built are the Severn (cost £1,410,000) and Trent (£1,060,000). For operations in shallow waters or confined space, the Severn carries a Y-class inflatable on the wheelhouse roof. For half the cost, the boat may be named but lesser donations would be acknowledged on a plaque in the lifeboat or lifeboat station, detailing names of donors and their gifts. The name is put on the boat, and a plaque in the lifeboat station commemorates the generous bequest (an example is the *Joy and John Wade*, an Arun-class lifeboat, moored in Yarmouth Harbour). The accompanying plaque in Yarmouth Lifeboat Station reads, 'This lifeboat was given by the Wade Foundation together with other generous gifts and bequests'.

People often leave money to a particular station as they are worried it will get swallowed up in general funds. This is not so and it will go to the project requested. Specific pieces of equipment are always needed, and even modest bequests are extremely valuable; it costs about £200 to kit out a lifeboatman, and if this request was made it would be followed. A letter of thanks would record the purchase made with the bequest. If specifically required, a plaque would be provided in the station, given the constraints of cost. It is suggested that potential bequests are discussed with Anthony Oliver. In theory, it is possible to buy a lifeboat station. There are 214 round the coast at present but the society is always on the lookout for the right new locations.

Some bequests are very substantial. The round-the-world yachtswoman Susan Hiscock MBE, who died in 1995 aged eighty-one, left £1 million to pay for a lifeboat, named *Wanderer* after the *Wanderer* III, IV and V yachts in which she and her husband Eric circled the globe (their first circumnavigation was between 1952 and 1955 and their second between 1959 and 1962 – they were the first husband-and-wife team to sail round the world twice). Mr Oliver said that the £1 million would provide a new Trent-style lifeboat or a substantial part of a Severn-type lifeboat.

Prices: Up to £500, up to £10,000, up to £100,000, up to £500,000, up to £1 million and beyond

Anthony K. Oliver, Deputy Head of Fund-raising and Marketing, West Quay Road, Poole, Dorset BH15 1HZ. Tel.: 01202 671133

Scout Association

The Scout movement provides a comprehensive programme of activities for more than 600,000 young people between the ages of six and twenty. Since its formation in 1907 by Robert Baden-Powell, the aim of Scouting has remained to help young people to achieve their full physical, intellectual, social and spiritual potential both as individuals and as members of their local, national and international communities. The modern Scouting programme has spread to inner-city areas and remote rural areas, where there may be problems of poverty, unemployment and a lack of community activities. The Scouts welcome members regardless of their religious beliefs or ethnic origin and also introduce Scouting activities to groups of young people who may be in an area of deprivation and are not members of the Scouting movement.

Because of the widespread nature of its activities, the Scout Association can offer a wide choice for suitable memorials to its benefactors. According to suitability, these may bear either the name of or a plaque to the donor. All Scout groups have charitable status. Benefactors can identify a particular area or troop. Bequests and in memoriam donations could range from: training centres, £500,000; seminar rooms, £100,000; campsite overnight accommodation, £50,000; camping lodges, £25,000; campsite entrances with gates (with plaque), £25,000; garden areas (with plaques), £5,000; memorial trees (individual or avenues), various prices; Scout training equipment, various prices; flags (with inscriptions on poles), £250; plaques on a variety of indoor accessories, £100–£500. Roadways in campsites can be named in memory and, including upkeep, cost around £100,000. Bedrooms in hostels can be provided and equipped from around £15,000 and a plaque can be placed on the door. Training manuals and instruction books cost between £500 and £5,000 to produce. Boats, yachts, canoes, dinghies and safety motor-boats cost between £1,500 and £15,000 and can be named or inscribed. A wing on a building or a building can be named. Camping areas or fields, set aside for Scouting use are also a welcome bequest, especially where such land has been used by Scouts or for outdoor activities.

Prices: Up to £100, up to £500, up to £1,000 up to £5,000, up to £10,000, up to £50,000, up to £100,000, up to £250,000, up to £500,000

Bryan Lees, Director of Finance/Marketing, Baden-Powell House, Queen's Gate, London SW7 5JS. Tel.: 0171 584 7030

Welsh Rugby Union (Undeb Rygbi Cymru)

There is a whole range of ways in which Welsh rugby clubs have remembered former players, committee members or supporters. A number of clubs have memorial seats; Penarth RFC, for example, has a row of seats in commemoration of former members.

Many clubs play memorial matches, including Llanelli RFC who each year stage a match in memory of their former coach Carowyn Jones. Cardiff RFC have the most famous memorial in Wales, in that the gates to the Cardiff Arms Park are in memory of E. Gwynn Nicholls, who played for Cardiff RFC and Wales at the turn of the century. There are 220 affiliated clubs in Wales. The Union has close association with two charitable trusts. The Welsh Rugby Union Charitable Fund has been established to assist players who are financially disadvantaged as a result of injury. Currently, it caters for more than twenty-five players or former players who have been seriously injured as a result of playing rugby. The Dragon's Trust was established some years ago to assist the development and promotion of the game at under-nineteen level. Both funds and the Welsh Rugby Union itself would happily accept donations or bequests. That donation or bequest could be for any amount and could be directed by the donor to an area of Welsh rugby that might be of special interest. In the past the Union has not agreed to place commemorative plaques at Cardiff Arms Park but such a view might change if the gift was sufficiently large.

Prices: Unspecified
Peter Owens, Administration Executive, Cardiff Arms Park, PO Box 22, Cardiff CF1 1JL. Tel.: 01222 390111

West Bromwich Albion Football Club Limited

West Bromwich Albion is opening a new administration wing, partly funded by the sons of a former director who was killed in tragic circumstances. This will bear his name. The club is also interested in developing other types of memorial, perhaps a wall on which the names of past fans might be inscribed. Ideas for memorials are welcome and John Evans can be consulted about all possible in memoriam gifts and bequests.

Prices: Unspecified

Dr John Evans, Secretary, The Hawthorns, Halfords Lane, West Bromwich, West Midlands B71 4LF. Tel.: 0121 525 4714

Worcestershire County Cricket Club

The only forms of memorial at present in the county ground are benches engraved with a loved one's name. These cost approximately £340 and an extra charge is made if a brass plate is put on the back rail. However, space is limited and in the future another form of memorial may be introduced. The cricket club is always willing to discuss bequests and memorials. If it had a request to build and name a new stand at the county ground after a particular person, sympathetic consideration would be given, although space is very limited. In the past, the club has named hospitality facilities after former players, for example the Don Kenyon Suite, the Foster Room and the Perks Room. Worcestershire County Cricket Club is planning to erect a cricket school at the ground, at an estimated cost of £1,200,000.

Prices: Up to £500
Pauline Boyce, Cricket Secretary, County Ground, New Road, Worcester WR2 4QQ. Tel.: 01905 748474

Index